G Suffredini
10 Hoag St
Seneca Falls NY 13148-2018

THE DAY JOHN DIED

THE
DAY JOHN
DIED

Christopher Andersen

WILLIAM MORROW

An Imprint of HarperCollins*Publishers*

Grateful acknowledgment is made to the following for permission to reprint the photographs in this book:

Paul Adao/Corbis Sygma: 53, 55, 59
Paul Adao/Sygma: 42, 43
David Allen/Corbis: 50
Archive Photos: 3, 14
Associated Press: 1, 2, 22, 28, 32, 34, 44, 45, 57, 58, 68, 70
Bettmann/Corbis: 6, 13, 20, 21, 25
The Coqueran Group: 36, 40, 46, 47, 48, 49, 62
Corbis/Bettmann-UPI: 8, 10, 15, 16, 17, 18, 19, 23, 26
Corbis Sygma: 9, 11, 12, 65, 66, 67, 71
Michael Ferguson/Globe Photos: 56
Gamma Liaison: 30
Globe Photos: 7, 24, 31, 33, 35, 60, 61, 69
JFK Memorial Library: 4, 5
David McGough/DMI: 27, 29
New York News Service/Corbis Sygma: 63, 64
Alex Oliveira/Sygma: 39
Denis Reggie: 51
Reuters/Corbis: 38
Reuters/Corbis-Bettmann: 37, 41
Lawrence Schwartzwald/Corbis Sygma: 52, 54

HarperCollins books may be purchased for educational, business, or sales promotional use. For information please write: Special Markets Department, HarperCollins Publishers Inc., 10 East 53rd Street, New York, NY 10022.

FIRST EDITION

Printed on acid-free paper

Designed by Jo Anne Metsch

Library of Congress Cataloging-in-Publication Data has been applied for.

ISBN 0-688-17203-2

00 01 02 03 04   QW   10 9 8 7 6 5 4 3 2 1

For my father, Edward Andersen

He had a legacy, and he learned to treasure it. He was part of a legend, and he learned to live with it.

—*Ted Kennedy, in his eulogy for John*

If Jack turned out to be the greatest president of the century and his children turned out badly, it would be a tragedy.

—*Jacqueline Kennedy Onassis*

PREFACE

Where were you the day John Kennedy died? For thirty-five years, there was no need to be more specific: so profoundly shocking was the assassination of JFK that Americans born before 1960 will never forget the moment they heard the news. So it was all but inconceivable that, on July 16, 1999, the nation and the world would again be plunged into an ocean of grief along with the plane that carried John Kennedy Jr., his wife, Carolyn Bessette, and her sister Lauren to their untimely deaths.

It was all too painfully familiar. The world had scarcely recovered from the shock of Princess Diana's death in the summer of 1997 when John took off on his final, fatal flight. Once again linked by the omnipresent media that had hounded both Diana and John throughout much of their lives, people around the world shared the heartache of losing someone they felt they knew. Here at home, John's death cut even more deeply because he was so quintessentially American: We believed he was one of us. His sudden, senseless demise, more than that of any other figure in recent memory, struck like a death in the family.

Indeed, parallels between Britain's fairy tale princess and America's Prince Charming abounded. They were both impossibly attractive, outlandishly wealthy, elegant, headstrong, *exciting*. Youth, glamour, sex, power, and money—not to mention the dreams and aspirations of their generation—were embodied in Diana and John. And though he was born to fame while she acquired it through marriage, both handled the pressures of public life and personal tragedy with a special, instinctive grace. As James Stewart said of Katharine Hepburn in *The Philadelphia Story,* John and Diana, unlike so many others born to wealth and privilege, seemed lit from within.

We were mesmerized by their beauty, unquestionably. But what impressed us most was their humanity—and their shared desire to lead something approaching a normal life. Diana was—as Jacqueline Bouvier Kennedy Onassis was before her—the cynosure of style. Yet she drove herself to the gym, took her children to McDonald's and to Disney World, and broke with royal tradition by unabashedly enjoying herself. John eschewed limousines for the subway, played Frisbee in Central Park, stood in line outside movie theaters, and more often than not biked or Rollerbladed to work.

Like Diana, John made an effort to connect with people. Even as a young prosecutor in the Manhattan district attorney's office, he agonized over sending young offenders to jail. "Every time I sent a kid to jail," he told a friend, "part of me just wanted to take him home with me. I often felt that all these petty criminals needed was a mother like the one I had, a job, a drug counselor. My first instinct was to help them, not just punish them."

There were, predictably, the endless black-tie benefits, ribboncuttings, and photo ops for worthy causes: Diana cuddled crack babies, consoled battered women, and strolled through minefields; John cheered on competitors at the Special Olympics, served on the boards of several charities, and with his sister, Caroline, presented Profile in Courage awards to public servants who swam against the political tide.

We would learn only after their deaths of other, unsung acts of kindness—secret visits to gravely ill children, gifts of time, money, and compassion to families and neighborhoods coping with crime, poverty, and drug addiction. Perhaps it was because both lost parents at an early age—Diana's mother abandoned the family when she was six, John was not yet three when his father was cut down in Dallas—that they felt other people's pain so keenly.

Their own foibles and failings made them even more appealing. When Diana went public with the sordid details of her disastrous marriage, her suicide attempts, her bulimia, and her depression, the public sympathized. When John failed his bar exam twice, fought with his future wife in the park, dodged the paparazzi, and struggled to find his own career path in the looming shadow of his legendary parents, we wished only the best for him. Although Americans may have always seen John as the Crown Prince of Camelot, he was more than royal. He was real.

Surreal was the word most often applied to Diana's sudden, violent death at the age of thirty-six. Those same feelings of shock, dismay, and grief were compounded exponentially by the plane crash that killed John at thirty-eight. It seemed all but impossible that, in the span of twenty-two months, the world had lost two of its most beloved icons.

Yet there was an important difference. John seemed as grounded as Diana was high-strung—no mean feat for a member of the star-crossed Kennedy clan. Unlike so many of his cousins, John did not abuse drugs or alcohol. Nor did he run afoul of the law. As a bachelor he cut a wide swath through New York's female population, but even ex-girlfriends had only nice things to say about him. And while other Kennedys made headlines with their reckless and boorish behavior, John was universally regarded as a gentleman.

This was, of course, no accident. Even though Jackie allowed her children to share in the Kennedy legacy by showing the flag at family gatherings in Hyannis Port, she went to considerable lengths to shield John and Caroline from the influence of Aunt Ethel's reckless brood. When she died of lymphoma in May 1994, Jackie took comfort in the belief that JFK's children had escaped the Kennedy curse.

Sadly, she was mistaken. The events of July 16, 1999, were, above all else, an American tragedy—one that seemed all the more heartbreaking in light of the unique bond John shared with Caroline and Jackie. No one experienced what they experienced, or could imagine what it was like to endure what they endured. Yet for all the strength and dignity she marshaled in the weeks and months following her husband's assassination, it is doubtful that even the resilient Jackie could have survived this final blow—the death of her cherished only son.

Like so many others who bore the name Kennedy, John seemed blessed by the gods. So it should come as no surprise that his brief, remarkable life took on the dimensions of a Greek tragedy. Yes, remarkable—not for what he did, but for what he *was*, for the special place he occupied in our national psyche.

From history's most famous salute to the plane crash that, in a bizarre twist of fate, took place within sight of his mother's beachfront estate, John's story is both poignant and inspiring—a bittersweet saga of love, loss, fate, and promise unfulfilled. That is why his stunningly brutal death, so unthinkable and yet in retrospect somehow so inevitable, touched us all—and why none of us will ever forget where we were and who we were with THE DAY JOHN DIED.

You know just enough about flying to be dangerous.

—*John Perry Barlow to*
his friend

To Flight Safety Academy,
The bravest people in aviation
because people will only care where
I got my training if I crash.
Best, John Kennedy.

—*JFK Jr.'s inscription on photo*
given to his flight instructors
in Vero Beach, Florida

John wasn't afraid to face danger. In fact, he loved the
challenge. This was his great escape.

—*Charlie Townsend,*
JFK Jr.'s mountain-
climbing guide

Flying is the most fun I've had with my clothes on.

—*John*

1
=

He gripped the controls tightly with both hands, trying to keep his tiny aircraft from being overturned by a stiff wind blowing in off the Atlantic. Two years earlier, in 1997, John had been warned by veteran pilots not to take off in blustery weather like this, and he had heeded those warnings. But now he was feeling more confident of his abilities as an aviator—confident enough to take a calculated risk in the skies over Martha's Vineyard.

In the distance, he could make out the silhouette of Gay Head's white, gray, and red chalk cliffs standing in sharp relief against the darkening sky. Gliding closer, he had a gull's-eye view of Red Gate Farm, the 474-acre estate left to him and his sister, Caroline, by their mother, Jacqueline. On one side was Squibnocket Pond, on the other 4,620 feet of private oceanfront. In between was a wonderland of Scotch pines, sand dunes, scrub oaks, and marshes. "It was a dream place, a sunlit place," Kennedy family friend George Plimpton had once observed. "It's hard to explain the effect it all had on you—all the variations in color, water sparkling like diamonds everywhere you looked."

From his vantage point high above it all, John was no less transfixed—until a sudden gust jolted him out of his reverie. He squeezed the controls even more tightly, but another gust pushed him sideways, and yet another seemed to slam down from above like a sledgehammer. He was heading toward open water, and losing altitude rapidly.

The situation would have been dire enough if John had actually been piloting a plane. But on this Memorial Day weekend he had taken to the skies in his $14,300 Buckeye ultralight powered parachute, a flimsy contraption that resembled a small go-cart with an engine-driven propeller at the back. Behind the propeller was a parachute that, once filled with air, acted like a wing, bearing the craft aloft.

"He was a natural for his first time flying," said Buckeye Industries' Ralph Howard, who sold John his first ultralight, a $13,000 Falcon 582 powered parachute, and trained him in its use. "John was literally at a loss for words, he was so excited."

Toward the end of his maiden flight, he pleaded with Howard to stay airborne. "The sunset is so beautiful," John said. "Can I go around one more time?" Once Howard had taken his student up for a few more runs, he was confident John was ready to solo. There was no need for any formal certification; piloting an ultralight does not require a license.

At first locals "didn't know what it was," said Brenda Hayden, who managed the sandwich shop where John often stopped before taking off. "It made this weird noise, like a flying lawn mower. But he really seemed excited about it, because he was always in it."

Others that afternoon in late May of 1999 were alarmed by the sight of the "flying lawn mower" whisking by high-tension power lines. "Is he that stupid?" said one. "If a gust of wind pushes him in the wrong direction, he'll get fried." Nor was he equipped to survive a plunge into the chilly Atlantic. Wearing pants, a shirt, and a cap instead of a wet suit, John would probably not have survived the forty-degree water temperature for long.

As John tried to bring his ultralight in for a landing, police lines lit up with frantic calls from onlookers who feared the young man in the odd-looking contraption would be killed. On the ground, Carolyn's aquamarine eyes widened in horror as John's flying machine careened wildly out of control. At the last minute, an updraft miraculously halted his descent, and instead of plummeting to earth he collided with one of his mother's beloved Scotch pines. Carolyn ran toward the crumpled ultralight, only to see John hopping on one foot in her direction before crumpling to the ground. "I'm okay!" he shouted. "It . . . it's just my ankle. I think I broke it . . ."

Carolyn, relieved but still shaken, knelt down beside her husband in the grass and shook her head. "Don't ever," she told him as she brushed a tear from her cheek, "scare me like that again. Do you hear me? *Ever.*"

He was in a fine state of mind.
He was at the height of himself.

—A friend

Please don't do it. There have been too many deaths in
the family already.

—Jackie to her college
student son when she
learned he was secretly
taking flying lessons

Thursday, July 15, 1999

A collective gasp went up from the crowd of forty-nine thousand people at Yankee Stadium—not because of Roger Clemens's pitching against the Atlanta Braves, but because a new television crew broadcasting the game had zeroed in on a single fan. There, smiling over the throng, was the tanned, movie-star-handsome face of John F. Kennedy Jr. Thousands of heads swiveled as spectators frantically searched the stands for a glimpse of John in the flesh—to no avail. Inured to the sort of commotion his mere presence often caused, John leaned back in his box seat near the dugout (courtesy of Yankee owner George Steinbrenner) and washed down a Lemon Chill with Deer Park bottled water.

John, crisply attired in a white dress shirt rolled up at the sleeves, rose with his three friends to leave when Anthony Hahn, a securities trader from Staten Island seated a few rows away, bounded to his feet and walked toward him. "If I don't get your autograph," he said, "my sister Karen will kill me. John," Hahn asked sheepishly, "would you mind signing?" Kennedy smiled and scribbled his name on one of the pink menus handed out to box seat holders. It would be one of his last autographs.

Then John grabbed the two white metal crutches that had been propped up against the seat next to him and began the difficult climb up the stairs leading to the nearest exit. It had been six weeks since he broke his left ankle flying his Buckeye powered parachute on Martha's Vineyard, and the itchy, uncomfortable cast had come off only hours before. But he still needed both crutches to walk, and winced noticeably whenever he put the slightest bit of weight on the injured leg.

Attending the Yankee–Braves game that night was worth the discomfort, if only to get his mind off other, weightier things. For the last few weeks, John had been courting new financial backers for *George,* the irreverent political magazine he had founded in 1995. Executives at Hachette-Filipacchi, the French publishing conglomerate that bankrolled the magazine from the outset, were no longer in awe of Jack and Jackie Kennedy's only son. After a wildly successful beginning—fueled largely by JFK Jr.'s celebrity megawattage and personal charisma—the magazine had taken a steep dive in both circulation and advertising revenues. By the summer of 1999, Hachette had lost tens of millions on the venture and was now ready to pull the plug.

John was now pleading his case before Armani-clad investment bankers and high-rolling entrepreneurs—anyone with pockets deep enough to keep *George* alive. "I know the sons-of-bitches he had to deal with," journalist Michael Wolff later wrote. "He was paying serious dues."

The previous Monday, John, unable to man the controls because of his injured ankle, had flown from Martha's Vineyard to Toronto—this time with his flight instructor—to meet with potential investors Keith Stein and Belinda Stronach. As Stein drove him north to his offices in Aurora, Ontario, his passenger was decidedly upbeat and inquisitive, sticking his head out Stein's car window "like a dog sort of looking around, taking it all in. He was obviously someone who was keenly interested in his surroundings. He had questions about everything."

Stein had a few questions of his own. Why, for instance, was he traveling to Canada when the deepest pockets were in his hometown of New York? "I like to operate," John said slyly, "below the radar screen."

"If John was stressed out about the magazine," Stein said, "he certainly didn't show it. He struck me as a guy who just didn't let things get to him." But John, who told Stein he had flown up with his instructor because he could not operate the plane's foot pedals, was becoming increasingly impatient to have the cast removed from his ankle. "He was hopping around and couldn't put any pressure on his foot," Stein later recalled. "He was clearly passionate about flying."

Indeed, John's only real complaint was that his broken ankle had kept him from doing the things he loved—Rollerblading, biking, and most of all, flying. "I've loved airplanes ever since I was a little kid," he told his Canadian hosts. "Because of this ankle, I won't be able to do the flying when we go back to New York tonight, and that's too bad—I really love the challenge of navigating at night. Besides, it's so much prettier when you approach New York and look down at all the lights."

The conversation then turned oddly philosophical. "How old are you?" Kennedy asked Stein.

"Thirty-five. You?"

"Thirty-eight," Kennedy replied, shaking his head. "God, how time flies." Then they discussed fate, and "how none of us knows how much time there is left."

Kennedy shrugged. "Don't worry," he said, "about what you can't control."

At another point, John asked about charismatic former Prime Minister Pierre Trudeau, the Canadian politician most often compared to President Kennedy. When Stein told him that Trudeau's son had recently been killed in an avalanche, John's mood shifted dramatically. "He suddenly went very quiet. It obviously affected him."

Then John invited Leslie Marshall, the American businesswoman who had arranged the meeting with Stein, to fly back with him. Stein objected. "I flew you up here commercial, Leslie, and you're flying back commercial!" Stein insisted.

"Something told me I shouldn't let her get on that plane," Stein said. "Later Leslie asked me why I was so adamant. But she has three kids, and I just felt uncomfortable letting her fly with John Kennedy that night."

John and his co-pilot did make it back to New York safely, and on Tuesday night Kennedy seemed to be in high spirits when he showed up at a British advertising agency party in downtown Manhattan. He only stayed forty minutes, apologizing to the ad agency president that he was worried he might fall on the slippery dance floor. "It would be just my luck," he joked, "to break my ankle again just before the cast is supposed to come off."

On Wednesday morning John and Carolyn played host in his office to the board of the Robin Hood Foundation, a group of well-connected Manhattanites who raise money for neighborhood projects in places like Harlem and the Bronx. As it often did, talk turned to John's political future. Before First Lady Hillary Clinton expressed interest in seeking the U.S. Senate seat being vacated by New York's Daniel Patrick Moynihan, Democratic leaders had sounded John out. Unbeknownst to those sitting at the table, it was John who, as early as January of 1997, actually approached New York State Democratic Chairwoman Judith Hope and told her he was interested in running for the Senate in 2000. John, aware that his hypersensitive wife might suffer a breakdown under the strain of a heated political campaign, never followed through.

Even though he was now thirty-eight—eight years older than his father when JFK was first elected to Congress—John told the Robin Hood Foundation board that he still was not quite ready to make the commitment. Furthermore, when he did feel ready to run, he would probably seek a position in the executive branch rather than in Congress; he admitted that he would rather be governor—presumably of New York—than a senator.

But for the moment, John hastened to insist, he was pouring all his energy into *George*. "I like things the way they are now," he said as his stunning thirty-three-year-old wife beamed. "I love my life."

That afternoon John met Carolyn again, this time for lunch with her sister Lauren at the Stanhope Hotel's Café M. As they dined on sea bass and salmon, the trio chatted about the upcoming wedding of John's cousin Rory Kennedy at Hyannis Port. A few months before

John had traded up from his single-engine Cessna to a faster, more luxuriously appointed Piper Saratoga, and was looking forward to showing the Bessette sisters how smoothly it handled. They would fly to Cape Cod after work Friday, depositing Lauren on Martha's Vineyard before making the short hop to Hyannis.

To a diner seated within earshot, it was clear that Carolyn was reluctant to fly up with her husband and that John had enlisted Lauren's help in talking her into it. "Oh, come on now," thirty-four-year-old Lauren chided her little sister after John asked for the check, "we'll have fun."

Carolyn, clearly, was not entirely convinced. Even before his paragliding mishap on the Vineyard, she had harbored serious reservations about John's flying. Just as Jackie had forbidden her son to take flying lessons, Carolyn repeatedly tried to talk him out of getting his pilot's license.

Given the Kennedy family's track record when it came to flying, there was ample cause for concern. Joseph P. Kennedy Jr., John's uncle and the eldest of Joseph P. Kennedy's sons, was killed when his bomber exploded over the English Channel during World War II. Four years later, in 1948, John's aunt Kathleen "Kit" Kennedy Hartington was flying from Paris to Cannes with her lover, Earl Fitzwilliam, when their plane crashed into the Cevennes Mountains, killing all aboard.

In 1964 tragedy struck when another of John's uncles, Edward Kennedy, insisted on flying to Springfield, Massachusetts, in bad weather to accept his party's nomination for a second Senate term. The small plane in which he was flying crashed into an apple orchard, killing Ted's aide and the pilot. Ted's back was broken in the accident. "Somebody up there," Robert F. Kennedy prophetically commented to Jackie when he reached the hospital, "doesn't like us." His wife, Ethel, lost her parents in a plane crash in 1955; her brother George Skakel Jr. was killed in a plane crash in 1966. Seven years later John's own stepbrother, Aristotle Onassis's only son Alexander, would also perish when his plane crashed after takeoff.

Just four days after John started attending a Florida flight school in December of 1997, his cousin Michael was killed playing a reckless game of football on skis. It was then that Uncle Ted joined Carolyn in pleading with John to drop out of flight school. He did, but was back within a matter of weeks.

For John, flying was far more than a pastime, more than a hobby—it was an escape. "When he flew on commercial aircraft, fellow passengers would ask questions, seek autographs, exchange memories," said longtime Kennedy family intimate Arthur Schlesinger. "John understood that they were people of goodwill, and he could not bear to be impolite, but the benign interest of others was a burden. Once he got his flying license, he seemed a liberated man, free to travel as he wished without superfluous demands on time and energy."

John's college buddy Richard Wiese put it more simply. "You know," Wiese mused, "it was just him up there, away from everybody and it made him feel free." What's more, added John's longtime friend John Perry Barlow, "He just wanted to prevent all those neck injuries suffered by other airline passengers straining to get a better look at him."

Not everyone shared young Kennedy's enthusiasm for flying—at least not with him in the pilot's seat. After he got his license in April 1998, John joked often and openly about how family and friends simply refused to fly with him. Uncle Ted, remembering how Jackie feared for her son's safety, not only declined every invitation to fly with his nephew, but tried to talk John out of it every chance he got.

So did former heavy heavyweight champion Mike Tyson, with whom John, an avid boxing fan, had managed to strike up a curious friendship over the course of researching an article for *George.* In March 1999, John had flown with his instructor to Maryland, where Tyson was serving a one-year sentence at Montgomery County Detention Center for assaulting two motorists.

"You're crazy to fly," Tyson told John through the Plexiglas partition.

"You don't know what it's like up there alone," John tried to explain. "You don't know what the feeling is like." John knew that Tyson had narrowly escaped death after a 1997 motorcycle accident that left him with a fractured back and punctured lung. "So why don't you give up motorcycles?"

Tyson held his ground. "It's not the same. Flying a small plane is stupid. There isn't enough metal up there for me. I'd rather be knocked out in the ring than be in a one-engine plane made of tin-foil and wood."

John laughed, but Mike asked him to promise one thing: "I told my wife and kids to stay away from small planes. John, if you are going to go up there, don't take anybody you love with you."

John ignored his friend's advice. "The only person I've been able to get to go up with me, who looks forward to it as much as I do, is my wife," John told one writer. "The second it was legal she came up with me. Now, whenever we want to get away, we can just get in a plane and fly off."

Carolyn had flown with John, but she was far from enthusiastic. Although he seemed to be a conscientious flyer determined not to take any unnecessary risks, Carolyn knew how much her husband enjoyed pushing the envelope. "There was a sense of testing his lim-its that was a little like his father's," said Douglas Brinkley, who worked with John at *George*. "If John was on a boat, he wanted to be in front with his face in the wind."

Carolyn had heard stories—like the time years earlier when a group of his friends watched as John swam out to sea off the coast of Baja California and—vanished. John's horrified companions had begun to panic when, in the words of one, "all of a sudden he just reappeared." On kayaking trips into the wilderness with friends, he would venture off alone for days at a time, then materialize back at base camp, exhausted and exhilarated.

"There were many times I've been with him in difficult situa-tions," said JFK's friend Billy Straus, "and he's always come out the other side." So many times, in fact, that most of his friends had to concede that John—though by no means as reckless as his Kennedy cousins—liked to live on the edge. "John had a certain daredevil quality to him," Kennedy family friend John Whitehead said. "He had great self-confidence in his ability to come through these things."

Indeed, only a few days before he broke his ankle, John was in South Dakota and asked authorities if he could rappel down the sixty-foot face of Mount Rushmore. His request was denied. Those few discreet buddies who tagged along on John's adventures had no doubt that, whatever the physical challenge, he would somehow prevail. Their nickname for John: "Master of Disaster."

Carolyn had her doubts. Although she had gone up with John in his ultralight and flown with him in the Cessna on numerous occasions, she had been in the new Piper Saratoga only once—two weeks earlier when they flew to Martha's Vineyard for the Fourth of July, and then only with an instructor in the cockpit.

In fact, this summer, they had spent nearly every weekend at the Vineyard. John was a familiar sight out by the airport hangar, where he obviously took pleasure just washing his new plane. "You know how it is when you get a new car?" asked Arthur Marx, who had started giving John flying lessons as far back as 1988. "He was picking little pieces of dust off it."

Just the weekend before, John and Carolyn were at the Vineyard playing host to his old friend CNN correspondent Christiane Amanpour and her husband, State Department spokesman James Rubin. That time, John's flight instructor rode along in the cockpit.

Even with a seasoned professional along, Carolyn often preferred either to buy a seat on one of the regularly scheduled airline flights or to drive the five hours to Hyannis and take the ferry to the island. Joan Ford, who worked at the Martha's Vineyard airport café, served the couple coffee and chowder a half-dozen times. Each time, she noticed that they arrived and departed separately. Once while she was waiting for John, Carolyn told Ford why she would not fly with her husband. "I don't trust him," she said bluntly.

Carolyn's misgivings may have had less to do with John's supposed penchant for risk taking than what even he conceded was his chronic absentmindedness. John routinely misplaced things—his wallet, his gloves, his credit cards. Over the last eighteen months, John had lost his American Express card three times. And even though he kept his keys on a chain fastened to his belt loop, he still somehow managed to misplace them. This happened so often that he kept a spare set of keys to his apartment at 20 North Moore Street tucked in a hiding place under the front stoop.

To Carolyn, who was nearly as meticulous as her famous mother-in-law, this lack of attention to detail was particularly disturbing.

"We spend hours every day just looking for his stuff," Carolyn complained to a friend. "It drives me so crazy."

Yet Carolyn had been willing to bend. So long as a seasoned instructor was on board, she was all too happy to fly with John at the controls. Jay Biederman, the flight instructor who had recently helped John pass his written instrument test and was preparing him for his instrument flight test, had in fact been scheduled to accompany them to Martha's Vineyard this weekend. But a week earlier Biederman, twenty-six, canceled to join his parents on a hiking trip in Switzerland.

There was ample time to find a replacement for Biederman—JFK Jr. could have had his pick of qualified instructors to tag along—but John made the decision to pilot the plane without a co-pilot. He did not have an instrument rating, but if the weather was good enough John could still fly under visual flight rules (VFR). That meant he could fly any route he wanted to Martha's Vineyard and he wouldn't have to file a flight plan—so long as, for all intents and purposes, he could see where he was going.

John spent the rest of that Wednesday afternoon at his forty-first floor office at Paramount Plaza, but returned to the Stanhope Hotel that evening at eight and checked into room 1511. Hobbling to the front desk on his crutches, his foot still in a cast, John told the assistant manager why he was not spending the night at his two-million-dollar TriBeCa loft. "My wife," John told him with a wink, "kicked me out."

In truth, things of late had been rather dicey in the Kennedy–Bessette household, and John and Carolyn needed to take a breather from each other. It was with Carolyn's blessing that John had taken his financial plans and magazine dummies to the Stanhope, where, undistracted, he could give *George*'s fate his full attention. This particular hotel was a logical choice: since *George*'s inception the magazine had maintained a corporate account at the Stanhope, and interviews and photo shoots as well as staff conferences were often held there. But even before he went into the magazine business, John had thought of the Stanhope, situated on Fifth Avenue directly across from the Metropolitan Museum of Art and just down the street from the apartment building where his mother Jacqueline had lived and died, as something of a sanctuary. When a room service waiter delivered a turkey club sandwich and mineral water an hour later, John was still poring over financial records and dummies of cover subject Harrison Ford spread out on the floor.

Not long after, a tall, striking brunette named Julie Baker knocked on the door of his room. John had dated the leggy lingerie model in the early 1990s, and even after their romance ended in 1994 she remained one of his closest confidantes. It was Baker, thirty-seven, to whom he often turned in times of crisis. Ostensibly he had invited "Jules," as he affectionately called Baker, to his hotel room to watch a video. But over the course of his marriage to Carolyn, Baker knew what this really meant. "Not sex," she explained to a friend. "He just wants somebody he can talk to. We've always been there for each other."

As he had so many times in the past, John unburdened himself to Baker—this time about the strains on his marriage and his financially beleaguered magazine. Baker left shortly before midnight, but only after promising to return to the hotel the next morning for breakfast.

On Thursday, the *New York Post* reported that the publishing industry was rife with rumors that Hachette-Filipacchi was about to pull the plug on *George*. But John was upbeat. If nothing else, today was the day that doctors at Lenox Hill Hospital were scheduled to remove his cast.

At 8 A.M. John walked into Café M at the Stanhope and slid into a corner banquette toward the rear of the restaurant. Ten minutes later, Julie Baker joined him, strategically sitting with her back to the other diners. Over pancakes and eggs Benedict, John and Jules picked up where they left off the night before. At one point, she reached over and tenderly touched his hand. "It's all going to turn out okay," she said soothingly. "Now go get that cast taken off your foot."

Shortly after 10:30 A.M. John, wearing a white T-shirt, gabardine pants, and a black beret, arrived back at his 20 North Moore Street apartment—still on crutches but with the hard white plaster cast replaced by a pale blue bandage encased in an open-toed rubber boot. He went upstairs, put on a dark blue business suit, removed the bandage on his foot and somehow managed to slip into black patent leather business shoes.

When he emerged two hours later, John was still using crutches and had to be helped into a waiting Lincoln Town Car by the driver. "He made a face every time he put pressure on the foot," said a neighbor. "He was clearly still in a lot of pain and it took him a while to ease into the backseat of the car."

Shortly before 1 P.M. a hush fell over the lunchtime crowd at San Domenico, the red-awninged Central Park South restaurant where John often dined. Wearing dark glasses and moving quickly despite his crutches, John was escorted to his customary table in the back. He waved hello to his longtime friend ABC newswoman Diane Sawyer and then dined alone on spaghetti with tomato and basil, followed by grilled sea bass. A friend of Maurice Tempelsman, the man who shared the last fifteen years of Jackie's life, leaned toward her dining companions and whispered, "Maurice worries about him flying that plane. He's afraid John is too . . ."

In truth, Tempelsman was carrying out Jackie's dying wish that he look after her children. The wealthy diamond merchant had helped Jackie parlay her twenty-six-million-dollar settlement from the estate of her late husband Aristotle Onassis into a fortune valued in excess of one hundred million dollars. Continuing to follow Tempelsman's sage financial advice after their mother's death in May 1994, John and Caroline watched their inheritance double. By the summer of 1999, each was worth in excess of one hundred million dollars.

Yet for all his considerable financial acumen, Maurice felt powerless to protect JFK Jr. from himself. Since the threat of assassination eased following her marriage to Aristotle Onassis, Jackie made a point over the years of indulging, even encouraging, John's instinctive adventurous streak. Whether he was scuba diving, skiing, mountain climbing, Rollerblading, playing football at Hyannis Port, or just weaving in and out of Manhattan traffic on his bicycle, Jackie took unabashed pride in her son's fearless athleticism. She did not even object when he disappeared into the wilderness for days at a time.

Flying was another matter. She forbade John from getting his pilot's license, and on her deathbed made Maurice promise that he would discourage John from pursuing his interest in aviation. She did not want to alarm John, but confided to Maurice the primary reason for her concern: In the latter years of her life, Jackie had a recurring premonition that John would be killed piloting his own plane. She pleaded with Maurice to do whatever it took to keep John from becoming a pilot.

Out of respect for his mother's feelings, John had put aside his own dream of becoming a licensed aviator during her lifetime. But now neither Maurice nor Uncle Ted could talk him out of it, and Caroline had long ago given up trying to influence her headstrong brother. "John just won't listen," a frustrated Tempelsman told a friend. "His mother would have been frantic. But I don't know what more I can do . . ."

Late that afternoon John headed for La Palestra, the exclusive West 67th Street gym owned by his friend Pat Manocchia. Undeterred by the injury to his foot, John spent the next two hours on a grueling upper body workout. Another member of the gym watched as John climbed down off one of the machines and "winced the minute he put weight on his left foot. Later on I saw him hobbling" toward the showers. After the Yankee game that night, John returned to North Moore Street to spend time with Carolyn. By 2 A.M., he was back at the Stanhope.

The next morning, John limped into the Stanhope's restaurant around 9 A.M., grimaced as he stretched out his leg, and ordered a breakfast of strawberries, orange juice, and oatmeal. An hour later he was meeting at Paramount Plaza with Jack Kliger, newly appointed president of Hachette. They both agreed that *George* had lacked a "well-thought-out business plan" from the beginning.

"So let's figure out how to go forward," Kliger said. John, relieved that his magazine was getting a stay of execution, nodded in agreement. Kliger believed Kennedy felt "fairly positive" about the future as he left the meeting. "Both of us came out of that meeting," Kliger said, "feeling good." Another friend John spoke with that day concurred: "He was in a fine state of mind. He was at the height of himself."

Kennedy returned to the Stanhope to collect his papers, and shook hands with the same desk clerk who had checked him in. "See you," the hotel staffer quipped, "the next time your wife kicks you out." John smiled and then, again with some difficulty, maneuvered his way into his waiting Lincoln before realizing he had forgotten to pay the bill. Slowly, he managed to pull himself out of the car, limp back inside the hotel on his crutches, and sign the check. The car dropped John off ten minutes later for lunch at Trionfo Ristorante on West 51st Street, where throughout the meal with several of his editors he kept his leg propped up on a chair.

Determined not to wind down early on this Friday afternoon, John followed his lunch with a flurry of phone conversations, story conferences, and layout sessions. He had originally planned to have dinner on Nantucket with his friend Billy Noonan, but since he was now going to be dropping Lauren Bessette off in Martha's Vineyard, he called Noonan to cancel. By the time Attorney General Janet Reno's office phoned that afternoon to say she had agreed to be interviewed by John for *George*'s fall Women and Politics issue, colleagues noticed that he was able to get around the office using only a cane.

Still, most of New York's publishing industry had long since left for the weekend by 4 P.M., when John sent an e-mail consoling his friend John Perry Barlow on the death of his mother. Like John, Barlow had been at his mother's bedside when she died. "I will never forget when it happened to me, and it was not something that was all that macabre," John wrote. "Let's spend some time together this summer and sort things out." Barlow would not read John's e-mail until the next day, when it would seem "like a voice from the grave."

Shortly after five, John placed a call to literary agent Sterling Lord telling him *George* would not be publishing a previously unpublished poem by Jack Kerouac. "I'm really sorry," John said, "but I'm afraid it's just too literary for us."

Lord was surprised that John had called at all. "I had a feeling," he said, "we were the only two guys working in town."

After speaking with Lord, John placed one last phone call to his sister's cell phone. Caroline was off on a white-water rafting trip in Idaho with her husband, Edwin Schlossberg, and their children, Rose, Tatiana, and Jack. John knew how much his nieces and nephew had looked forward to the wilderness trip, and urged his sister not to cancel their plans. In keeping with Jackie's wish that her branch of the family be represented at all major family gatherings, John and his wife would show the flag at Rory Kennedy's wedding.

Since their mother's death five years earlier, the bond between brother and sister had grown stronger. "She's an older sister, you know," John once mused. "We're obviously very close. And as a young brother, you look up to your sister."

Caroline "worried about John a lot," said a family friend. "She sort of took up where Jackie left off, telling him to watch himself, not to take any chances. But Jackie was not the smothering type, and neither is Caroline." When Jack told her he was flying his new plane up to Martha's Vineyard and then on to Hyannis Port, Caroline did not try to talk him out of it.

"Well, be careful," she told her brother.

"Don't worry," John reassured her. "I won't take any chances. I plan on living to a ripe old age."

Then he turned to his computer and logged onto www.weather-tap.com to check on weather conditions on Martha's Vineyard and the surrounding area. "No adverse conditions," read the weather report. "Visibility six to eight miles." No fog, no clouds, light winds.

A few blocks away at the NBC studios in Manhattan, another pilot who was going to fly roughly the same route as Kennedy on his way to Nantucket that night checked the same Web site and got the same information. NBC correspondent Dr. Bob Arnot, who was staying at the office later than usual crashing a piece for *Dateline,* went several steps further and called the Federal Aviation Administration's flight service twice. "I was told I had eight to ten miles visibility," recalled Arnot, who was also assured that there would be no fog that evening in the region. "No adverse conditions," he was told emphatically. "Have a great weekend."

But what John did not know was that no human had checked the skies around Martha's Vineyard that day. The data on visibility was coming from one of the FAA's newly mandated Automated Surface Observation Systems—an odd-looking electronic eye that the agency had installed around the country to save on manpower and money. But rather than scanning the sky, the device is pointed straight up, permitting it to report only on the air directly above it. "It's only looking at a very small slice of the sky," said Kyle Bailey, another pilot who planned to fly out of Essex County Airport that night. "If the area all around the monitor is blanketed in dense fog and there is a tiny spot of clear sky above it, then the machine will report that whole area has nothing but clear skies and perfect visibility. No pilots like these machines. They're worse than useless, they're dangerous because they can lull you into a false sense of security."

While John was checking the weather report—and being given false information—Carolyn was busy taking care of last-minute details. Their dog Friday, a frisky black-and-white Canaan John had purchased for 500 dollars from Illinois breeder Donna Dodson four years earlier, was dropped off with a friend for the weekend.

It was just as well: Friday hated to fly. High-strung under the best of circumstances, the Kennedys' dog had to be dragged onto the plane, and once on board he was difficult to control. "You'd always know when they were bringing the dog," a Martha's Vineyard charter pilot said. "He'd bark like crazy from the moment they got out of their car until John would scoop him up in his arms and put him in the plane. Whenever I saw the dog get on the plane, John had an instructor along. I don't think he could have handled the distraction if he were trying to fly the plane alone."

Shortly after 4 P.M., Carolyn headed for Saks Fifth Avenue to shop for a dress to wear to Rory Kennedy's wedding. While she and a friend scoured the racks in Saks's third-floor designer section for two and a half hours, Carolyn told one salesperson that she was "not looking forward" to flying with John and Lauren that evening. "He just had the cast taken off his leg," she said. "I don't know if he's ready yet to fly again."

Carolyn tried on an Armani design before settling on a black, off-the-shoulder silk crepe cocktail dress from the fall collection of Yves

Saint Laurent's Rive Gauche line by Alber Elbaz. After she put the
$1,639 dress on her credit card, Carolyn started to leave when the
salesperson wished her luck on her flight that night.

"Thanks," Carolyn replied. "I'll need it."

An hour later, she was back at their sparsely furnished loft apartment on 20 North Moore, packing for the trip. Around 6:30 P.M.
John's wife climbed into a black Lincoln Town Car for the forty-
minute drive to Essex County Airport in Fairfield, New Jersey.

They had spent their married life in TriBeCa, decidedly a neighborhood in transition, where movie stars and moguls walked past abandoned warehouses and seedy tenements on the way to their
multimillion-dollar apartments. But lately both Carolyn and John
were confessing to friends that they had grown weary of the noise,
the pollution, and—most of all—the constant hounding by the press.

Life in the media fishbowl was nothing new to John, of course. He
had long since come to terms with his place in his countrymen's collective consciousness. More than any celebrity of his stature, he handled the constant intrusions on his privacy with an uncommon
grace.

Conversely, Carolyn, who had grown up among the mansions and
country clubs of Greenwich, Connecticut, was ill-equipped to cope
with the blinding flashbulbs and the unending blizzard of tabloid
headlines. Insatiable reporters notwithstanding, Carolyn was by all
accounts as mercurial as she was beautiful. "She was fabulous in
many ways," said a former boyfriend, "but she could also be hell to
live with. It was always hard to keep on top of Carolyn's shifting
moods. I wish him luck."

Even before their 1996 marriage, the couple was videotaped in
New York's Washington Square Park battling ferociously, then tear-
fully making up. Since their storybook wedding in a tiny Georgia
chapel—one of the decade's best-kept secrets—John and Carolyn
continued to quarrel bitterly in public. Amid reports of tension in the
marriage, Mrs. John F. Kennedy seldom seemed to smile—not even
at charity events when her husband stood beside her grinning ear-

to-ear for the cameras. In much the same way that Princess Diana's body language left little doubt about the state of the royal marriage, Carolyn's icy demeanor signaled problems in the Kennedy–Bessette union.

By 1999, the Kennedys had reached a pivotal moment in their relationship. John was telling friends that for months Carolyn, unhappy despite a steady diet of prescription antidepressants, had simply refused to sleep with him. Frustrated and confused, the couple began seeing a marriage counselor in March.

Over the course of that spring, John and Carolyn appeared to make great strides in repairing their marriage. Perhaps the most serious disagreement, as it turned out, revolved around the question of when to start a family. John had wanted children almost from the start. If they had a son, he told friends on several occasions, he would name him Flynn rather than saddle him with the burden of being JFK III. But Carolyn worried about the inevitable tabloid frenzy and what effect it might have on a child. "She had always been in awe of John's ability not to just survive but to *enjoy* his life despite the lack of privacy," John Perry Barlow said. "It was something he had to deal with all his life, but to her it was all new—and understandably frightening. She could only imagine how much worse it would become if there was a child in the picture."

It had taken four years, but at last Carolyn had come to terms with life under the proverbial microscope. Now, as she climbed into her waiting limousine, John's wife was seriously considering motherhood and perhaps a new life raising children in the suburbs.

During his trip to Toronto just days earlier, John had told Keith Stein that he was looking forward to fatherhood. "He talked about having kids as if it were imminent in their future," Stein said. "He mentioned his wife a lot. She was a real reference point. It was clear they had a very strong relationship."

Two blocks down Broadway from *George*'s headquarters, Lauren Bessette was wrapping up another hectic week at Morgan Stanley Dean Witter & Co. With a Wharton MBA and a command of Mandarin Chinese, Lauren was a rising star at the investment firm, heading up a formidable team of young dealmakers. The year before, the willowy brunette had returned from a stint working for Morgan Stanley in Hong Kong and purchased a two-million-dollar penthouse apartment just two blocks from John and Carolyn. Although Lauren had naturally formed a unique bond with her twin sister, Lisa, she was now closer to Carolyn than she had ever been. She hit it off with John, and was in the process of landing a Kennedy of her own—John's cousin Robert Shriver.

The plan that day was for Lauren to walk over to the *George* offices and then ride with her brother-in-law to the airport in his white Hyundai convertible. Since John would be flying under visual flight rules, he wanted to take advantage of whatever light was available. If he and Lauren left for the airport at 6:30 they could be in the air by 7:15. Given the Piper's cruising speed of 180 miles per hour, that would put them in Martha's Vineyard by 8:30 at the latest—just before nightfall.

When he had called Billy Noonan on Nantucket earlier to cancel their dinner plans, John said he was running behind schedule because his sister-in-law had to work late. As it turned out, according to one of her staffers, Lauren spent much of the afternoon "just hanging out." At 6:20 P.M., she picked up her black garment bag, said goodbye to her co-workers, and left to meet John at his office.

Everyone was on the road, heading for the airport by the agreed-upon time of 6:30 P.M. But they had all underestimated how long the trip would take on a Friday afternoon in July. Pedestrians and motorists turned their heads as John's car crawled through Times Square traffic with the top down, and then headed west toward the inevitable bottleneck at the entrance to the Lincoln Tunnel. Carolyn was experiencing the same frustrating gridlock fifty blocks to the south; she slunk in the backseat behind tinted windows and flipped through a copy of *Vogue* as her limousine inched through the fume-filled Holland Tunnel.

Emerging on the opposite side of the Hudson River into an odd, yellowish summer haze, both cars then struggled west along traffic-clogged Route 3 toward Fairfield and the Essex County Airport. John's usual routine was to stop in at Jack's Friendly Service and Sunoco Station across from the Essex County Airport some time between 5 P.M. and 7 P.M. But Mesfin Gebreegziabher, who was manning the cash register Friday, noticed that it was already 8:15 when John arrived after dropping Lauren off at the airport. His sister-in-law used the time to freshen up in the airport rest room.

At about the same time, the man who had sold him the Piper Saratoga, furniture manufacturer Munir Hussain, landed at Essex after a harrowing flight from Long Island. Not only was visibility not five to ten miles, as the FAA had been insisting, but fog and pollution had combined to create a strange, opaque haze that made flying treacherous.

Taxiing in, Hussain saw Kennedy's plane being gassed up by airport operations worker Ricardo Richards. "Is John going to fly?" Hussain asked.

"Yes," Richards answered.

"Well, the visibility is bad, very bad." Hussain searched for John but couldn't find him. "If only I'd seen him," he would later say, "I would have told him, 'Don't go up.' "

Hussain was not alone. Two hours before, charter pilot Robert Hine landed his King Air 90 Twin-Turbo Prop at Essex County Airport. As he approached, the plane ahead of him tried to land but told air traffic controllers he had "lost" the runway in the haze. Instead, the plane had to abort its landing, swing around and try again. Once safely down himself, Hine had to talk a student pilot out of taking a lesson that night.

While Munir Hussain looked in vain for his friend, Mesfin Gebreegziabher watched John, wearing white pants and a white T-shirt, pull up alone and struggle to get out of his car using a single crutch. "He took a long look up at the sky," Gebreegziabher said, "and seemed to take a deep breath."

Although the sun was setting rapidly, John took his time chatting with Gebreegziabher and others in the store. He bought the usual— one banana and a bottle of Evian—and this time tossed in a six-pack of Duracell AA batteries. "How is your leg?" Gebreegziabher asked.

"I just got the cast off yesterday," John answered, "but it's feeling a lot better." In characteristically high spirits, John cheerfully obliged when another customer nervously asked for his autograph. On the way out, he paused at a newsrack to check out the headlines in the New York Post and the New York Daily News.

"Have a good flight," Gebreegziabher said as his most famous customer made his way out the door.

John turned and looked him square in the face. "I'll be fine," he said, waving goodbye. "I'll be fine."

But even getting back into the Hyundai with his injured leg appeared be daunting for John. "How he drove the car with his foot in that condition," Gebreegziabher said, "I don't know."

Kyle Bailey watched as Kennedy drove up, got out of his "little white car," and hobbled toward his red-and-white-striped Piper Saratoga waiting in the hangar. The plane's registration number, N92539A, was painted in large white letters along the fuselage. John was in the process of transferring the registration number of his old Cessna to the new plane. That number—N529JK—was a reference to his father's May 29 birthday.

Ten minutes later Carolyn, dressed in a black blouse and black pants, emerged from her Lincoln Town Car. Lauren, clad in the same taupe dress she had worn all day at her Morgan Stanley office, walked up and greeted her sister with a kiss. Then, slinging their garment bags over their shoulders, the two striking young women strode purposefully toward the hangar. Once there, they helped John load their luggage—including a one-man kayak and his single crutch—into the plane's small cargo hold. While John and his passengers struggled with their bags, two teenage girls spotted them and, according to Kyle Bailey, "started squealing, 'Look, it's John F. Kennedy! Wow!' "

Airport personnel and other pilots had become accustomed to seeing the couple standing on the tarmac, immersed in conversation. In fact, over the past year John had become a fixture at Essex County Airport, hanging around the small terminal with other weekend aviators trading flying stories. "We were all just used to him being there," said Larry Lorenzo, owner of the Caldwell Flight Academy. "You'd see him in his torn sweats and a baseball cap turned backwards, laughing and kidding around with the guys."

Kyle Bailey, who was still weighing whether or not to fly to Martha's Vineyard himself, watched as John went through his flight check in preparation for takeoff. The Piper had sixty-four gallons of fuel—more than enough to make the trip to and from Martha's Vineyard.

As earnest as John clearly was, it seemed to Bailey and others at the airport that Kennedy "was not always as careful as he might have been. He'd been careless in the past." More than once he had been asked to move his plane because he had parked it with the tail actually sticking out onto the runway.

Bailey had checked the same official weather reports that night but was skeptical about the accuracy of the automated observation systems. "There have been times when the official reading was clear," Bailey said, "and the fog was so thick you could barely see your hand in front of your face." So Bailey conducted a test of his own: He picked out a fixed point on the horizon—a ridge he knew he should be able to make out in the distance. "But I couldn't see it at all," he said. "There was this really strange, thick haze—heavy but sort of shimmering at the same time. I don't think I'd seen anything quite like it before. It was already getting dark, and the wind was picking up quite a bit. So I decided it wasn't worth the risk."

Only two weeks before, John Perry Barlow had warned his friend of this very danger. "John was perpetually late—and that meant he would take chances to get to the next appointment, the next destination. He was not an obsessive risk taker, but he had a sense of his own charmed ability to sort of skate the edge," Barlow added. "He loved skating the edge. So I said to him, 'You have confidence in the air, which could harm you. You're going to find yourself flying in instrument conditions because you think you can. Make me a promise: If you can't see the horizon, don't go for it.' He promised me he wouldn't."

For the most part, John impressed his fellow pilots as being cautious, thorough, and not one to take unnecessary chances. "He was such a conscientious guy," said Harold Anderson, a charter pilot operating out of Essex County Airport. Only two months before, John had taken off with Carolyn for Martha's Vineyard when he discovered an electrical problem aboard his Cessna and turned the plane around. Instead, he chartered Anderson's plane for the trip. On at least three other occasions, Anderson recalled, John had scrapped plans to fly to New England because of bad weather.

This time, however, John was determined to make the trip on his own. The giggling teenage girls watched as he gunned his engine to near-earsplitting levels—a routine instrument check procedure that is normally done at the end of the runway, since the propeller and whatever debris it might kick up pose an obvious hazard. "It struck me as really odd that he was gunning his engines like that right there in his parking spot next to the hangar," Bailey said. "You just don't do that, unless maybe there's something wrong with the plane. That's what I thought at the time: Maybe there's something wrong with the plane."

But John stopped revving up his engines after a few seconds, and Bailey walked back toward his car to leave. With John alone in the cockpit, Carolyn and Lauren belted themselves side by side into the luxurious tan leather seats. They faced forward, with two rear-facing seats opposite. Once everyone was settled, the Piper Saratoga rolled out onto the runway.

"John Kennedy is going to kill himself in that airplane," Bailey had told his parents a few weeks earlier. "The Piper Saratoga is a faster, more complex plane than he was used to. Sometimes I got the feeling that he didn't fully appreciate that. In some ways, he was like a little kid playing with a shiny new toy."

Doubts about John's seriousness aside, Bailey still had no reason to believe that Kennedy was taking any undue risk that particular night. Bailey hadn't actually seen Kennedy's flight instructor on the plane this time, but he knew John had never taken off in the new plane without an instrument-trained co-pilot on board. Otherwise, Bailey said, "it was a suicide mission."

As he walked toward his car, something made Kyle Bailey turn around. "It was so spooky," he later recalls, "but I watched as they taxied into position and waited to be cleared for takeoff." Lauren was on the opposite side of the plane and not visible to Bailey, but he could clearly see John and Carolyn in profile as the plane idled on the runway. "It was hazy but their silhouettes were so clear. I was struck at the time by how ethereal it looked, how eerie."

John was not required to file a flight plan, but he did inform the control tower that he intended to fly north to Teterboro, New Jersey, then east in the direction of the Vineyard. At 8:38 P.M.—twelve minutes after sundown—the tower cleared John for takeoff.

John advanced the throttle, and the plane rolled down runway 22.

Within seconds the wheels lifted off the tarmac and John's Piper Saratoga sailed smoothly into the twilight sky—heading south at first, over a golf course, then banking right to make a gentle turn toward the northeast. "North of Teterboro," he told the tower in his only radio communication that night. "Eastward . . ."

Bailey was impressed by the Piper Saratoga's graceful takeoff—apparently John's ankle wasn't giving him so much trouble that he couldn't operate the plane's foot pedals. "If he got into a spin, he'd need enough strength in that foot to get out of it," Bailey thought to himself. But that was scarcely likely to happen with a flight instructor on board.

As the plane soared eastward at about ninety knots (104 miles per hour), the engine noise was deafening. But inside the cabin, all three wore earphones that enabled them to chat. Where Lauren and Carolyn sat, there were adjustable reading lights and a small collapsible table where they spread out their magazines.

The Piper crossed over the Hudson and toward Long Island Sound as it climbed to its cruising altitude of fifty-six hundred feet. Suddenly, an air traffic controller on Long Island noticed that the small plane was coming uncomfortably close to an American Airlines passenger jet. Since John had not filed a flight plan, there was no way of knowing who he was, where he was from, and where he was headed.

The controller scrambled to alert the airliner's crew. Given the thick haze they were flying in, the American Airlines pilot was startled to see the Piper Saratoga off the end of his right wing. Promptly but smoothly, so as not to alarm his passengers, the American Airlines pilot altered his course to avert a midair collision.

John was clearly unaware of his proximity to the airliner. Oblivious to the narrowly missed catastrophe, he proceeded east. Hugging the coast, he could make out Greenwich, Bridgeport, New Haven, and New London—a shimmering necklace of lights strung along the Connecticut shoreline—off his left wingtip.

But forty minutes after takeoff, the haze had grown so thick John could make out nothing—not the stars or the sliver of moon that was out that night, not the reassuring string of lights along the coastline. Had he fully appreciated his new plane's capabilities, at this point John could have put the Piper Saratoga on automatic pilot and it

would have guided him straight to his destination. In fact, the autopilot could have flown the entire route from New Jersey and even
brought the plane in for a perfect three-point landing at Martha's
Vineyard Airport. But apparently no one had told him about this feature of the Piper Saratoga, or how to use it.

It was roughly at this stage of the flight that Dr. Bob Arnot, traveling with his young nephew, faced the same conditions only twenty
minutes ahead of Kennedy. "When I looked down at Martha's Vineyard," Arnot said, "I could not see it. I saw nothing. It's as if somebody put you in a closet and shut the door." In fact, Arnot wondered
if the Vineyard might have suffered a power failure. "There was no
horizon and no light," he recalled. "The night could best be
described as inky black.

"At the time I was perplexed," Arnot conceded. "I simply could
not explain why the visibility appeared so poor in what were supposed to be good VFR [visual flight rules] conditions." Arnot
switched to instrument flight rules (IFR) and landed safely at Nantucket. "I haven't been in conditions like that for years," Arnot said,
adding that he had five thousand hours in the air—compared to
John's three hundred hours—"and I had a problem."

Incredibly, all John Kennedy had to do was push two buttons to
turn on the autopilot. Instead, at 9:24 P.M—forty-six minutes into his
flight—Kennedy's plane passed Westerly, Rhode Island. Squinting
into the night, he tried but failed to make out Westerly's lights to the
left. Casting his gaze to the right, he searched for another reassuring
landmark, the tomahawk-shaped outline of Block Island. Nothing.

Normal procedure for pilots operating under visual flight rules
would have been to turn left at Point Judith and keep hugging the
coastline another thirty miles to Buzzard's Bay, then make a sharp
right turn and fly south to the Vineyard. That path would take them
out over eight miles of water.

But at this critical point, John decided to maintain his heading.
Instead of turning northeast and clinging to the coast, he would proceed straight ahead toward Martha's Vineyard—and across thirty-five
miles of open ocean. "Out there there are no visual reference points,
nothing at all to tell you where you are," said pilot Tom Freeman.
"Just this vast, black space. It can be very scary, and totally disorient-

ing. It's a route I wouldn't fly." And at the most, this shortcut over water would take Kennedy six minutes.

Without radioing anyone for assistance or—as many other pilots were doing that night—asking for permission to land at alternate airports inland, John pressed on. With no visual clues and only a cursory knowledge of the instruments before him, John's first instinct was to try and drop below the haze. So at 9:34 P.M., with the airspeed indicator at the upper left of his panel showing 150 knots (173 miles per hour), he began a faster-than-normal descent of seven hundred feet per minute before leveling off at twenty-three hundred feet. At last out of the haze, John was within sight of the familiar Gay Head Lighthouse—and the sprawling beachfront estate Jackie had left her children.

Whatever relief he may have felt soon evaporated. After five minutes, Kennedy and his passengers were again engulfed in a blinding haze. John had never flown alone in conditions quite like this before; it was as if the Piper Saratoga's windows had all been painted white. He remembered what he had been taught in flight school about spatial disorientation—how, without visual cues, the brain can be tricked into thinking up is down and down is up. But knowing about vertigo and experiencing it are two different things, and he was rapidly becoming confused.

John's head was swimming. Glancing back and forth between the control panel and the whiteout outside, he tried desperately to reconcile what his body seemed to be saying with the dials and indicators in front of him. A quick glance at the turn-and-bank indicator in the lower left-hand corner of the instrument panel would have shown that the red ball was not centered and, contrary to what his senses were telling him, the tiny white wings indicating the position of the wings were not level. The off-kilter reading on the directional gyro in the lower center of the panel would have also contradicted what he was feeling. At this point, John abruptly turned right and—presumably to get above a bank of haze—went back up three hundred feet.

"John, John, what's going on?" His passengers' concern by now would have turned to mounting panic—another thing JFK Jr. was ill-equipped to handle. During the instrument flight training he had not yet received, an instructor tries to distract his student with noise or any other way he can, all by way of teaching fledgling pilots to concentrate on handling an emergency. "They try and rattle you any way they can," explained fellow pilot Kyle Bailey. "Without warning, they'll yell, or grab you or pop a paper bag. They train you to have nerves of steel and screen out any and all distractions if you're trying to handle an emergency."

Pilot Tom Freeman put his training to the test when he lost an engine flying over the Caribbean. "My girlfriend and a friend of hers were flying with me," Freeman recalled. "Suddenly I was trying to bring us in and they were screaming, crying, pulling at me. It was pandemonium, but you have to be able to focus one hundred percent on your situation—*you have to*—or else."

At twenty-six hundred feet, with Martha's Vineyard Airport twenty miles straight ahead of him, John somehow managed to hold steady for about a minute. But he was not sure precisely where he was or where he was going. Uncertain of his bearings, at twenty seconds past 9:40 John turned right again. Then he began to descend. A quick check of the vertical speed gauge in the lower right of the panel showed that at twenty-two hundred feet the Piper Saratoga began picking up speed. Within seconds, it was hurtling toward the sea at a rate of five thousand feet per minute—ten times the normal speed.

"In a situation like that your body is playing all sorts of tricks on you," veteran military pilot Edward Francis explained. "You can be upside down and turning to the left and your body is telling you you're right side up and turning right."

Watching his wildly unwinding altimeter in the upper right-hand corner of the control panel, John's first instinct was to yank back on the yoke in an effort to slow the plane down and regain altitude. "But," explained Francis, "that is the worst thing you can do. *Before* you do anything else, you must get your wings level and straighten out the plane—*then* you pull up the nose."

But John did what most inexperienced aviators do and pulled up hard without first straightening his wings. The plane began turning clockwise like a corkscrew—rapidly accelerating into what aviators call a "graveyard spiral."

Even as the Piper Saratoga started to drop from the sky, there remained one slender hope. John might yet regain control of the plane. It had been done before. "If you believe what your instruments are telling you and focus on getting your wings level," Francis said, "you can recover—even at the last minute. But the degree of concentration it requires is *total*."

The plane spun wildly out of control now, turning and turning and turning in an ever-tightening spiral toward the surface of the Atlantic. Inside the cabin, John, Carolyn, and Lauren were riveted to their seats, their faces contorted by the G-forces pressing mercilessly against them. For fifteen seconds, they could hear the shrill, terrifying sound of the wind shrieking past the windows as they plummeted toward the unforgiving surface of the ocean at ninety-nine feet per second. . . .

It was clear that John was the light of his life.

—John's uncle Jamie
Auchincloss on JFK

It's hard to talk about a legacy or a mystique. It's my family. It's my mother. It's my sister. It's my father. We're a family like any other. We look out for one another. The fact that there have been difficulties and hardships, or obstacles, makes us closer.

—John

Now my wife and I prepare for a new administration, and a new baby.

—JFK's victory speech,
November 9, 1960

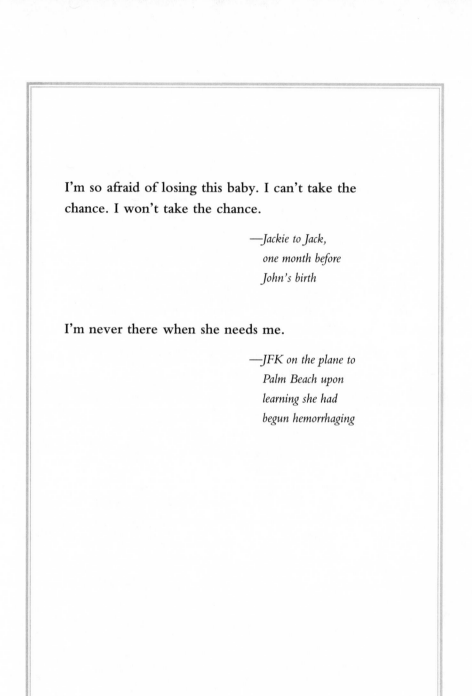

I'm so afraid of losing this baby. I can't take the chance. I won't take the chance.

> —*Jackie to Jack,*
> *one month before*
> *John's birth*

I'm never there when she needs me.

> —*JFK on the plane to*
> *Palm Beach upon*
> *learning she had*
> *begun hemorrhaging*

2
=

November 9, 1960

Okay, girls," Jack Kennedy said to Jackie and her equally pregnant friend Tony Bradlee the day after the presidential election. "You can take out the pillows now. We won."

Now that the election was over, Jackie prayed that her husband
might finally spend time with her and their daughter, Caroline. After
all, in the closing weeks of the campaign Jackie had—against doctor's
orders—finally relented and joined Jack on the campaign trail in
New York. She spoke Italian to crowds in Little Italy and Spanish in
Spanish Harlem.

The blitz climaxed with a ticker-tape parade through New York's
"Canyon of Heroes," with JFK and his eight-months-pregnant wife
balancing on the back of an open car as thousands of frenzied New
Yorkers reached out to touch them. At one point, the surging crowds
rocked the limousine so violently it threatened to spill its occupants
out onto the street.

After all Jackie had endured during her pregnancies, it was inconceivable that she would take such risks. At the beginning of their
marriage, she had suffered a miscarriage that was concealed from the

public. And later, when the young Massachusetts senator sought the vice presidential nomination at the 1956 Democratic National Convention in Los Angeles, Jackie had done everything he had asked of her. When he lost back then, Kennedy ignored Jackie's fervent pleas to stay by her side and flew off instead to cruise the Mediterranean with his brother Teddy and another womanizing senator, Florida's George Smathers.

On August 23, 1956, Jackie collapsed and doctors performed an emergency cesarean section to try to save the baby. The stillborn infant, a girl, was not named. Jackie nearly lost her own life in the process. After undergoing several blood transfusions, she was listed in critical condition. A priest was called to administer the last rites of the Roman Catholic Church.

Officially, the stillbirth was blamed on "exhaustion and nervous tensions following the Democratic National Convention." But Jack was still yachting with his friends, unreachable and unaware that his wife was forced to cope with the loss of their child alone.

JFK would later prove himself to be a doting father who reveled in the company of his children. But in 1956 he was merely following the lead of his father Joseph Kennedy, who was not present for the births of any of his nine children. Freewheeling Jack had never wanted to be a husband, much less a father, and like many men would only discover the joys of fatherhood once he had children of his own.

On November 27, 1957—the day before Thanksgiving—Jackie gave birth to a seven-pound-two-ounce girl at New York's Lying-In Hospital, Cornell University Medical Center. When the anesthesia wore off and Jackie came to, it was Jack who brought the baby to her. It was the first time Jackie laid eyes on Caroline Bouvier Kennedy.

Given his heartless reaction to the loss of their stillborn daughter only fourteen months earlier, Jackie was surprised by how naturally Jack took to fatherhood. Janet Auchincloss, Jackie's mother, was impressed by "the sheer, unadulterated delight he took in Caroline from that first day on. The look on his face, which I had never seen before, really, was . . . radiant."

Caroline was only eleven days old and still at the hospital when

British nanny Maud Shaw began caring for her. "He really loved Caroline," Shaw said of JFK. "And when he came into the house he always came straight upstairs to the nursery. That child always smiled for him when she never did for anybody else. Right from the very beginning he loved her and she adored him."

Yet by the time he became his party's standard-bearer, Jack had forgotten the lessons of the past. He had risked the health of his wife and their unborn child for votes, and, to her credit, Jackie had delivered. In an election that was decided by 118,550 votes—fewer than one-fifth of 1 percent—Jack's charming, glamorous wife may well have been a deciding factor.

Jackie was determined not to take any more chances now that the election was won. Just three weeks from her due date, she was under strict orders from her obstetrician, Dr. John Walsh, not to leave their red-brick Federal town house at 3307 N Street in Georgetown. Immediately after sharing a quiet Thanksgiving dinner there with Jackie and Caroline, Jack planned to fly to the Kennedys' winter compound in Palm Beach, Florida, to discuss cabinet choices with his father.

But Jackie, sensing that this delivery would not be as easy as Caroline's, begged her husband to stay by her side. He refused, leaving a wounded Jackie behind. An hour later, Maud Shaw heard a scream and rushed upstairs to find Jackie on the edge of her bed clutching her stomach. Blood stained the bedspread. An ambulance rushed her to Georgetown University Hospital.

Jack was savoring a daiquiri and cracking jokes with aides on board his campaign plane, the *Caroline*, when suddenly the news came crackling over the airwaves. "Jack was stricken with remorse," said aide Kenneth O'Donnell, "because he was not with his wife." Landing in Palm Beach, JFK commandeered the fastest plane available—the DC-6 press plane that trailed the *Caroline*—to get back to Jackie's side.

He clamped on the cockpit headphones and waited for news. Shortly before 1 A.M., November 25, 1960, Jack finally smiled for the first time in hours. He had just been informed that Jackie had given birth by cesarean section to a six-pound-three-ounce boy. When Press Secretary Pierre Salinger announced the birth of John Fitzgerald Kennedy over the plane's loudspeaker, the reporters cheered. JFK, assured by doctors that mother and son were doing fine, lit a Panatella and took a deep bow.

Notwithstanding the glowing reports issued to the press, Jackie and the baby remained in guarded condition. Once she came out from under the anesthesia, Jackie, still in considerable pain, demanded to see her son.

She was allowed to see John, but *only* see him. The baby spent his first six days of life in an incubator. His mother would take months to fully recover from the ordeal, and both would suffer a near-fatal setback along the way.

Making matters worse was the press, which now turned its full attention to Jackie and her beautiful children. "I feel as though I've turned into a piece of public property," Jackie said. "It's really frightening to lose your anonymity at thirty-one."

Even as the Kennedy family's private nurse, Luella Hennessey, wheeled Jackie in to see her son in his incubator, a photographer leapt out of a storage closest and began shooting. A half-dozen flashbulbs popped before Secret Service agents, caught completely off guard, finally wrestled the man to the ground and ripped the film out of his camera.

Jack, meanwhile, was determined to make up for earlier absences. As soon as his plane touched down, he rushed to Jackie's third-floor hospital suite and then dropped by the nursery to see his son. "Now that's the most beautiful boy I've seen. Maybe," he joked, "I'll name him Abraham Lincoln."

Determined to prove to Jackie that he was there for her, he visited her and the baby three times a day—in the morning, at lunch, and again after dinner. "The atmosphere was buoyant and joyous, almost carnival-like," recalled *Life* magazine reporter Gail Wescott of the scene at Georgetown Hospital. "Security was minimal and President-Elect Kennedy would wave from his wife's hospital room and then stop and talk with us all when he came downstairs. Back on N Street, we took marvelous pictures of him wheeling Caroline in her stroller. It was innocent and exhilarating. It did not seem that anything could ever go wrong."

It was a particularly happy time for Caroline, whose baby brother had arrived on November 25—just two days before her third birthday. John was presented to the little girl "as a birthday present," Maud Shaw said. "Caroline thought for a long time after that he *belonged* to her."

When John was a week old, Jack and Caroline arrived at the hospital for the baby's christening. As Jack wheeled mother and baby toward the hospital chapel, they spotted press photographers lying in wait at the far end of the hall. "Oh God," Jackie said. "Don't stop, Jack. Just keep going." But Jack was not so willing to disappoint the press, or the American people. He paused for a moment, allowing a few photos to be taken of the infant wearing his father's forty-three-year-old baptismal gown before they moved on.

Later, as they left the chapel, Jackie looked down at her son and said, "Look at those pretty eyes. Isn't he sweet?" JFK, preoccupied with cabinet appointments, nodded halfheartedly.

The diametric opposite of Jackie—with the exception of a similarly steely will—the incumbent First Lady was more dowager than empress. Now that she was about to decamp after eight years, Mamie Eisenhower had graciously offered to give her successor a tour of the White House—on the day Jackie was to be released from the hospital. "I don't want to go, Jack," she told her husband. "I'm not up to it." But JFK insisted, and Jackie did not want to disappoint him.

White House chief usher J. B. West was impressed with how pale and drawn Mrs. Kennedy looked when she arrived at 11:30 that morning. For the next two hours Jackie and Mamie schlepped through every room in the White House. Jackie nearly passed out several times, but managed to steady herself. Her hostess showed no sign of concern as they marched up and down staircases and later posed together for photographers.

A few days later, after Jackie's exhausting White House tour, the *Caroline* departed for Palm Beach with the president-elect's family aboard. While Jack held forth with his advisors, a cloud of cigar smoke enveloped John's bassinet.

A chain-smoker herself, Jackie had puffed on cigarettes through-out all of her pregnancies despite Dr. Walsh's repeated warnings. Determined to hide her habit from public view, she had actually encouraged Jack's cigar smoking to mask the smell of her own ciga-rettes. This time, however, she ordered JFK and his cronies to take their cigars to the other end of the cabin.

Still feeling the effects of her long march with Mamie Eisenhower through the corridors of the Executive Mansion, Jackie spent the next two weeks bedridden inside Joseph P. Kennedy's Palm Beach mansion. At the same time, her son John took a dramatic turn for the worse. "John's health really wasn't doing so well," she later said. "There was, thank God, this brilliant pediatrician in Palm Beach who really saved his life, as he was going downhill." In fact, John was being treated for an inflammation of the lung's hyaline membrane, a mild form of the respiratory problem that would later kill his infant brother, Patrick.

"It was kept quiet," said JFK's physician, Dr. Janet Travell, "but Jackie came perilously close to dying after John Jr.'s birth—and so did the baby. Jackie was very emotional about losing her son—it was the thing she feared more than losing her own life."

Just forty-eight hours after the "brilliant" Palm Beach pediatrician pulled John back from the brink of death, Richard P. Pavlick was parked outside the Kennedys' Palm Beach estate waiting for the president-elect to emerge and head for Sunday mass at St. Edward's Church. Pavlick, a would-be suicide bomber armed with seven sticks of dynamite in his car, planned to crash into JFK's car as he left the house.

But before Pavlick could step on the accelerator, Jackie and three-year-old Caroline came out to say goodbye. Luella Hennessey also appeared, carrying John Jr. Touched, Pavlick did not go through with his grisly plan. Later claiming to police that he "did not wish to harm Mrs. Kennedy or the children," Pavlick said he decided instead to "get" Jack "at the church or some other place." A few days later a drunk-driving arrest led police to uncover his assassination scheme.

Pavlick was charged with attempted murder and eventually sent to prison.

Jackie was horrified. "We're nothing but sitting ducks," she said, "in a shooting gallery." But Jack could not afford the luxury of worrying. With just a month to go before taking office, he was busy putting together the pieces of a new administration. During the campaign, Jackie often felt overwhelmed by the hordes of political operatives and back-room cronies who swirled around her husband at all hours of the day and night. Still convalescing and with two small children to watch over, Jackie found the conditions in Palm Beach equally intolerable.

"It was so crowded that I could be in the bathroom, in the tub," she said, "and then find that Pierre Salinger was holding a press conference in my bedroom."

To add to the confusion, Caroline kept upstaging her father at press conferences. At one point she careened between reporters' legs on her tricycle; at another she hobbled around in her pajamas and Mommy's size ten and a half stiletto heels.

Since Jackie, like millions of other women in the 1960s, did not even consider breast-feeding her children, it was left to Luella Hennessey to prepare the formula, change diapers, and get up in the middle of the night to rock John back to sleep.

John's mother, meanwhile, lay motionless and alone in her darkened bedroom. "I couldn't hold food down," she later said. "I guess I was just in physical and nervous exhaustion because the month after the baby's birth had been the opposite of recuperation."

Before fleeing to Palm Beach, Jackie had hired her old friend Letitia Baldrige, who was then working as publicity director for Tiffany's, to be her social secretary. After the tour with Mamie, Jackie told Tish that the White House looked like "a Statler Hotel that had been decorated by a wholesale furniture store during a January clearance." She told another friend, "It's the worst place in the world. So cold and dreary. I've never seen anything like it . . . I can't bear the thought of moving in. I hate it, hate it, hate it."

Jackie was still weak, but determined to put her stamp on the White House when she returned to Georgetown on January 14, days before the inauguration. Caroline and her baby brother remained behind in Palm Beach with their father, Maud Shaw, and Elsie Philips, the new nanny hired to take care of John Jr. Given the questionable state of her health, Jackie explained to Jack that there was no way she could help the children settle into their new home and unpack at the same time.

At precisely noon on January 20, 1961, Jackie, seemingly impervious to the bone-chilling twenty-degree temperature, gazed at Jack in practiced wonder as he took the oath of office from Chief Justice Earl Warren. At that moment, forty-three-year-old Jack became the youngest elected president in U.S. history, succeeding the oldest, seventy-year-old Ike. Jack was also the first president born in the twentieth century and the first Roman Catholic to hold the office.

Jack's inaugural address, with its enduring "Ask not what your country can do for you" message, stirred the nation. But Jackie had no opportunity to congratulate her husband on the dais. He did not follow tradition by kissing his wife immediately after taking the oath. And as soon as Marian Anderson ended the ceremonies with a rousing rendition of the national anthem, he bounded up the red-carpeted stairs and off the platform—inexplicably leaving Jackie behind.

Despite the arctic conditions, the new President and his First Lady led off the inaugural parade, riding in an open car from the Capitol to the White House. After an hour on the reviewing stand, Jackie—tired, freezing, and facing a long night ahead—excused herself. "I'm exhausted, Jack," she said. "I'll see you at home."

"Home" for the Kennedys was now 1600 Pennsylvania Avenue. While painters and carpenters put the finishing touches on John's second-floor nursery and a newly renovated family dining room, Jackie moved into the Queen's Room (so called because five queens had slept there). Jack, meanwhile, would sleep across the East Hall in the Lincoln Bedroom.

That evening, the dashing young President and his glamorous wife arrived at the first of five scheduled inaugural balls. Jackie was radiant, but by midnight she had begun to wilt. "I just crumpled," she later said. "All of my strength was finally gone." She made her apologies, and told Jack to go on to the two remaining inaugural balls.

Her inexhaustible spouse did not have to be told. The President soon hooked up with his friend Paul "Red" Fay and Fay's date, the striking blond actress Angie Dickinson. But when Fay asked if his other friend Kim Novak could join the party, Jack suddenly had a change of heart.

"I can just see the papers tomorrow," Jack told his old World War II buddy. "The new President concludes his first day speeding into the night with Kim Novak and Angie Dickinson while his wife recuperates from the birth of their first son."

Ironically, Jackie was suffering guilt pangs of her own—doubts that also sprang from John's difficult birth. "I always wished I could have participated more in those first shining hours with Jack," she said. "But at least I thought I had given him our John, the son he had longed for so much . . ."

After the inauguration, John and Caroline were at last allowed to join their parents at the White House. Jackie quickly became alarmed by the baby's inability to gain weight and his constant crying. She turned to Maud Shaw, who doubled the amount of formula he was getting and switched his morning meal of beef extract to lunchtime. By the time John was four months old, John's nanny was happy to report that he was no longer crying and that he had developed a healthy appetite for soup, cereals, fruit, and strained meats and vegetables.

"It isn't fair to children in the limelight," Jackie said, "to leave them to the care of others and then expect that they will turn out all right. They need their mother's affection and guidance and long periods of time alone with her. That is what gives them security in an often confusing world."

Perhaps. But to children of privilege like Jacqueline Lee Bouvier and John Fitzgerald Kennedy—neither of whom had hands-on mothers—nannies were an indispensable part of family life. Diaper-changing and bottle-feeding, Jack and Jackie agreed, were tasks best left to the professionals.

Even before her husband took office, Jackie's overriding priority was the children. In fact, their toys were the first things to arrive, secretly smuggled into the White House in boxes two weeks before the official transfer of power. "Oh, good," Jackie said when told Chief Usher J. B. West had hidden them in his closet, out of sight. "We'll bring them out as soon as the children's rooms are ready."

Before Jackie set out to transform the public rooms of the White House, the upstairs living quarters were the first to undergo a dramatic change. Opposite the Yellow Oval Room, with its doors opening onto the Truman Balcony, were the children's rooms. Jackie erased any trace of the hotel-modern decor favored by the Eisenhowers.

John's spacious nursery was white with blue crown molding. Caroline's room was done in pink and white, with matching rosebud linens and drapes, a white canopy bed, rocking horses, stuffed animals, a Grandma Moses on the wall—eventually to be joined by an elaborate dollhouse from Charles de Gaulle.

Between the children's rooms was a small room strategically occupied by their nanny. "Maud Shaw won't need much," Jackie wrote to J. B. West. "Just find a wicker wastebasket for her banana peels and a little table for her false teeth at night."

Within three months Jackie had accomplished all she wanted in the family living quarters. "She turned this drafty, cold old place," Tish Baldrige said, "into a warm environment for a young family overnight."

Just as quickly, the family settled into a routine that would vary little whenever they were in residence over the next thousand days. The President and the First Lady almost never saw each other in the morning. "That time," Baldrige said, "was the children's time."

Usually up by 8 A.M., Jack devoured a huge breakfast before poring over the morning papers and urgent cables in the tub. Maud Shaw then brought the children in to say good morning. After they kissed Daddy, Caroline turned on the television and sat on the floor watching cartoons. Jack LaLanne came on at 9 A.M., and the President laughed and clapped as Caroline, and later John, imitated LaLanne's exercise routine.

When he was dressed and ready, Caroline walked her father hand in hand to the Oval Office. Then she went off to the school Jackie had set up on the third floor for Caroline and the sixteen or so children of several White House staffers and a few close friends.

On the way to school, Caroline (and, when he was old enough to walk, John) dropped in on Mommy. Depending on how late she had stayed up the night before, Jackie ate breakfast on a tray in her room anytime between 8 A.M. and noon.

After giving dictation to her secretary, Mary Gallagher, Jackie took a brisk, hour-long walk alone around the White House grounds. Then she joined Caroline and John in what they called the "High Chair Room" while they ate lunch—usually a hamburger or hot dog served on a silver tray by a butler. At some point in the afternoon, Jackie made a point of pushing John's baby carriage, and later his stroller, up and down the circular drive.

John and Caroline were usually joined by their mother again when the children had dinner, though in the White House Jackie rarely ate with them. Instead, after drinks in the Yellow Oval Room, the President and First Lady usually dined upstairs with a small circle of close friends—but not before Maud Shaw brought the children in to say good night to their parents.

Frequently, the Kennedys' after-dinner ritual included the screening of a new Hollywood film. Not long after JFK's assassination, Caroline's religion teacher, Sister Joanne Frey, asked her students to put their heads on the table and think about Jesus. After a few minutes she asked the children what this little exercise made them think of.

Caroline raised her hand. "It made me think of how my mommy always watched cowboy movies with my daddy," she said, "because my daddy always liked cowboy movies. My mommy doesn't like cowboy movies *at all,* but she watched them because she loved my daddy."

During their early years, John and Caroline would witness very few overt signs of affection between their mother and father—a logical outgrowth of the First Couple's own upbringing. The marriage of Jackie's parents had ended in acrimonious divorce, and the chill between Joe and Rose Kennedy was palpable. And while Jackie adored her playboy father, Black Jack Bouvier, the lack of physical contact between the senior Kennedys and their children left Jack with a lifelong dislike of being touched in a nonsexual way.

Still, Jack and Jackie grew up in an era when egregious displays of affection were frowned upon—particularly among wealthy northeasterners who had been raised by nannies and then shipped off at an early age to boarding school. "Maybe they weren't always madly 'at' one another," Tish Baldrige allowed, "but there were plenty of tender moments when I'd catch him putting his arm around her waist, or she'd lean her head on his shoulder." At night in his room when his back was keeping him awake, a barefoot Jackie would brave the cold floor to put on the cast album of Lerner and Loewe's *Camelot*.

"Jack and Jackie had a very close, very romantic relationship," insisted Jackie's stepbrother, Hugh "Yusha" Auchincloss. "They enjoyed each other. They had *fun* . . . And that's what John grew up with. He was born into a house filled with love and fun and laughter, just like millions of other children."

Perhaps, but not *just* like millions of other children . . .

John was Lark. Caroline was Lyric. And their parents were Lancer and Lace. These Secret Service code names notwithstanding, Jackie worried less about their being harmed than the possibility that they might be emotionally scarred, robbed of their childhood. "I want my children to be brought up in more personal surroundings, not in the state rooms," Jackie insisted. "And I don't want them to be raised by nurses and Secret Service agents."

So, in addition to the school she set up in the third-floor solarium, Jackie designed a play area for John and Caroline just outside the President's Oval Office window. White House carpenters followed the First Lady's sketches precisely, installing a barrel tunnel, a slide, a leather swing, a rabbit hutch, a trampoline surrounded by trees ("All they'll be able to see is my head, sailing above the treetops," Jackie remarked), and, mounted inside the branches of Herbert Hoover's favorite white oak, a tree house with a slide.

"The slide comes down just exactly right," Jackie told J. B. West. "In fact, Caroline wants to push her baby brother down, carriage and all." In fact, John's earliest childhood memory was of watching a family pet make the trip down the slide.

"We had a dog who was named Pushinka, who was given to my father by a Soviet official," John later recalled. "And we trained that dog to slide down the slide we had in the back of the White House. Sliding the dog down that slide is probably my first memory."

Pushinka was just one of a dozen or more pets the Kennedy children juggled at any one time. They arrived at the White House with just one dog, their Welsh terrier, Charlie, but soon Pushinka joined the White House menagerie. Then came Wolf, an aptly named Irish wolfhound that was a gift from a priest in Dublin. Joe Kennedy then gave his favorite daughter-in-law a German shepherd, Clipper. "Get those damn dogs out of here" was the severely allergic president's usual reaction when he encountered them—although his allergy to cats was far more severe. Tom Kitten, Caroline's cat, eventually had to be given away.

Jackie built a stable for the most famous Kennedy pet of all, Caroline's pony, Macaroni. The First Lady, an accomplished equestrienne, also kept a pony named Leprechaun for John—until it became apparent that the boy, though not allergic to dogs, was in fact allergic to horses.

There were also pens on the White House grounds for the lambs, ducks, guinea pigs, and Zsa Zsa, the family's beer-drinking rabbit. Marybell and Bluebell, the children's hamsters, took up residence in Caroline's room along with her favorite pet, a canary named Robin.

"Jackie realized from the beginning," Tish Baldrige said, "that it was going to take more than toys and pets to give John and Caroline something remotely approaching a normal childhood. She did not want her children growing up in a fishbowl."

Fiercely protective of her children's privacy, Jackie ordered that trees and shrubs be planted at various strategic spots around the White House to foil gawkers. When Jack objected that the American people had the right to see the White House ("For God's sake, *they* paid for it, Jackie"), she backed down a bit.

"They're entitled to *some* view of the White House," Jackie conceded. "But I'm sick and tired of starring in everyone's home movies!" This became a familiar refrain. "I can't bear all those people peering over the fence," she complained. "I may abdicate."

As far as press coverage of John and Caroline was concerned, photo spreads in *Life* and *Look* magazines were fine—so long as she controlled the access and the circumstances. In the coming months, the public was treated to heartwarming shots of Caroline riding her pony, Macaroni, and sitting in a horse cart with her mother at bucolic Glen Ora, the family's rented getaway in the Virginia hills; Caroline and John dancing a jig in the Oval Office while their beaming daddy clapped; the kids showing off their Halloween costumes to delighted White House staffers. On Halloween night 1962, Arthur Schlesinger opened the door of his Georgetown home to find several goblins hopping up and down. "After a moment a masked mother in the background called out that it was time to go to their next house," Schlesinger said. The voice was unmistakably Jackie's. With the Secret Service lurking in the shadows, she was escorting John, Caroline, and their cousins on their trick-or-treat rounds.

Controlled glimpses into the lives of the First Family were one thing. Unauthorized shots by overzealous photographers were quite another. "Mrs. Kennedy," *Look* photographer Stanley Tretick said, "had a way that sort of strikes terror to your heart. She was a very strong-minded girl and very tough."

Tretick found out firsthand when he showed up at the Kennedy clan's annual Fourth of July celebration at Hyannis Port in 1961. Although he was there to shoot pictures for a story on the Shrivers, Tretick, who had been warned not to take any photos of Caroline playing with her cousins, could not resist. *Look* held off on publishing them for a year, hoping to get a nod of approval that never came.

When *Look* finally did use the photos, "Kennedy got very upset because he got the heat from Jackie," Tretick said. Pierre Salinger knew all too well how fierce the lioness could become when she felt her cubs were in danger. "Jackie was just ferociously protective of their privacy," Salinger said. "From the moment she set foot in the White House she wanted to keep them out of the spotlight."

"Jackie didn't want Caroline and John to be treated like stars," Tish Baldrige said. "But of course they *were* stars. The American people just fell in love with them."

"She became very paranoid about the press," photographer Jacques Lowe said. "But Jack knew the kids were a great asset for his administration. He was proud of them. He wanted to show them off. It got to be a game between the two of them, with me stuck in the middle."

One day JFK approached Lowe and said, "Jacques, take some pictures of Caroline and give them to Ben Bradlee." Bradlee was then with *Newsweek*.

"You know I can't do that, Mr. President," he replied. "You know Jackie doesn't want any photos of Caroline running around the White House."

JFK shrugged. "Then don't tell her."

"I took the pictures, and of course when they came out in *Newsweek* Jackie got all upset. Of course, the President played totally innocent. So naturally I took the rap."

Salinger was also a victim of the presidential squeeze play. When Jackie complained to him that yet another unauthorized photograph of the children had surfaced he tried to explain that JFK had requested the photograph be taken. "I don't give a damn," Jackie replied. "He has no right to countermand my order regarding the children."

Not even the President had the courage to face his wife when the subject of the children and the press came up, so much of the sub-terfuge took place when she was out of town. "As soon as she snuck out," Tretick said, "I snuck in."

Tretick, who had photographed JFK extensively on the campaign trail, was impressed with how affectionate he was with his children—particularly his young son. "His interest in the boy was incredible. It was almost sensual. John was sitting on the floor of the Oval Office one night and the President was talking to him. And he was saying something to the President and the President was looking down and talking to him. And then he just kind of reached for him—he reached for the boy and pulled his pajama up—you know, bathrobe and pajama—and he kind of rubbed his bare skin right above his rear end. He wanted to touch him.

"And then another time when he was sitting outside with John he put him over his knee like he was going to spank him, but you could see the way he was feeling him and was having fun with him. And you know, it was a genuine thing between the two of them. The boy also sensed his father. I think it would have really grown . . ."

This growing delight JFK took in his son was apparent to every-one. In the late afternoon, he would throw open the doors to the Rose Garden, clap his hands, and they would come running.

"The children could be playing all over him and he could still be conducting a conference or writing a speech," Baldrige said. JFK would also drop in on Caroline and her classmates at the school Jackie had set up in the White House. "He would be up there to see the children constantly. He would go out on the South Lawn and play with them and talk to them and they would all troop into his office at the drop of a hat whenever he gave the signal."

Jackie did her part to make sure John and Caroline did not grow up feeling isolated from other children, no matter how formal or weighty the occasion. "We had a reception for all the cabinet members and there were children there," she said. "Every time we could . . . I always tried to have their children there. Any time you knew of someone who had someone young, you tried to have them."

"So the house was full of children morning, noon, and night," Baldrige remembers. "You never knew when an avalanche of young people would come bearing down on you—runny noses, dropped mittens in the hall, bicycles . . ."

One of the antique treasures Jackie exhumed from the White House basement as part of her ambitious restoration project yielded one of John's favorite playthings. In 1878, Queen Victoria had given President Rutherford B. Hayes a mammoth desk carved from the timbers of the British warship H.M.S. *Resolute.* Woodrow Wilson had used it, and FDR sat behind it as he delivered his famous "Fireside Chats" on the radio. Jackie had it refinished and delivered to the Oval Office.

Presidential advisers, cabinet members, and even visiting heads of state might be locked in serious conversation when they would suddenly hear a strange scratching sound emanating from inside the desk.

"Is there a rabbit in there?" the President would exclaim in mock horror. Then a hinged door would swing open and out would pop John, who would proceed to laugh and whoop as he careened around the room. John, whose hide-and-seek games with his father beneath the Oval Office desk were immortalized by Stanley Tretick and other photographers, acquired the nickname "John-John" because whenever the President called the boy's name over and over again he dropped everything and came running. To family members, however, it was always just "John."

"John-John and JFK quite simply just break each other up," Ben Bradlee observed. "Kennedy likes to laugh and likes to make people laugh, and his son is the perfect foil for him."

Presidential adviser Theodore Sorenson remembered the time John lingered at a breakfast meeting in the Oval Office. "After shaking hands and bowing all around, John took over a proffered chair and very nearly took over the meeting," Sorenson recalled. "His father's suggestions to leave, accompanied by bribes to take him to the office later, were loudly resisted. Deciding to ignore him, the President opened his request for questions with the usual, 'What have we got today?'

"The first answer was John's: 'I've got a glass of water.' "

Caroline, though by far more well behaved, also had her moments. When the president's dinner guests got off the elevator one evening, they were nearly knocked over by a stark-naked Caroline as she dashed down the corridor with an abashed Maud Shaw in hot pursuit.

Whenever they weren't at the White House or one of the Kennedy compounds, at Palm Beach or Hyannis Port, the First Family unwound at Hammersmith Farm, the Newport, Rhode Island, estate of wealthy Hugh D. Auchincloss. Jackie's mother, Janet, had married Auchincloss after divorcing Black Jack Bouvier. Jackie called her stepfather "Uncle Hughdie."

During these outings, the President loved to tell his children stories. "Stories," Schlesinger recalled, "about Caroline—he called her 'Buttons'—hunting with the Orange County hounds and winning the Grand National, and about John-John in his PT boat sinking a Japanese destroyer. He would tell them about Bobo the Lobo, a giant, and Maybelle, a little girl who hid in the woods, and the White Shark and the Black Shark. The White Shark lived off people's socks, and one day, when the President and Caroline were sailing with Franklin Roosevelt Jr. off Newport, Kennedy pretended to see the White Shark and said, 'Franklin, give him your socks, he's hungry.' Franklin promptly threw his socks into the water, which made a great impression on Caroline."

Other guests were not immune to the same request. "We all

learned that when Jack began telling Caroline about the White Shark," longtime Kennedy family confidant Lem Billings said, "it was time to move to another part of the yacht."

John's favorite game with Daddy was "Going Through the Tunnel," which usually occurred en route to the office. "President Kennedy would have to stand tall," Maud Shaw remembered, "and John would go through his legs time and time again. John never got tired of this game. I'm sure the president did."

The President also tired of John's long, European-style hairstyle, which contrasted sharply with the crew cuts and close-cropped haircuts that were popular in the early 1960s. The White House was soon flooded with letters demanding that the President's son be given a haircut; some even sent in money to pay for it.

Jackie, who favored the Little Lord Fauntleroy look, stood her ground. Finally, JFK asked Miss Shaw to at least trim John's bangs. "If anyone asks you," he said, anticipating Jackie's reaction, "tell them it was an order from the President."

John's first years of life were counterpoint to the glamour, power, sex, and crisis that characterized JFK's thousand days in office. From their first triumphant tour of Europe, when JFK introduced himself as "the man who accompanied Jacqueline Kennedy to Paris," to the sixty-six glittering state occasions over which they presided like American royalty, to a succession of crises both foreign and domestic, the President and his First Lady led frenzied—albeit exhilarating— lives.

Victims of incomprehensible public pressures and private stress, the Kennedys had found a way to cope. They, like several other notable figures of the day, turned to New York physician Max Jacobson, the infamous "Dr. Feelgood" whose amphetamine cocktails— mostly Dexedrine, injected once or twice a day—gave them the energy boost they needed. At the time, amphetamines had not yet been declared by the Food and Drug Administration to be either harmful or addictive.

Jack and Jackie remained patients of "Dr. Feelgood" throughout his presidency—and in Jackie's case, beyond. By any clinical definition, they were dependent on the medication being dispensed by

Jacobson. The President and the First Lady of the United States were, unknowingly, addicted to speed.

Much to his wife's chagrin, the injections also enabled JFK to continue pursuing other women. Following in his own father's extramarital footsteps, Kennedy cheated on Jackie with scores of other women, among them Ben Bradlee's sister-in-law Mary Pinchot Meyer, Mob moll Judith Campbell, and of course, Marilyn Monroe. While Monroe sang "Happy Birthday, Mr. *Pres-i-dent*" to Jack before thousands at Madison Square Garden, Jackie was with John and Caroline in Virginia, competing in the Loudoun Hunt horse show. Her children watched as the First Lady, determined to shield herself and her family from public humiliation, took home a third-place ribbon.

Whatever the strains between them, Mommy and Daddy made it a point never to argue in front of the children. Given their hectic schedules, they lavished affection on John and his sister whenever they could spare the time to be with them.

The President was so eager to communicate with his son that when John was only ten months old, he impatiently asked Maud Shaw, "When's John going to talk?"

"Oh, but he does talk, Mr. President. It's just that you can't understand him."

"That's right, Daddy," Caroline added, "he does talk to me."

"I guess you'd better interpret for me," JFK suggested.

After a quiet dinner upstairs at the White House, Ben Bradlee wrote in his diary, "John-John has a big thing about coming up to you and whispering a lot of gibberish in your ear. If you throw your head back and act surprised, John-John roars with laughter until he drools."

As the boy grew older, the President was not above teasing him. "So how're you doing, Sam?" he'd ask.

"I'm not Sam, I'm John."

"What was that, Sam?"

"No, no, no," John would reply again. "I'm not Sam. I'm John. John, John, JOHN!"

"Oh, sorry, Sam."

But JFK also took the time to answer his son's questions. The President would take John into the hangar where the presidential helicopter was parked and, Maud Shaw recalled, "sit for quite a few moments—just sitting patiently inside the helicopter, putting the helmet on John and showing him how things work, moving gadgets for him just like a big boy." The Commander in Chief let "Captain John" issue orders from the pilot's seat, and even pretended to obey them.

Literally from the time he could walk, John was fascinated with aircraft, helicopters in particular. At thirteen months, he took his first public steps at the Palm Beach Airport seeing his father off to Washington. Three weeks later, as Jackie and the Kennedy children flew home, John delighted members of the press corps by toddling up and down the aisle and playing peekaboo with reporters.

By the time he was two, John was a familiar fixture waiting impatiently on the White House lawn for his father's helicopter to land. Heartwarming photos and newsreels showed the President climbing down the helicopter steps and waiting, arms outstretched, as the little boy ran toward his father—and straight past him to the chopper.

John was so heartbroken when the helicopter arrived on the South Lawn to take his father to Andrews Air Force Base ("Daddy, don't leave me") that JFK began taking the boy along. Once the chopper deposited him at Andrews, the President kissed his son goodbye and John, accompanied by a Secret Service agent, was flown back to the White House. Whether the presidential helicopter was coming or going, John enjoyed doing his own helicopter imitation, spinning around with his arms outstretched until he collapsed, laughing, from dizziness. The boy's new nickname: "Helicopter Head."

Not surprisingly, John's favorite plaything at the time was a toy helicopter. "I held his hand for him and helped him write his name on it," official White House photographer Cecil Stoughton said. "It was his first autograph."

Of course, Daddy was not always able to take John with him to Andrews Air Force Base. "I'm afraid you can't come with me this time, John," he would say, reaching into his pocket and pulling out a tiny plastic plane. "But here's a toy airplane for you until I get back. You fly this one, son, and as soon as you grow up Daddy's going to buy you a real one." John would then run up to anyone who'd listen, shouting, "My daddy's going to get me a real one when I grow up!"

Before *Look* published its first major story on John-John in the White House, Stanley Tretick gave the President a set of the photos. "He ran all over the White House with them, showing people," Tretick said. It was like a guy with a walletful of pictures more than anything else. When Jackie got back he showed them to her upstairs and she was pleased with them. She wasn't mad at all."

Jackie reveled in Jack's growing need to spend more time with John and Caroline. "Sometimes they even have lunch with him," she said. "If you told me that would happen, I never would have believed it. But after all, the one thing that happens to a president is that his ties to the outside world are cut, and the people you really have are each other."

"He was enjoying his kids," said Cecil Stoughton. "I think it was more enjoyable to him than he thought it would be. But he really came to understand them and he played with them in that marvelous way that some people have and others don't."

JFK and his namesake "were really great pals," Stoughton added. The President's longtime secretary, Evelyn Lincoln, kept a glass jar on her desk filled with pink and blue rock candy. JFK would, said Stoughton, "stop whatever he was doing, lead John over to a candy jar on his secretary's desk, and play with him for a few minutes . . . Little John was so endearing—his father couldn't get enough of him."

One thing did seem to bother JFK about his son. Although his own combat exploits in the Pacific were legendary, JFK fretted about the boy's overexposure to the trappings of war. "I'm concerned about John's fascination with military things," he told Stoughton. "He's right there when he sees guns, swords, or anyone wearing a uniform." Life in the White House was, to be sure, a blur of color guards, parades, wreath-layings, and twenty-one-gun salutes.

"Why don't you just stop letting him watch the parades?" Stoughton asked.

The President was hardly willing to deprive his son of one of his greatest pleasures. "I guess we all go through that phase," JFK allowed. "John just sees more of the real thing."

Not that John couldn't be, as Baldrige observed, "quite the handful." Writing to her grandmother Rose Kennedy about a recent sleigh ride on the White House grounds, Caroline described her brother as "a bad squeaky boy who tries to spit in his mother's Coca-Cola and who has a very bad temper."

When Iran's Empress Farah Diba paid a state visit with her husband, the Shah, on April 12, 1962, she bent down and handed a daffodil to the President's little boy. "No!" he shouted, pulling away. Miss Shaw was mortified.

With Jackie's blessing, the nanny took a firm hand with John. Whenever he behaved particularly well, Maud Shaw told JFK Jr., "You're my big boy." John, eager to win Miss Shaw's approval, became markedly more obedient, rushing up to his nanny and declaring "I'm your big boy!" whenever he had washed his hands, cleaned his plate, or successfully used the potty.

One of the things John was proudest of was his fearlessness in and around water. At the beach, he would head straight for the water and jump—often without bothering to change into a swimsuit. Then he would run up to his nanny with the same question.

"I can swim, Miss Shaw, can't I?"

"Yes, John," she said patiently, "you swim very well."

In truth, Secret Service agents and family members alike scrambled whenever the President's son was near the water. Jackie's half brother, Jamie Auchincloss, remembered his nephew at age two "not just going off the diving board and into the deep end at the swimming pool of Bailey's Beach in Newport, whether or not someone was right there to catch him. But actually asking for help to climb to the high diving board and just racing off the board to ten feet of free fall. His father was often there to catch him."

Once, John was headed up the ladder to the high board when his father reached up and pulled his swimsuit down, exposing his rear end.

"Daddy," said an outraged John. "You are a bad man!"

When he turned to go up a second time, the President yanked his trunks down again. Now John, searching for the most scathing epithet he could find, turned crimson and yelled, "Daddy, you are a poo-poo head!"

"John," JFK replied with mock indignation. "No one calls the President of the United States a poo-poo head."

"All the other Kennedy children were allowed to do pretty much as they pleased," Maud Shaw said. "What people did not expect, though, was that Caroline and John would be such unspoiled, nice kids. There was nothing 'bratty' about them."

It was no accident. Jackie had specific ideas about how her children were to behave, and that meant addressing all adults—from White House maids to cabinet members—as Mr., Mrs., or Miss. "The children were well behaved because," Baldrige said, "their mother would not have it any other way."

Jack would. "He was absolutely determined to spoil John from the beginning," Senator George Smathers said. "He could not deny that boy anything. If the President was having a cabinet meeting or talking to some head of state, it didn't matter—he'd stop everything if John came skipping into the Oval Office. Jackie didn't mind at all— she hadn't expected him to be such an adoring, affectionate father— but it did make her job of keeping John under control a lot harder."

Once when the President was having a particularly tense meeting with Soviet Foreign Minister Andrey Gromyko, John was barred from the Oval Office. Frustrated, the boy stood outside the door shouting "Gromyko! Gromyko!" at the top of his lungs until Miss Shaw led him away.

If Jack more often than not indulged his son, so did the rest of the often unruly Kennedy clan. On December 19, 1961, a massive stroke left the seventy-three-year-old Joseph P. Kennedy paralyzed on his right side and unable to speak. Jack and Jackie, who had always been particularly close to her father-in-law, were crushed by Joe's illness, which left him confined to a wheelchair and capable of uttering only one word: *No*, which he repeated over and over again in abject frustration.

John and Caroline were among the few pleasures he had left. Although Joe's face was now contorted and he drooled, both John and Caroline were comfortable around the old man. Ben Bradlee described one White House dinner with Joe in attendance: "Caroline and John were careening around during the cocktail hour, oblivious to Grandpa's condition, and obviously delighting him. At one point, John bumped into the small table holding Joe Kennedy's drink, spilling it smack into his lap." The spill was cleaned up instantly, and John continued reeling around the room while his father and grandfather laughed.

Fatherhood opened up Jack to all children, not just his own. This was most evident at the height of the Cuban Missile Crisis in October 1962, when U.S. intelligence discovered the presence of Soviet offensive missiles in Cuba. For a week, top-secret meetings went on behind closed doors at the White House as Kennedy decided what action to take. Without members of the White House staff ever knowing, State Department and Pentagon officials slept behind closed doors on couches and cots. Jack explained the gravity of the situation to his wife, and the importance of conducting business as usual in the White House.

Even though he was consumed with the mounting crisis, Jack squeezed out a few extra moments to spend with Caroline and John, who to make matters worse was in bed with a temperature of 104. In an uncharacteristically melancholy moment, Jack turned to Jackie and spoke of the distinct possibility of nuclear war. "We've already had a chance," he said. "But what about all the children?"

The next evening, the President addressed the nation, announcing that he had ordered a naval blockade of the island. The Cuban Missile Crisis lasted a total of thirteen days. Then, on October 24, Russian ships carrying missiles toward Cuba turned back. "We're eyeball to eyeball," Secretary of State Dean Rusk said, "and I think the other guy just blinked."

Now that the world had pulled back from the brink of nuclear war, Jackie planned a joint party to celebrate her children's birthdays—John's second and Caroline's fifth. Brother and sister stuffed themselves on creamed chicken, cake, and ice cream before joining their guests for cartoons in the White House theater.

In February 1963, John was running at his customary breakneck speed when he stumbled and banged his tooth on a concrete step.

The bloody tooth went flying, and John fell on the ground sobbing. Maud Shaw managed to calm him down, and after a few moments he suddenly leapt up and dove into the bushes. He emerged with the tooth, which he then happily displayed—along with his gap-toothed smile—to everyone. Not long after, he broke another tooth playing inside a large playhouse on the White House lawn. This time the President, who had been busy delivering the State of the Union address when John lost his first tooth, comforted the boy.

By the spring of 1963, John appeared for all intents and purposes to be the perfect little gentleman. He had been taught how to bow and Caroline how to curtsy in preparation for a state visit by Luxembourg's Grand Duchess Charlotte on April 30.

Miss Shaw promised the children that they could have a cookie and some ginger ale after they greeted the grand duchess, but John grew impatient as he watched adults helping themselves to goodies from the buffet table at the far end of the room.

Just as the First Lady began to introduce her son to the grand duchess, John threw a tantrum, falling to the floor and staying there, motionless.

"John," Jackie said, "get up this minute."

John did not budge.

"Would you ask Miss Shaw to come in?" Jackie instructed an aide.

A chagrined Miss Shaw came to Jackie's rescue, scooping the boy up and whisking him upstairs. "Now what on earth did you do that for?" she asked John. "That's not being my big boy, is it?"

"But, Miss Shaw," he tried to explain, "they didn't give me my cookie."

Perhaps John's biggest faux pas would come while he stood on the Truman Balcony watching a welcoming parade for Yugoslavia's president, Marshal Tito. While the Marine Band played, John stood waving two toy pistols and shouting "We want Kennedy! We want Kennedy!"

With the two presidents standing directly below him, John accidentally dropped one of the toy guns off the balcony. It narrowly missed Tito, landing inches from his feet.

JFK was happy that the sudden appearance of a gun—toy or otherwise—had not resulted in an international incident. "John has grown up," the President sighed to his longtime friend and aide Kenny O'Donnell, "to develop a colorful personality."

JFK was so smitten with his "colorful" son, Jackie told her friend Roswell Gilpatric, that "what he wants more than anything else in the world is another wonderful little boy." On April 18, 1963, Jackie made the official announcement from Palm Beach that she was pregnant.

Having already suffered through a miscarriage, a stillbirth, and two difficult pregnancies, Jackie refused to take any chances this time. She spent most of that summer painting, reading, and resting in their rented oceanfront home on Squaw Island, not far from the Hyannis Port compound.

On August 7, 1963—five weeks before the baby was due to arrive—Jackie took John and Caroline horseback riding at nearby Osterville. On the ride home, she began experiencing labor pains. At 11:10 A.M., Jackie was heading for the helicopter that would whisk her to the military hospital at Otis Air Force Base.

Jackie had been characteristically composed, but suddenly she became emotional. "Dr. Walsh," she said, turning to her obstetrician, "you've just got to get me to the hospital on time! I don't want anything to happen to this baby."

"We'll have you there in plenty of time," he said, trying to reassure her.

But Jackie kept pleading. "Please hurry! This baby mustn't be born dead!"

The helicopter arrived minutes later at the hospital, and at 12:52 Jackie gave birth by cesarean section to a four-pound-ten-ounce boy who was promptly placed in an incubator. The base chaplain immediately baptized the boy Patrick Bouvier Kennedy, after Jack's paternal grandfather and Black Jack Bouvier.

Forty minutes after Patrick's birth, Jack arrived. Before he had a chance to see either Jackie or his new son, the President was told the baby suffered from a severe respiratory problem involving the lung's hyaline membrane, which is not uncommon among premature infants.

The decision was made to transport the baby by ambulance to Children's Hospital in Boston, where he could receive better care. But first, Jack wheeled Patrick into Jackie's room and placed him in Jackie's arms. She held the baby for a few minutes before he was placed back in the incubator. It was the last time she ever saw her youngest child. "His hair was dark," said Jackie's secretary Mary Gallagher, who was standing a few feet away, "his features well formed."

Jack visited John and Caroline on Squaw Island while their little brother was being taken by ambulance to Boston. Then he returned to the hospital at Otis Air Force Base to check on Jackie before flying on to Boston.

That night, the baby was moved to Harvard's School of Public Health, where he was put in an oxygen chamber. Jack visited the baby four times the next day, flying to Otis in the afternoon to bolster Jackie's spirits and helicoptering back to Boston. He refused to leave the hospital that night, and slept in a vacant bed two floors above the room where Patrick lay fighting for his life in an oxygen chamber.

The nation prayed for Patrick's recovery. But at 5 A.M. on August 9, 1963, he died. Patrick was forty hours old. "He put up quite a fight," Jack told his friend Dave Powers. "He was a beautiful baby."

JFK rushed to his wife's side. When they saw each other they both broke down. "Oh, Jack, oh, Jack," she sobbed. "There's only one thing I could not bear now—if I ever lost you."

The baby's mother was still too weak to attend the funeral. JFK's brothers, Bobby and Teddy; Jackie's sister, Lee Radziwill; and Janet and Jamie Auchincloss were among the few who heard Boston's Cardinal Cushing say the Mass of the Angels. When the cardinal was finished, Jack placed a St. Christopher medal Jackie had given him on their wedding day into the tiny casket.

Jack was the last to leave the chapel. "I was behind him," the gravel-voiced Cushing remembered. "The President was so overwhelmed with grief that he literally put his arms around that casket as though he was carrying it out. I said, 'Come on, Jack. Let's go. God is good.' "

At Holyhood Cemetery, not far from his Brookline, Massachusetts, birthplace, an inconsolable Jack reached out to touch the coffin as it was lowered into the ground. Tears were streaming down his cheeks. "Goodbye," he said. "It's awfully lonely down there."

Jack was especially concerned about the impact of Patrick's death on John and Caroline, who had been eagerly anticipating their little brother's arrival. To cheer them up, he returned to Squaw Island with Shannon, a cocker spaniel puppy. When Jackie arrived home after a week recuperating in the hospital, she and Jack were greeted by the sight of John, Caroline, and the Kennedy canine menagerie—Shannon, Clipper, Charlie, Pushinka's puppies White Tips, Streaker, Butterfly, and Blackie—rolling around on the front lawn.

On September 12, a few close friends helped the President and First Lady celebrate their tenth wedding anniversary. Ben and Tony Bradlee rode with JFK in the presidential helicopter, and when they landed they were struck by the new closeness between the Kennedys. "This was the first time we had seen Jackie since the death of little Patrick," Bradlee said, "and she greeted JFK with by far the most affectionate embrace we had ever seen them give each other . . . they are the most remote and independent people, so when their emotions do surface it is especially moving."

Still, both were devastated by the death of Patrick. Lee Radziwill was searching for ways to boost her sister's spirits when Greek shipping tycoon Aristotle Onassis offered the use of his yacht *Christina* for an Aegean cruise.

"Lee had sort of a romance going with Onassis," Evelyn Lincoln recalled. "At first Jack didn't like the idea [of Jackie going on the *Christina*] but then he thought maybe it would do her some good."

While Mommy was sailing aboard the *Christina,* Caroline attended her classes in the White House school as usual. The President, meanwhile, was spending more and more time with his son. He even took the boy along to a meeting of the International Monetary Fund at the Sheraton Park Hotel. As they walked through the lobby, JFK looked down and saw that John's nose was running. As his treasury secretary and a score of foreign dignitaries looked on, the President of the United States pulled a handkerchief out of his back pocket, leaned down, and wiped his son's nose.

When she arrived home from her high seas adventure, Jackie was greeted by JFK, John, and Caroline. "Oh, Jack," she said, rushing to embrace him before scooping up the children in her arms. "I'm so glad to be home!"

Her first order of business was to begin the children's religious instruction. Questions raised by their tiny brother's death made it more imperative that they learn about God and his mysterious ways. That October, Caroline and her six Catholic schoolmates at the White House school began attending catechism class at the Georgetown Visitation Academy, a cloistered convent.

During one class the teacher, Sister Joanne Frey of the Mission Helpers of the Sacred Heart, asked the children to cut out pictures from a magazine and then tell the class the story the pictures told. "My mommy helped me," Caroline volunteered before showing her teacher a picture of a child about her age and a mother holding an infant. "This is Mommy," Caroline explained, "this is me, and this would have been Patrick, my baby brother. He's in heaven."

Jackie often brought John along to classes. One day in October 1963, John burst into a class with a stick over his shoulder. "He thinks he's a soldier," Caroline said, rolling her eyes, "and he doesn't even how to salute."

"A month later," Sister Joanne said, "like everyone else I cried when I saw him standing there saluting his father's coffin. It was a *perfect* salute. Ironic, isn't it? The most famous salute of all time."

Jackie, who was decidedly more devout than her husband, wanted John's religious education to begin earlier than Caroline's. On October 27, 1963, the President, Jackie, and Caroline took John to his first mass at the Church of St. Stephen the Martyr, near their weekend home in Middleburg, Virginia.

Two weeks later, on November 11, JFK took John with him to Veterans Day ceremonies at Arlington National Cemetery. After watching his father lay a wreath at the Tomb of the Unknown Soldier, John, mesmerized by the colorful uniforms and fluttering flags, drifted away from his father. JFK looked out over the thousands of headstones and markers rolling up and down the hillsides. "Go get John," he ordered a Secret Service agent. "I think he'll be lonely out there."

Sometimes I can't remember what really happened, and what I saw in pictures.

—*John*

Jack made John the mischievous, independent boy he is. Bobby is keeping that alive.

—*Jackie*

3
=

Jack and Jackie exchanged one final glance as the first of the three shots hit him in the back of the neck, severed his windpipe, and exited his throat. The expression on Jack's handsome, forty-six-year-old face that moment would haunt his widow's dreams the rest of her life. "He looked puzzled. I remember he looked as if he just had a slight headache," she later said. "I could see a piece of his skull coming off. It was flesh-colored, not white. I can see this perfectly clean piece detaching itself from his head. Then he slumped in my lap." As the motorcade sped toward Dallas's Parkland Memorial Hospital, Jackie cradled her husband's head. "Jack, Jack, Jack, can you hear me?" she told him. "I love you, Jack."

A half hour later, Dr. Kemp Clark, one of the attending physicians in trauma room 1 at Parkland Memorial, told Jackie it was over. Her husband, whose blood covered the floor of the trauma room, was dead. A sheet had been pulled up to cover his face, leaving one foot exposed. The foot, Jackie observed, was "whiter than the sheet."

She took the President's foot in her hand and gently kissed it. Then she pulled the sheet down, exposing his face. "His mouth was so *beautiful*," she recalled. "His eyes were open." Dr. Marion Jenkins, head of Parkland's anesthesiology department, remembered that "she started kissing him. She kissed his foot, his leg, thigh, chest, and then his lips. She didn't say a word." One of the doctors found his hand under the sheet and guided hers to it. She held his hand while Father Oscar Huber gave Jack Extreme Unction.

Only nine days earlier, Jack, Jackie, Caroline, and John had watched from the White House balcony as the kilted Black Watch pipers performed for an audience of seventeen hundred underprivileged youngsters on the South Lawn. Caroline squeezed into the chair alongside her father, her arm around him. John, excited as always, squirmed on his mother's lap. It was the last time this First Family was to be together.

"Those poor children!" Ethel Kennedy cried when her husband, Jack's brother Bobby, told her the news. As attorney general, Bobby had been among the first to learn of his brother's assassination. That afternoon, Caroline was chatting away in the backseat of a family friend's station wagon on the way to her very first sleepover. An unmarked Secret Service car with a single agent inside followed at a discreet distance. When the first news flash came over the radio, the mother of Caroline's friend had switched it off immediately. She was confident that Caroline, immersed in conversation with her daughter, had heard nothing.

But she had. Within minutes, they had pulled over to the side of the highway and transferred Caroline from the station wagon to the Secret Service car. Sitting in the passenger seat next to the agent, Caroline clutched her pink teddy bear and her small suitcase as they sped back to the White House. "There was no way of knowing," said the agent, "if someone was out to kill the whole First Family. We couldn't take the chance."

Another motorist thought the same thing. Spotting Caroline in the unmarked black Ford, an anonymous driver, who may well have thought the First Daughter was being kidnapped, began to pursue the car. After a breakneck chase through Washington streets during which the car carrying Caroline swerved in and out of heavy midday traffic, John's big sister was deposited safely back at the White House.

John, meantime, was happily playing with his toy helicopter as Maud Shaw looked on. When Jackie's mother, Janet Auchincloss, heard the terrible news, she made the unilateral decision to have her grandchildren brought to the Auchincloss mansion on O Street.

Jackie's sixteen-year-old half brother, Jamie Auchincloss, was scurrying between classes when a teacher told him that his brother-in-law had been shot. Rushing home to the O Street mansion, he found John and Caroline waiting for him in the living room, "expecting to spend a playful late afternoon with their uncle Jamie." Although Caroline knew something serious was going on, neither child had been told what had actually happened.

"Usually when we got together a lot of the chitchat revolved around the interesting things Daddy and Mommy did," Jamie said. "This time I steered them away from the subject, although I'm sure with all the excitement Caroline knew something was up. While we lay on the floor of the living room several of the Secret Service men were huddled around the TV set in the kitchen.

"I tried to keep her away from the news," Jamie recalled, "but at one point Caroline jumped up and ran into the kitchen for a cookie. The Secret Service men jumped up and switched off the set, but I think in that fleeting moment Caroline saw what was going on. When she came back into the room, we picked up where we left off, but her mood had changed. She turned very quiet."

At Bethesda Naval Hospital in Maryland, where an autopsy was conducted on her husband's body, Jackie seemed compelled to share the grisly details of what had happened in Dallas over and over again. Eyes wide with shock and still wearing her gore-spattered suit, Jackie nonetheless "never broke down," said the Kennedys' old friend Charlie Bartlett. "She was in complete control, remarkably poised, just unbelievable."

Now, for the first time, Jackie asked about the children. When Janet Auchincloss told her that John and Caroline were at the Auchincloss house on O Street, Jackie stiffened. "What are they doing there?" she demanded to know.

"Jackie, I had a message that you had sent from the plane that you wanted them to come there and to sleep there," Janet replied without missing a beat. Jackie looked, her mother observed later, "absolutely amazed."

"But I never sent such a message."

"You don't want them there, then?"

"No, I don't," Jackie said firmly. "The best thing for them would be to stay in their own rooms with their own things so their lives can be as normal as possible. Mummy, my God, those poor children. Their lives shouldn't be disrupted, now of all times!"

Janet rushed to the phone and called Maud Shaw. "Fortunately, they hadn't gone to bed yet," Janet said. "So they thought they had simply come to have supper with their grandmother."

The children were bundled into their winter coats and whisked back to the White House. "She was right, of course," a chastened Janet Auchincloss later conceded. "When it came to her children, Jackie was always right."

Ben and Tony Bradlee were at the White House when the children arrived. Before they left the White House to meet Jackie at Bethesda, they wondered aloud if it wasn't time someone broke the news of their father's death to the children. "I'm going to tell them myself," Bradlee had said, only to be pulled back his wife at the last minute. Instead, the journalist did his best to distract the children.

"Tell me a story! Tell me a story," John demanded, jumping up and down. Bradlee told him a story, and then another. The boy wanted more.

Bradlee thought for a minute. "Chase me around the house," Bradlee ordered John. Delighted to oblige, the President's son did chase Bradlee—around the Yellow Oval Room, down the hall, into the West Sitting Room, the family dining room, the kitchen, and back—squealing with joy the entire time.

Back at Bethesda, the children's grandmother asked Jackie point-blank, "What do you want to tell the children?"

Jackie paused for a moment, weighing her thoughts carefully. John was too young to understand what was happening, but what if Caroline was told by one of her little friends?

Jackie took a long drag on her cigarette. "I think Miss Shaw," she said, "should do exactly what she feels she should do." Her tone was businesslike, but that was just a defense. The very thought of having to look into her children's eyes and tell them their father had been murdered was too much for her. This was one burden someone else would have to shoulder.

"Miss Shaw will have to judge how much the children have seen or heard or whether they are wondering," Jackie said. "She will just have to use her own judgment."

As she watched the children play in the family quarters of the White House, Miss Shaw dreaded the assignment handed to her. Things got worse as more and more dignitaries arrived and departed via helicopter and limousine. Each time a chopper touched down, John leapt to his feet shouting, "Daddy's home! Daddy's home!"

It had been left to the nanny to break the news of their brother, Patrick's, death to them, but this was something she felt she could not muster the strength to do. "I haven't the heart to tell them," Miss Shaw kept saying. "Why can't someone else do this? I can't . . . I can't . . ." She tucked little John in his crib without mentioning anything about his father's death; that, it was agreed, could wait until morning.

After Caroline changed into her pajamas and climbed under the covers, Miss Shaw sat down on the edge of the bed and held the little girl's hand. There were tears in the woman's eyes. "I can't help crying, Caroline, because I have some very sad news to tell you," she said softly. "Your father has been shot. They took him to a hospital but they couldn't make him better. He's gone to look after Patrick. Patrick was so lonely in heaven. He didn't know anyone there. Now he has the best friend anyone could have. And your father will be so very glad to see Patrick."

Caroline burst into tears. "But what will Daddy do in heaven?" she asked.

"I'm sure God is giving him enough things to do because he was always such a very busy man. God has made your daddy a guardian angel for you and for Mommy and for John."

Miss Shaw stayed with the child for the next hour as Caroline buried her head in her pillow and cried herself to sleep. The nanny was confident she had made the right decision in not waiting until morning. "It's better for children Caroline's age to get a sadness and a shock before they go to sleep at night," she later explained to

Jackie. "That way it won't hit them hard when they wake up in the morning."

John was another matter. He was told the next morning that his father had gone to heaven to take care of Patrick. "Did Daddy take his big plane with him?" he asked Miss Shaw.

"Yes," she replied.

"I wonder," John said, "when he's coming back."

Not long after Miss Shaw broke the news to her uncomprehending little brother, Caroline woke up and bounded out of bed, convinced it had all been a bad dream. Grabbing the big stuffed giraffe Daddy had given her, the little girl in pink pajamas raced down the hallway toward Daddy's bedroom as she did every morning. John was right behind her, pulling a toy.

But when they pushed open the door, they saw Grandmother and Uncle Hugh Auchincloss propped up in their father's bed, unable to sleep. Jackie had asked her mother and stepfather to stay in Jack's room overnight.

Pushing the giraffe ahead of her—"sort of to ease her entrance," Janet Auchincloss later said—Caroline inched her way into the bedroom, with John following.

On the bed was a copy of the *New York Times* with JFK's black-bordered picture covering the entire front page.

"Who is that?" Caroline asked.

"Oh, Caroline," her grandmother replied sadly, "you know that's your daddy."

The little girl looked up. "He's dead, isn't he? A man shot him, didn't he?"

The normally talkative Janet was speechless. "Her little face was so extraordinary," she said. "It's hard for Caroline to . . . she's a very, very affectionate little girl and she's a very thoughtful child. And I think the behavior of both the children through the next days was a remarkable tribute to the way the President and Jackie had brought them up."

There was to be a brief mass that morning at the White House for family and friends. At 9:45, Maud Shaw brought John and Caroline to Jackie's bedroom. It was the first time she had seen them since the assassination. She hugged each child, then took them by the hand and marched downstairs.

The children, too young to attend the mass, watched from the Green Room next door. Then their uncle Jamie and Jamie's sister (Jackie's half sister), Janet, took them for an outing at Manassas Battlefield. "To take their minds off things, we brought along the German shepherd, Baron, and my mother's French poodle," Jamie recalled. "We let them walk the dogs for a while, and then took the leashes off so they could run."

A park ranger spotted the dogs and began yelling at the children, "No dogs allowed!"—until he realized who the children were. At the sight of John and Caroline, the burly park ranger burst into tears.

After the service in the East Room, where JFK's casket lay in state, Jackie walked over to the Oval Office where Evelyn Lincoln stood, bewildered, in the middle of the room. From there, she walked with White House usher J. B. West to the Cabinet Room and sat down.

"My children," Jackie said, "they're good children, aren't they, Mr. West?"

"They certainly are."

"They're not spoiled?"

"No, indeed."

That day, Jackie found the time to dash off notes to several of Jack's friends and colleagues—including his senatorial friend turned presidential rival, Richard Nixon. She told him to be thankful he had not won the 1960 election.

In turn, she was touched by the notes Lyndon Johnson penned to John and Caroline the night of JFK's murder. "It will be many years before you understand fully what a great man your father was," LBJ scrawled to the President's not-yet-three-year-old son. "His loss is a deep personal tragedy for all of us, but I wanted you particularly to know that I share your grief—you can always be proud of him."

Now Jackie wanted her children to do the same for their father. "You must write a letter to Daddy now," she instructed Caroline, "and tell him how much you love him."

DEAR DADDY, Caroline printed in large block letters. WE ARE ALL GOING TO MISS YOU. DADDY, I LOVE YOU VERY MUCH, CAROLINE. John scrawled a large X on his sister's letter. That night, Jackie sat down to write her own, rambling letter to her dead husband. It was dawn before she finished pouring out her heart, and the letter, now five pages long, was drenched in tears. Before JFK's body was moved to the Capitol Rotunda, where more than a quarter-million mourners would pay their respects, Jackie went to the East Room and placed both letters inside the casket, along with a pair of gold cuff links she had given him and a favorite piece of scrimshaw—the presidential seal carved on a whale's tooth—which had also been a present from Jackie.

That evening, millions of American families sat in dazed silence watching the President's family join mourners inside the Capitol Rotunda. While cabinet members and Supreme Court justices struggled to maintain their composure, Jackie leaned over and said softly to Caroline, "We're going to say goodbye to Daddy now, and we're going to kiss him goodbye, and tell Daddy how much we love him and how much we'll always miss him." Then they walked up to the catafalque, silently knelt, and in a gesture that would unleash what was left of America's tears, took the flag that covered the coffin in their gloved hands and tenderly kissed it.

John, meanwhile, was restless and fidgety. Miss Shaw took him into an office off the rotunda. Several tiny flags decorating a bulletin board immediately caught the little boy's attention, and a congressional staffer standing by offered him one.

"Yes, please," John said, "and one for my sister, please." As the man handed him two flags, John added, "Oh, and may I have one for my daddy?" The man handed him a third flag, and when John returned he proudly showed it to his mother.

For those days, so fraught with emotion, the eyes of the nation were on the beautiful widow and her beguiling children. Jackie wore the only black dress she owned—the same one she'd worn the night JFK announced his presidential candidacy—but she wanted John and Caroline to look their age as much as possible, not like miniature adults. Toward that end, she dressed them in powder blue children's coats and red shoes instead of somber mourning attire.

"It was wise not to put them in dark clothes and hats," Jackie's mother said. "They looked and behaved perfectly naturally, not like some wind-up dolls. That's what Jackie wanted."

Jackie also wanted, above all else, to do justice to her husband's memory by impressing on the American people the magnitude of the nation's loss. "She felt he should be in the pantheon of great leaders, alongside Lincoln and FDR," writer and friend Theodore White said, "and the state funeral was an important step in that direction." From the design of the printed mass cards to the black bunting in the East Room ("Find out how Lincoln was buried," she had instructed Bobby Kennedy), not even the smallest detail escaped Jackie's perfectionist eye.

Yet her thoughts never strayed far from her children. That Sunday, just two days after her husband's murder, Jackie walked into Pierre Salinger's office. "Pierre, there is only one thing I can do now," she said. "I have to take care of those kids day by day. I have to make sure they become intelligent. I have to make sure they do good work in school. I have to make sure when they get older that they have strong views on what they should be doing. This is the only thing I can do anymore."

That same day, eyes justifiably widened when Aristotle Onassis showed up at the White House less than forty-eight hours after the President's assassination. Jackie had formed a friendship with the Greek shipping tycoon during her cruise aboard the *Christina,* and now, on the eve of her husband's state funeral, she drew Onassis to her side.

Everyone had been so overcome by the events of the past few days that it was only at the last minute that Maud Shaw realized Monday, November 25—the day of John Fitzgerald Kennedy's state funeral— was also his only son's third birthday. Caroline was turning six two days later, so it had been agreed that there would be a joint birthday party midway between the two dates. But over breakfast that morning, Caroline and the nanny sang "Happy Birthday to You" to young John and handed him two presents, a children's book from Miss Shaw and a toy helicopter from his sister.

An hour later, a dazed Jackie took her children's tiny hands and walked them to a waiting limousine that would ferry John and Caroline to St. Matthew's Cathedral. Then, to the eerie, unforgettable cadence of muffled drums, Jackie, flanked by Bobby, Teddy, and the rest of the Kennedy clan, walked behind the horse-drawn caisson bearing her husband's body from the White House to St. Matthew's Cathedral. They were followed by a cortege that included 220 representatives from 102 nations, including French President Charles de Gaulle, Ethiopian Emperor Haile Selassie, German Chancellor Ludwig Erhard, Britain's Prince Philip, and Israeli Foreign Minister Golda Meir.

During the mass inside the cathedral, Jackie finally broke down. "You'll be all right, Mommy, don't cry," Caroline said, reaching up to wipe away her mother's tears. "I'll take care of you." With that, Jackie regained her composure.

"Caroline, she held my hand like a soldier," Jackie commented a few days later. "She's my helper. She's mine now . . . John is going to belong to the men now . . ."

At the service, John was again squirming. Jackie asked Bob Foster, the Secret Service agent assigned to the children, to take her son to a small room at the rear of the church. An army colonel took time to chat with the little boy, pointing to the medals on his uniform and describing what each one meant.

When it was time to return to the church, John saluted the colonel, but with his left hand instead of his right. "Oh, no, John," the colonel said. "That's not the way to salute. You salute with your right hand." The officer then patiently showed the boy the proper way to salute.

John returned to his mother's side outside the cathedral, watching the flag-draped coffin leave for the final journey to Arlington National Cemetery. Jackie, her tear-streaked face visible behind a fluttering veil of black lace, leaned down to her son and whispered, "John, you can salute Daddy now and say goodbye to him."

Then, remembering what the colonel had taught him only moments before, John snapped off a perfect salute that melted the hearts of millions. It was the moment that both symbolized a nation's grief and defined John's place in the collective psyche of his countrymen. (Sadly, as an adult John would try in vain to summon the memory of what transpired that historic day. "I've seen that photograph so many times, and I'd like to say I remember that moment," he said three decades later, "but I don't.")

After the funeral, Jackie returned to the White House and stood in an East Room receiving line while more than two hundred world dignitaries filed past. On the second floor, Maud Shaw put John down for his afternoon nap.

At the Georgetown Visitation Academy, meanwhile, Sister Joanne Frey was preparing for the afternoon religion class. "I was told by the White House that there would be a class," she recalled, "but of course that Caroline would not be there." Then, without warning, "in walked Caroline and a Secret Service man. Caroline was wearing a little trench coat."

"Sister, I know I'm early," Caroline said apologetically. "But we were just riding around and we didn't have anyplace to go."

"Caroline looked so lost and alone," Sister Joanne remembered.

"Oh, I'm glad you're here," the nun replied. "I've got so many things to do to get the class ready—you can help me!"

Caroline pulled out her religion book. "Mommy had lots of things to do," she said, "and I know I'm not supposed to, but she told me I could go ahead a few pages and work in my religion book. I'm sorry. Everybody else was so busy. I just needed something to do."

"Of course it's fine, Caroline," Sister Joanne said. Frey was moved by how alone the little girl seemed, but she was also struck by the activity her mother had chosen to keep her busy. "Here it is the day of the President's funeral—her husband's funeral—and Jackie could have told Caroline to do anything. But she wants Caroline to do something involving religion. It really says a lot about the woman, and how much she cared about the kind of people her children would become."

Later that same day, there was a small party celebrating John's birthday in the family dining room. "John knows today is his birthday," Jackie said, "and I did not want to disappoint him."

There was a little table piled high with packages, ice cream, and a cake with three candles on it. With his sister's help, John blew out the candles, and then he proceeded to tear the brightly colored wrapping paper off gift after gift.

Dave Powers led everyone in an a capella rendition of "That Old Gang of Mine" and "Heart of My Heart," and, as Jamie Auchincloss recalled, "everyone's emotions were strained to the very limit."

For Bobby, hearing "Heart of My Heart," one of Jack's favorite tunes, was unbearable. He fled the room.

At one point during the party, Jackie and Rose were having coffee in the Yellow Oval Room when Caroline ran up to her mother. "Mommy," she asked, "did they love Daddy?"

"Oh, yes. They did love Daddy," Jackie replied.

"No, Mommy," Caroline objected, shaking her head. "They couldn't have loved Daddy. If they had loved him, they wouldn't have done what they did to him."

Jackie could think of nothing to say. Then Caroline, looking concerned, asked, "Mommy, do they love you?"

It was obvious the question had been preying on Caroline's mind. Jackie answered, "Well, I think so, at least some." Seeing the look of confusion on the little girl's face, Jackie continued, "Maybe I should have told you that not everybody loved Daddy. Many more loved Daddy than loved me. But I think some of them love me, too."

Jackie could see that Caroline was not completely satisfied with the answers she was getting. "After all, not everybody loved Jesus, did they?" she said. That was enough for Caroline, and she scampered back to her brother's party.

Two days after her husband's funeral, Jackie and the children flew to Hyannis Port to spend Thanksgiving with the rest of the Kennedy clan. Arriving with the folded flag that had covered Jack's casket, she went straight to Joe's room and did not emerge for an hour. "When Jackie opened the door to leave," Secret Service agent Ham Brown recalled, "there was this sad, sad sight of Joe just sitting upright in bed, the triangle of flag still in his lap."

The day after Thanksgiving, Jackie summoned *Life* magazine's Theodore White to Hyannis Port. While John and Caroline slept upstairs, Jackie, dressed in a beige pullover sweater and black pants, poured out the gruesome details of the assassination to him between drags on her ever-present cigarette. She was angry at the "bitter people" who were already writing that JFK had been in office too short a time to have a lasting impact.

That, in fact, was why she had invited White to Hyannis Port in the first place—to create, with *Life*'s help, a new American myth. "I want to say this one thing," she told White. "It's almost been an obsession with me, all I keep thinking of is this line from a musical comedy, it's been an obsession with me."

Jackie told White that at night, when Jack's pain made it hard for him to sleep, she would play his favorite record—the cast album from *Camelot*. The song he loved most was the very last cut on the record. And his favorite line was the very last one in the song—the line that had been running relentlessly through Jackie's fevered mind. The melancholy lyric had been written by Jack's old friend and Harvard classmate, Alan Jay Lerner:

> *Don't let it be forgot*
> *That once there was a spot*
> *For one brief shining moment*
> *That was known as Camelot.*

"There will never be another Camelot," she told White wistfully. "There will be great presidents again—and the Johnsons are wonderful, they've been wonderful to me—but there'll never be another Camelot again."

"She was a keenly intelligent woman who had obviously thought long and hard about how she wanted her handsome, heroic husband remembered," White said. "She had always been described as a fairy tale princess, and now she wanted Jack Kennedy to take his place in history as a modern King Arthur."

Implicit in this was the notion of a Kennedy dynasty. "If JFK was a benevolent king," White later observed, "then by extension John was cast as a prince of the realm, and heir apparent to the throne."

For the moment, however, Lyndon Johnson wore the crown—and he was growing increasingly impatient for Jackie and her brood to move out so he could move in. Reluctant to leave it all behind, Jackie wound up staying a full eleven days—in contrast to the wife of the last president to die in office, Eleanor Roosevelt, who left the same day.

No sooner had she arrived back in Washington with her husband's body than Jackie was confronted with the question of where she and the children would live. "I'm not going to 'travel extensively abroad.' That's a desecration," she said, putting an end to the rumors that she planned to move to France. "I'm going to live in the places I lived with Jack. In Georgetown, and with the Kennedys at the Cape. They're my family. I'm going to bring up my children. I want John to grow up to be a good boy."

While she looked for a new place to live, Jackie stayed at the stately, art-filled Georgetown mansion owned by then–Undersecretary of State Averell Harriman. Over a two-day period, the Kennedys' personal possessions were packed up in boxes and moved by van to the Harriman mansion at 3038 N Street.

When John spotted a box marked "John's Toys—N Street," he burst into tears. Maud Shaw reassured him that he would see his toys again, and to ease the transition suggested he don one of his birthday gifts—a marine uniform made specially for the son of the fallen Commander in Chief. Afterward, the little boy and his nanny sat on the floor and together retrieved a few select toys—a cowboy gun, a helicopter, and some swords—from the cardboard moving box. Then Miss Shaw patiently helped pack them into John's small suitcase so that he would be able to carry them to the new house himself.

In the meantime, there was a flood of last-minute deliveries at the Harriman house. There was a briefcase emblazoned with the initials JFK, a bicycle, a tricycle, hatboxes, the children's two parakeet cages—one pink, the other blue—and several cases of French wine.

The last night they were to spend together at the White House as a family, Jackie threw the promised joint birthday party for John and Caroline. There was another cake—a big one this time—and the children took turns opening their presents. Caroline's favorite was a stuffed bear, John's a model of Air Force One.

The next morning, Secret Service agent Bob Foster took John for a last walk around the White House grounds while inside his mother bid a tearful farewell to the staff. John was thirsty, so Foster lifted him up to drink from a water fountain. At that moment, a photographer walked up and began snapping away.

John looked him square in the eye. "What are you taking my picture for?" he asked. "My daddy's dead."

"The poor photographer started to cry," Foster recalled. "I cried too."

Shortly after noon on December 6, 1963, John got ready to leave the White House with his mother and sister. Moments earlier there had been a small ceremony in the State Dining Room, where Lyndon

Johnson awarded a posthumous Presidential Medal of Freedom to JFK. Bobby Kennedy accepted the medal for Jackie, who was too distraught to attend. Before they departed, Jackie handed her son the black box containing the medal. "John," she said softly, "here's something else you can carry out of the White House. Keep it, and be proud of it always."

John tucked the box under his right arm and, waving a small American flag, walked with Jackie and Caroline toward a waiting White House limousine. A half hour later, the car pulled up in front of the Harriman house and out stepped Jackie and her children, followed closely by Bobby and Ethel.

For the time being, Secret Service agents kept vigil inside and outside the house. At first the law provided that Jackie, Caroline, and John would receive protection for two years—a period that was eventually extended to a presidential widow until remarriage or death. Under the new provisions, all presidential offspring are entitled to receive Secret Service protection until age sixteen.

They needed it. Outside the Harriman house, a carnival atmosphere prevailed. Drivers hoping to catch a glimpse of Jackie or the children slowed to a crawl. Sidewalks on both sides of N Street were packed shoulder to shoulder with gawkers.

Inside, Jackie felt like a prisoner—and worried about the impact all of this would have on Caroline and John. It had become apparent to family and friends that Caroline was in psychic pain. Her French teacher at the White House School, Jacqueline Hirsh, recalled that Caroline "looked ghastly. She was so pale and her concentration broken. She comprehended the assassination fully, absolutely. You could see that it was on her mind, that it was rough on her. But she never did complain, never."

Bobby became the dominant male presence in their lives, visiting the house every day. JFK adviser McGeorge Bundy, longtime friends Charlie and Martha Bartlett and Chuck and Betty Spalding, as well as a handful of others, made a point of dropping by at least once a week.

Dave Powers, once aptly described by Ben Bradlee as "JFK's leprechaun," also dropped by every day around lunchtime to play on the floor with John or—the little boy's favorite pastime—practice marching from dining room to kitchen to living room and back.

Although Mary Gallagher was coming to the house each day to work on Jackie's correspondence, it occurred to the little boy that he had not seen Daddy's secretary. He was told that Evelyn Lincoln had her own office now—the President's devoted secretary had been assigned a tiny room in the Executive Office Building to handle the formidable task of cataloging all of JFK's papers and belongings.

John asked to see Mrs. Lincoln, but Gallagher and Maud Shaw thought it wiser that he call. The nanny dialed the number, then held the receiver up to the boy's ear.

"Hello, Mrs. Lincoln," he said. "This is John."

"Why, John," she replied with delight. "What a wonderful surprise."

John then told Mrs. Lincoln that he and Miss Shaw would be dropping by for a visit a few days later.

"That would be lovely, John," she said. "I'm looking forward to seeing you."

"Me, too." Then he paused for a moment. "Mrs. Lincoln?"

"Yes, John?" she said. A few moments went by before the little voice on the line continued.

"Is Daddy there?"

I hate this country. I despise America and I don't want my children to live here anymore. If they are killing Kennedys, my kids are the number one targets. I have the two main targets. I want to get out of this country!

—*Jackie after the*
assassination of
Bobby Kennedy

There has always been just the three of us: my mother, Caroline, and me.

—*John*

4
=

J ohn pulled back the drapes and peered out the window at the commotion on the street. Instantly, a dozen flashbulbs went off. "What are all these silly people taking my picture for?" John asked his nanny.

In the wake of the assassination, John was viewed—even more than before Dallas—as America's beloved surrogate son. Jackie would have none of it, and was more determined than ever to make life as normal as possible for her young, impressionable, and highly vulnerable children.

Caroline wrote a letter to Santa asking for a Nancy Nurse doll and rehearsed for her Christmas pageant. It would be the first one without her father in the audience. "Mrs. Kennedy wanted the pageant to go on as usual," Sister Joanne Frey said. "Angier Biddle Duke, the White House protocol chief, had been in Paris but he flew back to handle the guest list, and Jackie would come in every now and then—sometimes wearing riding clothes—just to see how everything was going. Jackie came with her sister, Lee, and the Auchinclosses and everyone sang Christmas carols. But no one could forget that someone was missing."

Caroline was already showing signs of having inherited her

mother's taste. She went on a Christmas shopping expedition and picked out Van Gogh prints to give to her mother, her brother, and Maud Shaw.

As they had in previous years, Jackie and the children spent that first Christmas with the rest of the Kennedy family at Joe's Palm Beach estate. They decorated the tree on Christmas Eve, and while John hurled handfuls of tinsel at the branches Caroline asked about her father.

"Will Patrick be looking after him in heaven?" she wanted to know.

Before anyone could answer, John added, "Do they have fish chowder in heaven?" Fish chowder, as everyone in the room knew, had been a staple of JFK's diet.

That December, Jackie had asked her friends to scout local real estate opportunities for a permanent home. She hastened to tell them that cost was a major consideration.

Jack had, in fact, left his family far from destitute. At the time of his death, his estate was valued at $1,890,646.45 (the equivalent of at least twenty-five million dollars today) and did not include additional millions placed in trust for his wife and children.

JFK did, however, leave Jackie with a cash flow problem. She received a little less than seventy thousand dollars in cash—representing the presidential salary owed for the month of November, Navy disability pay, and Civil Service death benefits. The rest, about ten million dollars, was tied up in two trust funds for the widow and her children. Jackie was to be paid the income from one of the two funds—about $175,000 a year—as well as the standard annual widow's pension of ten thousand dollars and free lifetime use of the mails.

As she had done throughout her marriage, Jackie sent her bills to the Kennedy family offices in New York to be paid. But, now feeling vulnerable and alone, she began to fret about her own financial future and the financial future of her children.

In mid-December, Jackie paid $175,000 for a fourteen-room, three-story, beige brick colonial town house at 3017 N Street, just down from the Harrimans. What she failed to consider was that, unlike the Harriman mansion, the rooms in the front of her new house—including the living room, dining room, study, several bed-rooms, and bathrooms—were at street level and plainly visible to passersby.

"They actually sit there and eat their lunch and throw sandwich wrappers on the ground," she said of the gawkers who forced her to keep her drapes shut day and night. "I'm trapped in that house and I can't get out. I can't even change my clothes in private because they look in my bedroom window."

"The new Kennedy home," recalled decorator Billy Baldwin, whom Jackie had hired to do the interior, "had become a tourist site . . . She felt as if she were on permanent display."

"It's very upsetting," Jackie complained to Baldwin. "Women are always breaking the police lines and trying to hug and kiss my chil-dren as they go in and out. The world is pouring terrible adoration at their feet and I fear for them. How can I bring them up nor-mally? We never would have named John after his father if we had known."

Out of her overriding concern for her children, she showed Bald-win photographs of their bedrooms at the White House and asked that he make their new rooms look identical. "She wanted their lives to be disrupted as little as possible," Baldwin said. "She was trying for some semblance of constancy, continuity. Sadly, this was impossible."

Jackie was unable to overcome her grief even with the help of Max Jacobson's amphetamine injections. During one of his visits to the new house, she told Jacobson, "My life is over, Max. Just empty, meaningless."

Still, Jackie relied on her husband's loyal Irish "Murphia" to buoy the children's spirits. Dave Powers continued to show up each day to march around with John or give him piggyback rides as he had at the White House. Playing Davy Crockett to Powers's grizzly bear, John seemed blissfully unaware of his mother's sadness.

Not Caroline. "She was a very, very bright girl," Sister Joanne Frey said. "After her father died, she picked up on everything that was going on around her. She was very much attuned to her mother's pain."

"She seemed to age before our eyes," said Rita Dallas, Joe Kennedy's private nurse. "She stayed to herself, lost in thought, and her eyes, once so pert and dancing, were listless. Children seldom clench their fists, but her tiny hands were always knotted."

In late January, Sister Joanne was teaching her catechism class about Mary Magdalen washing the feet of Christ when suddenly Caroline said, "My mommy cries all the time."

The nun returned to the Bible story, but Caroline insisted. "My mommy cries *all* the time. My mommy cries all the time."

Frey tried a third time, but Caroline wanted to talk about her mother's anguish. So Caroline's teacher stopped everything to listen.

"After my daddy died, my mommy is always crying," Caroline said. "I go and get in bed with her and tell her everything is all right and tell her to stop crying. But she doesn't. My mommy is always crying . . ."

There were poignant reminders of Caroline's own sense of loss. Sharing a wishbone with Jackie's half sister, Janet, Caroline asked if she could have anything she wished for.

"Anything," Aunt Janet assured her.

"I want to see my daddy," Caroline said.

That February, Jackie decided to spend a few days with the children at New York's Hotel Carlyle, where for years JFK had maintained a penthouse suite. Although days were largely devoted to shopping with her sister, Lee, and lunching with old Park Avenue friends, Jackie entertained John and Caroline by taking them to play with the children of Deputy Peace Corps Director Bill Haddad.

Haddad joined the children playing on the floor when he noticed that John was lining up his cars in formation—"what he had grown up with—a Secret Service convoy," Haddad realized.

Suddenly, John asked Haddad, "Are you a daddy?"

"Yes, I am."

"Then," John said, scrambling to his feet, "will you throw me up in the air?"

Haddad did, fighting back tears.

Daddy's brother stepped in and tried to fill the void. Over the next six months, Bobby became a surrogate father to his brother's children. Nearly every day, Jackie took them to Hickory Hill to play with Bobby and Ethel's brood of eight.

"They think of Hickory Hill as their own home," Jackie said. "Anything that comes up involving a father, like Father's Day at school, I always mention Bobby's name. Caroline shows him her report cards."

"We used to think that if anything happened to us," Jackie went on, "we'd want to leave the children with Ethel and Bobby . . . now I want them to be part of that family. Bobby wants to look after his brother's children. There's John, with his brother's name. He's going to make sure John turns out as he should."

By late March, Bobby was picking John up nearly every day and taking him to his office at the Justice Department. There, John would spend the morning playing with his cousins Kerry and Michael.

There was also, predictably, a healthy dose of Kennedy roughhousing. At Hickory Hill, Bobby spent part of one afternoon trying to teach his nephew how to kick a football. John would kick the ball a few feet and he would fall to the ground.

"Get up, try again," Uncle Bobby said, and little John did. Again, the ball rolled a few feet and John plopped down.

"Get up, try again," Bobby repeated. John did, again—and again. And again.

The sixth or seventh time, John fell to the ground and stayed there.

"Get up, try again," Uncle Bobby said.

John didn't budge. "Come on, a Kennedy never gives up," Bobby told the boy.

John looked up from the ground. And he said, "Hmmph, here's one that does."

Jackie became so convinced that Bobby could replace Jack in her children's lives that she asked him to legally adopt John and Caroline. Ethel, growing jealous of the attention Bobby was lavishing on Jackie, suggested that would not be a good idea.

Bobby was not the only male John had formed something akin to a father–son bond with. He grew so close to Secret Service agent Bob Foster that he began calling Foster "Daddy"—something the flustered agent repeatedly tried to correct, but to no avail. Worried that John was becoming too attached to Foster as a father figure, Jackie reluctantly asked that he be reassigned. As a token of their admiration and affection, Jackie and the children gave the departing agent Charlie, one of their seven dogs.

On St. Patrick's Day, Sister Joanne had just finished teaching her religion class when Caroline came up to her and pointed to a magazine on her desk. On the cover was another photograph of JFK. "Can I take it home, Sister?" she asked. "My mommy saves every picture she can find of my daddy. She told me that whenever I see one I should bring it to her. Then she puts them in these big books. I don't know why, but it makes her smile."

Lee Radziwill had been lobbying her sister to move to New York, where she could escape the painful memories that surrounded her in Washington. She even paved the way by having her husband, Prince Stanislas "Stas" Radziwill, buy an eleven-room co-op at 969 Fifth Avenue.

That Easter, Jackie fled again to Palm Beach. There she hosted an Easter egg hunt for forty local children at the palatial oceanfront home of her wealthy friends Charles and Jayne Wrightsman. The Manhattan toy store FAO Schwarz provided the prizes, which included one of the first popular action toys for boys, G.I. Joe.

Suddenly, the Easter egg hunt was interrupted by the crash of a wrought-iron table being overturned and the sound of two little boys yelling at each other. To her horror, Jackie saw John and another little boy named Richard slugging it out over ownership of a G.I. Joe. Jackie rushed up and pulled the boys apart, but John kept on swinging. Jackie gave that particular toy to the other boy, and got another one for her son. But John's behavior did not go unpunished. Jackie took him inside and spanked him. "My mother was very strict with me," John later told a friend. "Caroline could do just about anything, but if I stepped out of line, I got a swat."

On May 29, what would have been her husband's forty-seventh birthday, Jackie and the children attended an emotion-filled mass at St. Matthew's Church. They then drove to Arlington and placed flowers on JFK's grave as more than a thousand visitors looked on. John had been given something special to leave behind—a tie clasp in the shape of PT-109. Following his mother's instructions, he removed the clasp from the lapel of his white linen coat, reached over, and placed it on the boughs that covered his father's final resting place.

From there, Jackie flew north to Hyannis Port. Still worried that her husband would somehow be forgotten, she made a televised appeal on behalf of the John F. Kennedy Library that was broadcast on both sides of the Atlantic. The broadcast over, she retreated into what she called her "shell of grief."

Finally, in June of 1964, Jackie went apartment-hunting with Lee in New York. She wound up paying two hundred thousand dollars for a five-bedroom, five-bathroom, fifteenth-floor apartment at 1040 Fifth Avenue. The apartment boasted its own elevator and, more important, sweeping views of Central Park and the reservoir.

Family and friends, most of whom lived in New York, were ecstatic. They would, in the end, provide the grieving Jacqueline with a built-in support group—not to mention playmates galore for John and Caroline. In addition to Lee, who lived just down the block, in-laws Peter and Pat Lawford resided at 990 Fifth, Steven and Jean Kennedy Smith lived at 950 Fifth, and stepbrother Yusha Auchincloss lived nearby on Park Avenue. All, much to the delight of JFK's son and daughter, had children.

To completely sever her ties to Washington, Jackie sold Wexford for $130,000 and leased a house not far from Bobby's summer rental in Glen Cove, Long Island. Soon Bobby would relocate permanently to New York and announce his candidacy for the U.S. Senate.

While more than $125,000 worth of renovations to her new apartment were under way, Jackie took a suite at the Carlyle. John and Caroline, meanwhile, took full advantage of the playgrounds, zoo, bike paths, lakes, and carousel located just across Fifth Avenue in Central Park.

But before JFK's family could officially make their move north to Manhattan, disaster struck again. On June 19, 1964, Uncle Ted's small plane crashed in Massachusetts, killing his aide and the pilot and breaking Ted's back. "Oh, Bobby," Jackie said when she met him in the hospital cafeteria, "we have such rotten luck."

The week following Ted's plane crash, Bobby posed for the cover of *Life* with six of his extended brood crawling all over him. Caroline, touchingly, sat on her uncle's knee wearing an expression that fell somewhere between wistful and melancholic. In the foreground John, wearing shorts and missing his left front tooth, smiled broadly for the camera.

There was no underestimating the political appeal of JFK's children, John in particular. When he paid a visit to the World's Fair in Flushing Meadows, Queens, that September, the boy's every move was chronicled by a small army of reporters. Riding on the back of one of his four bodyguards, John cheerfully answered questions tossed at him by the press.

"Where's Caroline?" asked one reporter.

"She's in school," he answered, "but I'm too young."

At the Magic Skyway, part of the fair's futuristic Walt Disney exhibit, a Disney executive presented John with a toy car. "Hi, everybody!" he said to the assembled crowd as he got down on all fours. "I'm going to play car!"

John's mood was more subdued when he emerged from Sinclair Oil's Dinoland. The *Tyrannosaurus rex* exhibit was a bit too realistic for a not-quite-four-year-old. "The lights and the dinosaurs," he said, left him "a little bit scared."

Two weeks after Bobby trounced Keating by a seven-hundred-thousand-vote margin, John finally moved with his mother and sister out of the Carlyle and into their new home at 1040 Fifth Avenue. "I think she saw her return to the city," Nancy Tuckerman said of her best friend, "as coming home."

Even before they moved into their new home, Caroline was enrolled in second grade at the prestigious Convent of the Sacred Heart just a few blocks up Fifth Avenue at 91st Street. At first, she was conspicuously excluded from other girls' birthday parties. Jackie called one of the mothers to find out why.

"Of course we'd love to invite Caroline," the woman stammered, "but we all felt it might be presumptuous of us to ask."

"Please invite Caroline to everything!" Jackie pleaded. "She's dying to come!" Not surprisingly, from that point on Caroline was the most popular student at Sacred Heart.

For John, the adjustment to life in New York went smoothly. He would not be attending St. David's School until the following February, so for now he made do pedaling his tricycle through Central Park, going on the swings at the nearby playground, and riding the merry-go-round under the watchful gaze of ever-present Secret Service agents.

The place John and Caroline would call home for the next two decades was an elegant reflection of their mother's irrefutable good taste. Nearly all the furnishings had been in the family quarters at the White House.

The private elevator opened onto a long entrance hall with gilt mirrors and nineteenth-century French architectural studies hanging on the walls. In the living room, there were white sofas with floral throw pillows, velvet-upholstered Louis XVI chairs, and on an ornate French chest half a dozen Greek and Roman busts—part of the antiquities collection begun by JFK.

John would proudly lead visitors to the dining room to look at a world map covered with pins, each pin indicating a spot their father had visited during his presidency. From the living room windows, the view was dominated by Central Park and the reservoir, with the Hudson River and New Jersey beyond.

In the kitchen, there was another reminder that this was, if not exactly typical, an American home. On one wall was a bulletin board covered with family snapshots, along with the children's artwork.

After several happy weeks in their new home, John noticed that his mother's mood had suddenly darkened. The first anniversary of the assassination was approaching, and the memories were all flooding back. Mommy was crying again.

In late November, black-bordered photographs of JFK went up in store windows everywhere. Walking down Fifth Avenue on the way to Kenneth's hair salon, Jackie passed a dozen of these sad reminders. Closing the door of the salon behind her, she stood at the receptionist's desk and wept.

Jackie was plunged into such black despair that she told a friend she had actually considered suicide. "She said she had enough sleeping pills to do it," Roswell Gilpatric said. "But of course she wouldn't because of the children. Everyone who loved her was very concerned about her state of mind."

"On so many days—his birthday, an anniversary, watching his children run to the sea—I have thought, 'But this day last year was his last to see that,'" Jackie said. "Soon the final day will come around again . . . What was lost cannot be replaced. Now I think that I should have known he was magic all along . . . Now he is a legend when he would have preferred to be a man."

Three days later, John was blowing out the four candles on his birthday cake as two dozen cousins and playmates looked on. They played pin-the-tail-on-the-donkey and musical chairs and, for a fleeting moment, it seemed to John's mother that things might turn out all right—that John F. Kennedy's children might be allowed to lead normal, happy lives.

For that to happen, Jackie was convinced that the Secret Service would have to be reined in. She spelled out what she expected them to do and what she demanded they *not* do in no uncertain terms.

"Mrs. Kennedy feels very strongly," wrote the head of the Secret Service Children's Detail in a confidential memo, "that though there are two children to protect, it is 'bad' to see two agents 'hovering around' . . . If Mrs. Kennedy is driving the children, she still insists that the follow-up car not be seen by the children . . .

"Mrs. Kennedy is adamant in her contention that agents must not perform special favors for John Jr. and Caroline or wait upon them as servants. Agents are not to carry clothes, beach articles, sand buckets, baby carriages, strollers, handbags, suitcases etc., for Caroline and John Jr. and the children must carry their own clothing items, toys etc. . . ."

Furthermore, Jackie wanted the agents to perfect the art of hiding in plain sight: "The agent must drift into the background quickly when arriving at a specific location, and remain aloof and invisible until moment of departure . . .

"Mrs. Kennedy," the memo continued, "is inclined to believe that the agents are doing too much for the children, and feels 'it is bad for the children to see grown men waiting upon them.'" Jackie wanted the agents to "demand" that John and Caroline "pick up their own discarded clothes, shoes, toys, accessories, etc.'"

Jackie insisted on remaining her children's first line of defense at the beach. "Drowning is my responsibility," she told the agents, insisting that the Secret Service "is not responsible for any accident sustained by the children in the usual and normal play sessions."

She did, however, expect the government agents to act as a shield against the general public. One day she took John to a local newsstand in Hyannis Port and encountered what the agent on duty described as a small group of "harmless onlookers—mostly elderly ladies with cameras." Jackie "turned a cold shoulder and refused to permit any photographs," the agent recalled. As they left, she turned to the agent and blasted him. "Do something," she said, "when there are people around like that!"

The day after Christmas 1964, John and his sister were whisked off by their mother for a ski vacation with Uncle Bobby and his brood, this time in Aspen. A battalion of photographers followed them on the slopes, snapping away as Jackie struggled with John's boots and the children threw snowballs at each other. Over the next few weeks, Jackie would take John and Caroline on two more ski trips, to the Catskills and New Hampshire.

By February, Jackie decided it was time for John to start school. A Secret Service agent went along when Jackie walked John to his first day at St. David's, the Catholic boys' school located at 12 East 69th Street. But the agent was powerless to protect the boy from his classmates—and vice versa. His first morning at the school, John punched another student in the nose.

Over the next few years, John would get into several fights with fellow students—the result, said one of his teachers, of his "naturally high spirits" and the fact that, despite his mother's discipline, he had always been accustomed to being the center of attention.

Nevertheless, John was soon one of the most popular kids in class. "John, well, he's something else," Jackie observed. "John makes friends with everybody. Immediately." Added his uncle, Jamie Auchincloss, "John Jr., from the earliest age, was a natural politician, a diplomat, a person who lit up a room." The strongest and most enduring friendship John formed at St. David's was with his own cousin, William Kennedy Smith.

On May 12, 1965, England's Queen Elizabeth walked over to the little boy and smiled. "Pleased to meet you, Your Majesty," John said, bowing at the waist. Maud Shaw sighed with relief; she had spent nearly an hour explaining to him that England's monarch was to be addressed as "Your Majesty," not "*My* Majesty."

The royal encounter took place at Runnymede, the meadow beside the Thames where the Magna Carta was signed in 1215. In this historic setting, Jackie was reduced to tears as the queen dedicated a memorial to JFK. After the ceremony, John joined Caroline and his mother for tea with Her Majesty at Windsor Castle.

For the next few days, Jackie and the children took up residence at Stas and Lee Radziwill's elegant house in Regent's Park. They took in the Changing of the Guard at Buckingham Palace, and posed to have their picture taken with the gold-helmeted, frozen-faced cavalrymen at Whitehall. In both cases, John departed only after offering an enthusiastic salute.

The relentless English press were a constant presence—so much so that Jackie pleaded with them to back off. "In view of the full coverage given to the children already," she said, "it is very much hoped that the remainder of the visit can be kept private."

Not likely. Even when they tried to sneak out the back door of the Radziwill house, press photographers popped out of the bushes and began clicking away. At one point, John was running down a path in Regent's Park, fell, and began wailing. "Crybaby," Caroline said in full view of reporters. Miss Shaw had to restrain John from taking a swing at his sister. All was duly recorded by reporters, who stood nearby scribbling in their notebooks.

Jackie, John, and Caroline pressed on. At the Tower of London, Secret Service agents and Beefeaters watched John clamber into the barrel of a black cannon as Mommy and Caroline gazed at the crown jewels. Castles and pageantry notwithstanding, John seemed happiest taking a boat ride with his cousins Tony and Christina Radziwill on Regent's Park Lake. (As he would with Kennedy cousin Willie Smith, John would go on to form a special bond with his Bouvier cousin Tony).

Maud Shaw was, as always, a constant presence in the lives of John and Caroline. On this first trip to England, she held John's hand as he crossed the street, watched carefully as he played with Caroline and their cousins, and made sure that he was fed, bathed, and properly dressed—freeing Jackie of such mundane matters. Miss Shaw had, in truth, been as much of a loving mother figure to John and Caroline as Jackie had been.

Unbeknownst to John and Caroline, Miss Shaw had decided to retire to her native England. She would not be returning with the family to New York. Neither child was told the truth, only that she was staying behind and would be rejoining them later.

The children had settled back into their lives on Fifth Avenue when the news of Miss Shaw's retirement was finally broken to them a few weeks later. To be sure, there were still plenty of familiar faces around. Jackie's maid since 1955, Providencia "Provi" Paredes, had moved to 1040 Fifth with the family, and the familiar faces of Jackie's chauffeur and cook—not to mention the ever-present Secret Service detail—provided a warming sense of continuity.

That spring, Jackie became a glittering fixture on the social scene. Night after night, invariably swathed in ermine or mink, she emerged from hotels, restaurants, concert halls, and nightclubs to a fusillade of popping flashbulbs. Even her social mentor, millionaire Paul Mellon's wife, Bunny, confessed she became exhausted "just looking at Jackie's calendar."

Yet each morning she walked Caroline up Fifth Avenue to the Convent of the Sacred Heart, then returned to walk John down the avenue to St. David's. "They are," she said, "the center of my universe, and I hope I am the center of theirs. I intend to always be there for them."

In August 1965, Jackie staged an elaborate party for Caroline and forty of her daughter's friends at Hammersmith Farm. "Jackie wanted the party to be a treasure hunt," recalled longtime friend George Plimpton, "so she went to the Coast Guard station and got a longboat, then she went out and bought all this fake jewelry for the treasure and a big chest to put it in."

Jackie then had Plimpton write a pirate's log giving clues that led to the treasure. But included with those clues was a warning that if anyone disturbed the treasure, the pirates who buried it would return to claim it for themselves. Plimpton and several other men in pirate garb waited just out of sight in the longboat. "When the children found the treasure, Jackie gave the signal and we rowed into view shouting and yelling and waving our rubber swords."

The result was pandemonium. "A lot of the children began weeping," Plimpton recalled. "Others ran for the nannies. Caroline and John looked puzzled, but they didn't run away."

Plimpton stepped off the boat, slipped, and fell into the water. Caroline walked straight up to him and said, "I know who *you* are." John, meanwhile, asked to borrow one of the pirates' rubber swords and began waving it above his head. But, said Plimpton, "nobody had more fun that day than Jackie. She was doubled over with laughter."

Later that month, John, Caroline, and fifteen of their Kennedy cousins attended Cardinal Cushing's seventieth-birthday party in Boston. They joined the other Kennedy grandchildren again that October, when the whole clan went trick-or-treating in Hyannis Port. Caroline went as a Dutch girl, with pigtails, Dutch cap, and wooden shoes. John was a dirty-faced hobo with holes in his shoes and torn pants.

Once again, as the second anniversary of the assassination approached, John's mother was plunged into a pit of despair. This time, however, she bounced back quickly. In fact, for Jackie and for the children life had come to resemble one long vacation interspersed with occasional bouts of schoolwork.

That winter of 1965 there were long weekends at their leased farmhouse in Bernardsville, New Jersey, where Jackie rode with the tony Essex Hounds Fox Club. There was a trip to Antigua, where they stayed at the luxurious Mill Reef club estate of Paul and Bunny Mellon and swam in the warm waters of the Caribbean. And there were the ski vacations, usually with Uncle Bobby, to places like Aspen, Stowe, and the exclusive Swiss resort of Gstaad. On the way back from Gstaad, Jackie stopped in Rome to visit with Fiat chairman Gianni Agnelli and Pope Paul VI, then skipped down to Argentina so that John and Caroline could spend time with some real gauchos.

That May of 1966, Jackie jetted off alone to catch Seville's famous *feria*—another "vacation" that would rival her official visits as First Lady to Paris and New Delhi. Two weeks after returning from Spain, Jackie made up for her absence by presenting John with the one thing he had always wanted. At Hyannis Port on what would have been JFK's forty-ninth birthday, Jackie kept the promise her husband had made years earlier. She gave John a reconditioned—albeit engine-less and propellerless—World War II vintage Piper Cub observation plane. Understandably thrilled, John climbed into the cockpit and took off on an imaginary flight. "Jack always said he was going to give John a real plane when he grew up," Jackie told JFK's friend Chuck Spalding. "Well, it's a little early, but now he has it—a real airplane."

No sooner had she given John his very own plane than Jackie took off once again. This time she, John, and Caroline were joining Jackie's former brother-in-law Peter Lawford and his children on a Hawaiian vacation.

For the next seven weeks, Jackie and the children stayed at an oceanfront house near the base of Diamond Head, which they rented for three thousand dollars a month. Just down the beach was Peter's cottage hideaway at the Kahala Hilton, with its teak floors and dol-phin pools. Kindred spirits—Peter had spent much of his boyhood in France, and often felt overwhelmed by the loud Kennedy clan—Lawford and Jackie often whispered conspiratorially to each other in French.

John, meanwhile befriended three local boys—fourteen-year-old Gary Miske and his brothers Michael, thirteen, and Tommy, eleven. "You would think that we'd get annoyed with a little five-year-old tagging along," Tommy Miske remembered. "But we found him to be a fun and adventuresome little kid."

"We slid down mudslides in Nuuanu," Tommy said. "We hiked through huge boulders at Sacred Falls . . . Caroline got coral cuts that had to be bandaged." John routinely broke up his new friends by pretending to be a pirate peering through a make-believe spyglass.

"John had no fear of the ocean," Gary Miske said. Nor, apparently, did he have a healthy fear of fire. Toward the end of their Hawaiian sojourn, Jackie accepted an invitation from San Francisco architect John Warnecke to take the children on an overnight trip to the big island of Hawaii.

The outing nearly turned to tragedy when John fell into a cook-ing pit during preparations for a luau and burned his buttocks, hands, and arms. Rescued from the flames by quick-thinking Secret Service agent John Walsh, John was treated at a local hospital and released after a few hours. "That brave little kid," Tommy Miske recalled, "never once complained."

When he arrived back in New York, little John was sporting a new badge of honor—a white glove he wore over the second-degree burns on his right hand. The glove was off by the time he accompanied his mother and sister to the wedding of Jackie's half sister, Janet Auchincloss, in Newport.

Only thirteen years earlier, thousands clogged the streets of Newport to catch a glimpse of the dashing young senator from Massachusetts and his regally beautiful bride. The crowds were back again—to see Jackie, not the bride. Janet, all but eclipsed by her big sister on what was to be the most important day of her life, turned to their mother and wept.

John, resplendent in satin shorts and a blue velvet sash, was also grabbing his share of the limelight. While Caroline, earnestly clutching a small bouquet, took her role as flower girl seriously, pageboy John tugged at the collar of his ruffled powder blue shirt and squirmed throughout the ceremony. When someone called John a "sissy," the Secret Service moved quickly to stop JFK's son from bloodying the boy's nose.

No matter. During the reception at Hammersmith Farm, JFK Jr. wound up rolling in the dirt with another page—and at one point had to be stopped from trying to run two of the Auchincloss ponies through the reception tent. Jamie Auchincloss insisted that his high-spirited nephew was merely "having a little fun. Jackie was very strict, and both Caroline and John were incredibly thoughtful, polite children. But you just can't expect a five-year-old to behave like a little adult all the time. John was never a brat, but he was all boy."

Back at St. David's, that meant the occasional fistfight with one of his classmates. But Jackie was still more concerned with threats to her son's safety, not the other way around. "I'm nerve-racked about the safety of the children," she told one teacher. "There are so many nut cases about."

Jackie had cause for concern. Walking hand in hand out of Manhattan's St. Thomas More Church on All Saints' Day, Jackie and Caroline were accosted by a woman who grabbed the little girl and began shouting, "Your mother is a wicked woman who has killed three people! And your father is still alive!"

A terrified Caroline tried to free herself from the woman's grasp but couldn't. "It was terrible, prying her loose," Jackie said. The woman was hustled off to Bellevue for observation. "I still," she told a friend over lunch at Schrafft's more than a year later, "haven't gotten over that strange woman."

As the third anniversary of Jack's death approached, Jackie was surprised at how well John seemed to be handling his situation. She was, in fact, impressed with her son's strength, and not at all bothered by the fact that he had already gotten into several fights at school.

"He surprises me in so many ways," Jackie said of her brown-eyed son. "He seems so much more than one would expect of a child of six. Sometimes it almost seems as if he is trying to protect me instead of just the other way around."

St. David's headmaster, David Hume, thought Mrs. Kennedy was "a sensible, affectionate mom who had a straight relationship with her son. Some people coo over their children. But by the time children are seven or eight, you shouldn't coo. When they reach out a hand, you should hold it. When they want to let go, you should let go. She understood that."

"There was no one sweeter than John," St. David's assistant headmaster, Peter Clifton, later said. "He had no guile in him. He's still like that. I have to give Jackie a lot of credit for that."

On the afternoon of November 22, 1966, Jackie picked John up at the school as usual. But this time, she noticed that several of his classmates were following him. Without warning, one of them shouted, "Your father's dead, your father's dead!"

Jackie was shocked and upset, but it was not the first time she had heard words like that from children at her son's school. "You know how children are. They've even said it to me when I run into them at school, as if . . . Well, this day John listened to them saying it over and over, and he didn't say a word."

Instead, John took his mother's hand and squeezed it. "As if he were trying to reassure me," Jackie said, "that things were all right. And so we walked home together, with the children following us."

John was no less attentive to Caroline. "You never had to urge him to be kind to his sister," Maud Shaw said. "He shared things with her and remembered her when he was given anything . . . John treated his sister with a sensitivity far beyond his years."

Still, Jackie constantly fretted over the children's emotional well-being. In early 1967, she was particularly concerned about what impact her headline-making battle with William Manchester over the publication of his book *The Death of a President* might have on John and Caroline. Jackie had actually approached Manchester to write the book and had cooperated fully—until she read the manuscript. Many of the details she had shared so freely with the author now seemed shockingly personal in print.

But the front-page free-for-all only served to focus attention on the very things Jackie thought to keep private, gruesome details of the assassination and its aftermath she did not wish her children exposed to. "We didn't talk about it, of course," she said. "But children pick things up. A word here, and a word there, and they knew something was happening that involved them. There was no way to keep them from passing newsstands going to and from school. It was natural for them to look at the magazine covers and the headlines. Or be told something at school or on the street. It isn't always easy for the children."

Jackie expressed concern that perhaps Caroline was "too withdrawn." But it was clear to those around her that John was Jackie's number-one concern; she was fixated on what would become of him.

"I sometimes say to myself, 'He'll never remember his father. He was too young.' But now I think he will," she mused. "He'll remember his father through associations with people who knew Jack well and the things Jack liked to do. He will be getting to know his father. I tell him little things like, 'Oh, don't worry about your spelling. Your father couldn't spell very well, either.' That pleases him, you can bet.

"Then there will always be a Dave Powers to talk sports with him. John seems to know an awful lot about sports. He talks about someone named Bubba Smith, and about Cassius Clay . . . I want to help him go back and find his father. It can be done . . . This coming summer at Hyannis Port, John will sail in his father's favorite boat, with Ted. And that will help, too. And even smaller things that bring him closer to Jack. The school insists that children even as young as John must wear neckties to class. That was all right with him. It gave him a chance to wear one of his father's PT-boat tie pins.

"I don't want the children to be just two kids living on Fifth Avenue and going to nice schools," she went on. "There's so much else in the world, outside this sanctuary we live in. Bobby has told them about some of these things—the children in Harlem, for instance. He told them about the rats and about terrible living conditions that exist right here in the midst of a rich city. Broken windows letting in the cold . . . John was so touched by that that he said he'd go to work and use the money he made to put windows in those houses. The children rounded up their best toys last Christmas and gave them away.

"I want them to know about how the rest of the world lives, but also I want to be able to give them some kind of sanctuary when they need it, some place to take them to when things happen to them that do not necessarily happen to other children. Caroline was knocked down by a charge of photographers when I took her out to try to teach her how to ski. How do you explain that to a child?

"And the stares and pointing, and the stories . . . the strangest stories that haven't a word of truth in them, great long analytical pieces written by people you never met, never saw. I guess they have to make a living, but what's left of a person's privacy or a child's right to privacy?"

For his part, John seemed to enjoy the attention. In June 1967, John, his mother, and his sister made a six-week pilgrimage to Ireland, where they paid a visit to the Kennedy ancestral home in Duganstown. "I am so happy to be here in this land my husband loved so much," Jackie said when they arrived at Shannon Airport. "For myself and the children it is a little bit like coming home, and we are looking forward to it dearly."

So were their Irish hosts, who understandably took immense pride in JFK and harbored immense affection for his family. "The Kennedy family has a huge role in Ireland's heritage," said Brian Barron, one of the photographers who covered the visit, "and John had inherited the mantle of clan chief."

During their stay, the Kennedys took up residence in Woodstown House, a sixty-room Georgian manor rented for them by their wealthy New Jersey neighbors Marjorie "Peggy" and Murray McDonnell. Much of the Kennedys' time was spent, in fact, with the McDonnells, who had eight children of their own.

The Duganstown relatives were impressed that young John knew the words to "When Irish Eyes Are Smiling," and gave him credit for trying, albeit unsuccessfully, to play Irish football on the Fourth of July. They even laughed at his impression of the Beatles, who had popularized the hairstyle for which John had been so fiercely criticized during the White House years.

There were moments, however, when John seemed anything but charming. On their visit to Woodstown Beach in Waterford, two busloads of reporters and photographers showed up to chronicle the famous visitors' every move. In front of all of them, John sat with a bucket and shovel making sand castles but simply refused to join his sister in the water. Instead, he broke away and ran into a nearby candy store.

"What do you want, dear?" the woman behind the counter asked.

"Everything."

"Now, you know you can't have everything," she replied.

"I can too!" John barked back. Jackie, mortified, led him outside.

Later, John was dashing through a potato field when suddenly he ran back to Jackie. "There's electricity in the grass," he yelled. "I got a shock! Electricity!" As accustomed as he was to playing on the manicured lawns in Newport, Hyannis Port, and Palm Beach—not to mention Central Park—John had never been stung by nettles before.

Understandably, Jackie wanted time away from the children—not only hers, but the McDonnells' as well. Their third week in Ireland, she began to slip away alone in the evenings to swim. One night, she was caught in a strong undertow and, struggling against the current and the cold, nearly drowned. As she was about to give up hope,

Jackie suddenly felt "a great porpoise at my side"—Secret Service agent John Walsh, who miraculously appeared in the water just in time to pull her to safety. Unbeknownst to her, Walsh had followed Jackie every evening.

Jackie did not share the details of her near-fatal accident with the children, but in Ireland that night John and Caroline had come perilously close to becoming orphans. At Jackie's insistence, Walsh, who had also pulled John from the fire in Hawaii, was cited for valor by the Secret Service. Later, she succeeded in having him promoted to head up her detail in New York.

The children were accustomed to seeing Kennedy family members, including themselves, on television. But they were glued to their set in January 1968 when one of their Bouvier relatives, Lee Radziwill, made her disastrous acting debut in David Susskind's ABC production of the murder classic *Laura*. Lee threw a party, and Jackie showed up to lend moral support, but John and Caroline stayed home at 1040 Fifth and watched the critically panned show with their uncle Jamie Auchincloss. John jumped up several times and clapped whenever Lee appeared. "They were so excited," Jamie said, "at seeing their aunt Lee kissing on the screen."

Jackie made another trip abroad in March of 1968, this time to visit the ancient Mayan ruins on Mexico's Yucatán Peninsula. This time, her escort was former deputy defense secretary Roswell Gilpatric, and again rumors flew. But on the trip Gilpatric, who had fallen in love with Jackie, was astounded to learn that she had someone else on her mind.

"Even at the most romantic moments," Gilpatric said, "she kept mentioning Aristotle Onassis's name—what did I think of him? Was he as rich as they said he was? She also said she felt he was very protective toward her, and that he cared about the children and their welfare."

Behind the scenes, Onassis had in fact been secretly bombarding Jackie with letters and phone calls. But for now Bobby Kennedy remained the most important man in her life—in large part because of his continued role in raising John.

While she was still in Mexico, Jackie learned that Bobby had decided to seek the Democratic presidential nomination. Two weeks later, Lyndon Johnson stunned the nation by going on television to announce he would not seek reelection.

At first, Jackie was heartsick at the news. "Do you know what will happen to Bobby?" she asked Arthur Schlesinger. "The same thing that happened to Jack. There is so much hatred in this country, and more people hate Bobby than hated Jack . . . I've told Bobby this, but he isn't fatalistic, like me."

By this time, Jackie was involved in a clandestine affair that, if made public, would almost certainly scuttle Bobby's presidential ambitions. Not even John and Caroline were aware of Jackie's increasingly intense relationship with Onassis.

Already in the throes of a highly publicized affair with the legendary diva Maria Callas, Onassis had been intrigued with Jackie ever since he met her and JFK in 1955. And like JFK, the shipping tycoon who began with sixty dollars in his pocket and built it into a five-hundred-million-dollar shipping empire had affairs with dozens of glamorous women, including Paulette Goddard, Evita Perón, and even Gloria Swanson, who had been Joe Kennedy's mistress for years.

When he was forty-six, Onassis married the seventeen-year-old Athina "Tina" Livanos, daughter of the biggest ship owner at the time, Stavros Livanos. The union, which produced two children, Alexander and Christina, ended in 1959 after Tina took a stroll on the deck of the Christina and saw Onassis and Callas making love in the bar.

A great believer in maintaining appearances, Onassis splurged on penthouse suites, limousines, and helicopters. He owned Olympic Airways, the Greek national airline, and a five-hundred-acre private island, Skorpios. But his favorite toy was the 325-foot frigate he christened Christina, after his adored only daughter, in 1954. On board were a five-passenger Piaggio seaplane, four motorboats, two kayaks, a small sailboat, three dinghies, a glass-bottomed boat, and a small car. There were gold-plated bathroom fixtures, lapis lazuli balustrades, Baccarat crystal chandeliers, a ballroom, several bars, an Olympic-sized swimming pool, and mosaic floors throughout depicting scenes from

Greek mythology. The children's playroom was decorated by *Madeline* creator Ludwig Bemelmans, and contained a kid-sized slot machine from Monte Carlo and dolls dressed by Dior. A crew of sixty catered to their employer's every whim.

To Bobby, Onassis was "a rogue on a grand scale." When RFK announced his intention to run for the White House, Onassis took it as a clear signal that Jack's younger brother could no longer tend to Jackie's personal life—or function, as he had, as surrogate father to John and Caroline.

Knowing that word of Jackie's romance with the notorious Greek could derail his campaign, Bobby dispatched Ethel and Ted's wife, Joan, to 1040 Fifth. The Kennedy wives pleaded with Jackie not to marry "The Greek."

Not quite sure how to proceed, Jackie then went to Cardinal Cushing, asking what the Vatican's attitude might be toward her marrying a divorced man. Privately horrified, Cushing chimed in with the Kennedy clan and advised against marriage—at least not at the moment. For Bobby's sake, Jackie agreed to wait until after the 1968 presidential elections to make a decision.

On April 4, 1968, the world reeled at the news that Martin Luther King had been shot to death outside his motel room in Memphis. At Bobby's urging, Jackie attended King's funeral and stood beside the slain civil rights leader's widow. "I was looking at those faces," she later told one of Bobby's closest advisers, Frank Mankiewicz, "and I realized that they know death. They see it all the time and they're ready for it . . . in the way a good Catholic is. We know death . . . As a matter of fact, if it weren't for the children, we'd welcome it."

A few weeks later, there was rejoicing in the Kennedy camp over polls that showed Bobby overtaking Vice President Hubert Humphrey in the race for the nomination. "Oh, Bobby," Jackie said, "won't it be wonderful when we get back in the White House?"

"What do you mean, 'we'? " Ethel snapped. It was obvious that she wasn't kidding.

"Jacqueline Kennedy looked as if she'd been struck," said Joe Kennedy's nurse Rita Dallas, who was standing just a few feet away.

"She flinched as though a blow had actually stung her cheek. I'll always remember the look of pain in Jackie's eyes."

Jackie knew the children would always be Kennedys, but she also felt her own ties to Jack's family slipping away. In May 1968 she managed to elude the press and board the *Christina* for a four-day Caribbean cruise—and spent part of the time throwing up in her cabin.

At 3:45 on the morning of June 6, 1968, Jackie was jolted awake by a phone call from her brother-in-law Stas Radziwill. She had gone to bed just a half hour earlier, after staying up to watch Bobby win the California Democratic Primary.

"Jackie," asked Stas, "how's Bobby?"

"He's fine, terrific. You heard that he won California by 53 percent, didn't you?"

"But, Jackie, he's been shot. It happened just a few minutes ago."

There was a silence, and Jackie screamed, "No! It can't have happened! No! It can't have happened!"

But it had, in the pantry of the Ambassador Hotel in Los Angeles, after Bobby spoke to reporters in the hotel ballroom. A young Palestinian named Sirhan Sirhan, apparently angered over the recent defeat of the Arabs in the Six-Day War with U.S.-backed Israel, fired six shots at Bobby, hitting him in the head, neck, and right side.

Jackie caught the first plane to Los Angeles, and went straight to Good Samaritan Hospital. In an eerie replay of November 22, 1963, Jackie was among those closest to Bobby who accompanied his body on the plane ride home.

For Caroline, the death of her beloved uncle Bobby was merely the latest in a series of emotional blows that would leave her reeling. Once again, she reacted not with tears but with quiet, withdrawing more inside herself.

For John, Bobby's death and its aftermath would also be a reprise of Dallas, but with an important difference. This time, at age seven, he would more fully comprehend what was going on—and he would always remember.

President Johnson led the two thousand mourners who jammed St. Patrick's Cathedral to pay their last respects to Bobby. Ethel, pregnant with Bobby's eleventh child, remained stoic even as Teddy, delivering the eulogy just a few feet from his brother's flag-draped casket, began to crack. "As he said many times in many parts of this nation," Ted said, "to those he touched and to those who sought to touch him, 'Some men see things as they are and say, why? I dream of things that never were and say, why not?' "

Jackie, ashen-faced and shrouded in a black mantilla, "was in a trance," recalled Pierre Salinger. "Just completely in shock." John, his tie held in place by his cherished PT-109 tie clasp, joined Caroline and several Kennedy cousins in taking part in the mass. Occasionally he glanced at his mother, clearly concerned for her welfare.

Later, Jackie and the children boarded the funeral train bound for Washington, where Bobby was to join his brother Jack at Arlington. Two million people lined the 226-mile route. But as if to validate the growing sense that there was a Kennedy family curse, a passing train killed two people and injured six others who had come to pay their respects—a gruesome scene witnessed by several of John's cousins.

Jackie's first concern now was for John and Caroline. She could no longer allow her destiny to be charted by the Kennedys. Craving seclusion and terrified for her children's safety, she turned to the one man who could provide both—on board the *Christina,* behind the gates of his guarded homes in Athens and Paris, and on his private island of Skorpios.

John's mother actually had more faith in Onassis's private army than she did in the U.S. government. The four-man Secret Service detail assigned to Jackie and her children was dwarfed by Ari's machine-gun-toting, seventy-five-member private security force, supplemented by trained-to-kill attack dogs.

There was, of course, another reason for becoming Mrs. Aristotle Onassis. By marrying a man whose fortune was often compared to those of J. Paul Getty and Howard Hughes, Jackie would no longer be treated like the poor relation.

Even though Bobby had come closest to replacing their father, Jacqueline took special care in reminding both John and Caroline that no one ever really could. At age eleven, Caroline still cut out photos of her father and added them to her collection, which now literally papered the walls of her room.

John had a different way of keeping his father's memory alive. In his room, along with his extensive collection of toy airplanes and helicopters, he kept a record player and several LPs of his father's speeches. Whenever he'd have another child over to play, he invariably asked the same question. "Would you like to hear my father?" he would ask as he carefully removed one of the records from its sleeve. Without waiting for an answer, he put the LP on and listened to JFK's "Ask not what your country can do for you" and "Ich bin ein Berliner" speeches before returning to the floor to play.

Now, more than ever, Ari "had to have her," said columnist Aileen Mehle, a friend of both Onassis and Jackie. Ari and rival Greek ship owner Stavros Niarchos were "in constant competition," Mehle recalled. "Jackie was a great big feather in Ari's cap. She was the widow of the President of the United States, the most famous woman in the world. Jackie was a tremendous trophy for Ari."

By way of winning her hand, Onassis knew he needed the children in his corner. Thus, whenever he paid a visit to 1040 Fifth or to Hyannis Port, Ari always came loaded down with expensive gifts from FAO Schwarz. But Onassis was also careful to invest something else—his precious time—to forge a bond with Jackie's son and daughter. Ari took long walks with them on the beach at Hyannis Port, played games with them, and made sure they understood their mother needed someone to take care of her.

Realizing that Jackie was most concerned about the impact Bobby's death would have on John, Ari focused special attention on JFK's only son. Onassis took John Jr. to baseball games and on fishing trips. "Here," he said, handing the little boy two hundred-dollar bills. "Go buy some worms."

More important, when John invited him into his room and asked if he wanted to hear the prized recordings of JFK's speeches, Ari hung on every word. Onassis stressed one thing above all else: that he had great respect for the children's father, and that he would never try to replace him in their lives.

That August, Ted Kennedy accompanied Jackie to Skorpios, where he and Onassis began hammering out the terms of a prenuptial agreement. Ted began by pointing out that, once Jackie remarried, she lost both the two hundred thousand a year she received from her trust and her ten-thousand-dollar annual presidential widow's pension. A final deal would be negotiated between Jackie and her financial adviser, Andre Meyer: three million dollars for Jackie up front, and the interest on a one-million-dollar trust fund for John and a one-million-dollar trust fund for Caroline.

For John there were other—and, from the perspective of a seven-year-old, more pressing—matters to attend to. In September, Jackie transferred John from St. David's to the 330-year-old Collegiate School after teachers at St. David's suggested that he repeat first grade.

Affiliated with the Dutch Reformed Church, Collegiate catered to the sons of the rich and famous—Leonard Bernstein's, Jason Robards's, Ford Foundation chief McGeorge Bundy's among them—but also to a fair share of students from the city's poorer neighborhoods attending the school on full scholarship.

Every morning at 7:45, a yellow Collegiate school bus pulled up in front of 1040 Fifth—not to pick up John, but one of his young neighbors. For security reasons, John did not take the bus. Instead, at 7:55 he would emerge from a side door and, clutching a large brown leather briefcase covered with travel stickers, walk toward a waiting unmarked cream-and-tan Oldsmobile with his new governess, Marta Sgubin, in tow. Cigar-chewing Mugsy O'Leary, who for years had been Jack's chauffeur, was at the wheel; a Secret Service agent stood at the curb, holding open the rear passenger door.

Invariably, someone would be standing outside waiting to catch a glimpse of a Kennedy. "There he is! There's John-John!" was a refrain that would often greet him as he departed for school. According to writer Nancy Moran, "John, depending on his mood, frowns darkly, smiles shyly, or darts back inside the building. The governess fetches him out again."

Seven minutes later, the beat-up Oldsmobile would pull up in front of the entrance to Collegiate, at 241 West 77th Street, and John, wearing the school's navy blue blazer with its orange, purple, and gold crest, would dash through the massive wooden front doors. The Secret Service agents would follow, and become, as Jackie had instructed in her secret letter to the agency, "invisible" as they kept tabs on John. The agents accomplished this by playing cards or napping in the basement, then periodically coming up to spy on the boy from an unseen vantage point.

Ironically, the haircut that had drawn such criticism when John lived in the White House had launched a trend. Now John was indistinguishable from many of the other skinny, dark-eyed, shaggy-maned boys who attended Collegiate. On more than one occasion, a passerby asked John to point out John-John, or quizzed him on "what John-John is really like." More often than not, John would earnestly respond that John-John was nice, a great football player, and "very, very smart."

"I used to stand by my window and try to pick him out," a young woman who lived across the street from Collegiate said. "I'd think I'd found him, and then out of the school would come two more little boys who looked exactly like the one I thought was John-John. I got so confused I gave up looking."

Once seated in their green-carpeted homeroom with students' drawings covering the cinder-block walls, John and his classmates studied math, reading, spelling, English, French, and geography. After lunch, John's class either went to the gym to play basketball or to nearby Central Park—like most private schools in New York, Collegiate did not have its own playing fields—to play baseball, football, or soccer. All the while, the Secret Service lurked in the shadows. Precisely at 4 P.M. each weekday, O'Leary materialized outside Collegiate in the battered Oldsmobile and, with at least one Secret Service agent riding shotgun in the front passenger seat, drove John home.

John quickly established himself as an athlete, although his mother's insistence on dressing him in shorts when most of his classmates wore long pants made him the frequent butt of jokes. John's response to teasing was always the same: He lunged at the offender with clenched-fisted fury.

On his first day at Collegiate and several times after that, John got into fistfights with other boys, just as he had at St. David's. Typical was the boy who went home with a bloody nose claiming "John Kennedy did it. I called him John-John and he socked me. But don't worry. I hit him back."

The Secret Service may have been the main reason John was so quick to punch anyone who taunted him. The agents, all of whom had taken a fatherly interest in John to one degree or another, thought it advisable to give John boxing lessons. "I guess," one said years later, "he was just eager to put them to good use."

As always, John still managed to make friends quickly. Two of his closest friends were among the handful of African-Americans at Collegiate, Geoffrey Worrell and Hans Hageman. John had asked to be introduced to Hageman after he spotted the school's star ten-year-old runner and wrestler sprint around a Central Park racetrack. It made perfect sense that John asked to meet Hans and not the other way around. "At Collegiate," wrote Nancy Moran, "being a good athlete is more prestigious than being the son of a president."

In addition to fisticuffs and sports, John also showed early talent as a storyteller. He wrote a short pantomime about kite flying that was acted out by his class before an audience of parents. He had one of the boys tug too hard on the string—so hard that the string broke and the kite drifted away. The mother of the boy later recalled that the pantomime, given all that John had already gone through in his short life, was "charming and poetic."

That autumn of 1968, everyone in both the Kennedy and Onassis camps was so immersed in working out the details of their secret marital pact that no one noticed a possible tragedy in the making.

At the weekend house in Bernardsville, New Jersey, the Secret Service detail in charge of protecting John and Caroline followed the wrong car out of the driveway and lost the children.

For two frantic hours, agents radioed back and forth trying to locate John and Caroline. At Secret Service headquarters in Washington, panic set in. After the assassinations of Jack and Robert Kennedy, the disappearance—the *abduction*—of JFK's children was the sort of blow the agency might not survive.

Dark had already fallen by the time the Kennedys' neighbor Peggy McDonnell drove up to Jackie's farmhouse with John and Caroline in the back seat. They had been playing at the McDonnell house, and when no Secret Service agent showed up, Peggy thought it best to deliver them to Jackie personally. In doing so, she left her own eight children unattended—a fact that would particularly rankle Jackie. The incident, which remained hidden from the public, confirmed Jackie's feeling that Onassis could better protect her children.

Neither child could be shielded from the hysteria triggered by Jackie's official announcement confirming her intention to wed Aristotle Onassis. But no one took it harder than Maria Callas, who raged behind the scenes but managed to contain her anger in public. "She did well," Callas said slyly of her rival for Ari's affections, "to give a grandfather to her children."

As the wedding date approached, several of John's schoolmates joined the chorus of taunts. "You know, John's mother explained to him why she's marrying a frog instead of a prince," one said. " 'Because when he croaks, we'll all be rich!' " John responded, as usual, by decking the other boy with a quick right to the chin.

At times the boisterous, flamboyant Onassis seemed remarkably sensitive—particularly when it came to John's feelings. A few days before they all left for the wedding ceremony on Skorpios, Ari took John aside and reminded him of one thing. "Don't forget, John," he told the boy who was about to become his stepson. "We will always be *filaracos.*"

John smiled. *Filaracos,* as Ari had explained to him the day they first met, is Greek for "buddies."

She has not made us look at our father's life to worship
it at the expense of our own. Whatever Caroline or I
choose to do, she supports.

—John, on his mother

I can't very well marry a dentist from New Jersey.

*—Jackie, on her decision
to wed Aristotle Onassis*

They look just right to me now. I would like to
remember them at this age, as they are, just now.

*—Jackie to artist Aaron Shikler,
explaining why she wanted him
to paint John and Caroline in 1968*

5
=

John stood with his sister and their mother in the eye of the storm. "The reaction here is anger, shock, and dismay," reported the *New York Times*, though, oddly, reaction was even stronger abroad. JACKIE, the *Stockholm Express* asked on its front page, HOW COULD YOU? A London paper sniped: JACKIE WEDS BLANK CHECK. JACK KENNEDY DIES FOR A SECOND TIME TODAY, blared the headlines in Rome's *Il Messagero*.

On October 25, 1968, Jackie's children were among the twenty-two family members and friends crammed into Skorpios's white-washed neoclassical Chapel of Panayitsa (the Little Virgin). Wearing a beige chiffon dress by Valentino, Jackie towered at least four inches above the five-foot-five-inch-tall groom.

John and Caroline, grasping long white candles, were positioned on either side of the bride and groom. "The flames eerily lit up their serious and nervous faces," Onassis's personal secretary, Kiki Feroudi Moutsatsos, recalled. "I could imagine how scary this all was to them . . . Caroline and John had to be worrying about what would happen to them now that their mother was marrying a man they hardly knew."

When the wedding party emerged in the driving rain forty-five minutes later, the bride was beaming. A reporter asked Ari how he was feeling. "I feel very well, my boy," he replied. The same reporter asked John if he was happy. He turned away without answering.

John was not the most solemn person at the ceremony. Ari's children, Alexander, twenty, and Christina, eighteen, were heartbroken. They vehemently opposed the marriage, making it clear that they regarded Jackie as nothing more than an American gold digger. "My father needs a wife," Alexander protested openly to reporters, "but I don't need a stepmother." On the day of the wedding, said Ari's friend Willi Frischauer, Christina and Alexander "wept bitter tears."

After the ceremony, John, Caroline, Jackie, and Ari then piled into a gold-painted Jeep and, with Ari at the wheel, drove off to the reception aboard the *Christina*. There, in the glass-walled sitting room, Jackie sipped champagne while her new husband lavished gifts on nearly everyone present—$1.2 million in jewels to his bride, a diamond-and-platinum ring for Jackie's mother, gem-encrusted gold rings to Lee Radziwill and Kennedy sisters-in-law Jean Smith and Pat Lawford.

The little girls—Caroline and her cousins Sydney Lawford and Tina—each received diamond bracelets. And John's face brightened noticeably when he and cousin Tony Radziwill each opened their presents: one-thousand-dollar Swiss-made wristwatches.

Marta Sgubin, who had replaced Maud Shaw as the most constant, nurturing presence in John's life, watched over the children that night aboard the *Christina,* as she would until they left for boarding school. Kiki Moutsatsos went up to chat with John and Caroline. "There was no doubt that the children were overwhelmed by what was going on around them," she recalled. "Yet it was also obvious that they were polite, well-brought-up, adored children."

In a curious way, Jackie's marriage to Onassis made the bond between mother and son that much stronger. "The reaction of Ethel Kennedy and her children was horror," Pierre Salinger said. "That made John and Caroline even closer and emphasized for all of them that they were three against the world: Bouvier-Kennedys, as opposed to their garden-variety Kennedy cousins."

While her new husband indulged his consuming passion for making money, Jackie indulged hers for spending it. By way of repaying

Billy Baldwin for standing by her during those dark days following the assassination, she hired him to redecorate the house on Skorpios, Onassis's villa nineteen miles outside Athens at Glyfada, and the *Christina*.

For now, she would put plans to redecorate Ari's opulent Paris pied-à-terre on Avenue Foch and his mansion in Montevideo, Uruguay, on hold. Not that she spent all that much time at any of Onassis's residences; for Jackie and her children, life would continue to revolve around 1040 Fifth, the farm in New Jersey, and Hyannis Port.

Marrying Ari gave her dominion over more than seventy servants—not counting the sixty-member crew of the *Christina*. But becoming Mrs. Onassis also, Jackie explained, "liberated me from the Kennedys—especially from the Kennedy Administration. None of them could understand why I'd want that funny little squiggly name when I used to have the greatest name of all . . . Well, I like seeing all these politicians dealing with Ari's squiggly name."

John reveled in his mother's newfound happiness—and in his stepfather's generosity. By any standards, John led a life of luxury and privilege in Manhattan. But their stepfather's world lent a whole new meaning to those words.

In addition to the cruises to exotic ports of call aboard the *Christina* (where JFK Jr. preferred to eat belowdecks with the crew), John and Caroline spent weeks at a time swimming, sailing, and hiking on Skorpios, their new island paradise. Here the hills were covered with oleander, fig trees, and cypress, and the air was redolent with the scent of bougainvillea and jasmine.

Understandably, Onassis was less than excited when his presence was required at Jackie's New Jersey farmhouse. In late November, he joined Jackie and the children in Bernardsville. Before he arrived, she had a French photographer arrested for trespassing and put up barricades blocking the road leading to her house. Once there, Onassis kept to himself. While Caroline and John joined their mother riding to the hounds—John nearly toppled from his pony when the animal snagged one of its hind legs jumping a fence—Ari stayed inside juggling deals on the phone.

Since John did not share his mother's and sister's fondness for horses, what Onassis did have to offer appeared to suit him just fine. On trips abroad, Jackie, John, Caroline, and their guests now simply commandeered an Olympic Airways jet. In April 1969, John flew to Greece to spend Easter on Skorpios. When he brought his pet rabbit on board, John was informed that animals were not allowed in the passenger compartment and that the pet would have to be put in the cargo hold.

Jackie intervened, demanding that the rabbit fly first class alongside her son. The pilot refused to break the rules regarding animals in the passenger cabin. He did, however, allow the rabbit to be brought up to the cockpit, where it stayed in its cage under the pilot's watchful eye for the rest of the trip.

As determined as Jackie was to keep John from being spoiled, she would not deny him all that his stepfather had to offer. Just as Ari had routinely raided FAO Schwarz during his courtship of their mother, he continued to shower the children with expensive gifts.

To keep John entertained on Skorpios, Onassis bought him his own mini-Jeep, a jukebox, and a red speedboat with his name emblazoned across the bow. He bought a sailboat for Caroline, and Shetland ponies for each. When Caroline admired a horse that was not for sale, Onassis bought the horse's parents and siblings for her. Then there were the small but thoughtful gestures—like the Coney Island hot dogs, a favorite of Jackie and the kids, that Ari had flown from New York to Skorpios.

It was more than just the money. From the beginning, Onassis made a determined effort to be a father to John. When the children visited Greece, Ari often canceled business plans in Athens and rushed to Skorpios to spend time with them. Taking John tightly by the hand, Ari would take long walks through the woods with him, patiently pointing out the birds and animals that inhabited the island. On fishing excursions, Onassis entertained John with yarns about his own Greek boyhood and made sure that, if the fish weren't biting, a crewman would be on hand to put a live one on John's hook and make him think he'd caught it. Onassis, said Moutsatsos, "always acted as if there was no other place he'd rather be" than with John and Caroline.

Like JFK, Ari was afraid of defying Jackie when it came to press photographers snapping pictures of the children. Once when she returned to New York and left John in Ari's care, Onassis kept the boy a virtual prisoner on board the *Christina* for several hours rather than let him venture outside, where a small armada of press boats swarmed around the yacht waiting to take his picture.

Finally, Onassis ordered one of his crewmen to board a speedboat and zigzag among the unwelcome visitors, swamping each boat and sending one cursing photographer after another into the shallow water. Then John and Ari appeared on deck for the first time, tossed towels to the drenched members of the press, and sped off on their own tour of Skorpios's neighboring islands aboard Ari's Chris-Craft.

In New York, Ari maintained his own suite at the Pierre Hotel, some twenty blocks south of Jackie's apartment. But he often spent time with Jackie and the children at 1040 Fifth, and continued to work diligently on building a bond with John.

Although he cared little about sports and understood nothing about American baseball, Ari took John to Shea Stadium to watch the Mets play the Baltimore Orioles in the third game of the World Series. More to Onassis's liking were excursions to John's favorite ice cream parlor, Serendipity, for hot fudge sundaes, and marathon walks around Midtown or through Central Park.

Once Jackie and Kiki Moutsatsos looked out the window of Jackie's fifteenth-floor co-op apartment and watched as Ari and John walked hand in hand down Fifth Avenue. Onassis was, as usual, bending down to talk into John's ear and gesturing with his free hand.

One day Jackie asked Onassis what it was he and John talked about. "I am teaching him," Ari said.

"Teaching him what?"

"To be a successful man," Onassis answered.

She wondered what he meant. Ari's secretary tried to reassure Mrs. Onassis that her husband was probably teaching him to how to "act like a grown-up person, not a little boy."

Jackie's eyes widened. "Oh dear," she said, "I just hope he isn't spending all their time together telling John how to get a woman." Then the two women burst out laughing.

The other parents at Collegiate were impressed by Jackie's near-perfect attendance at school events. "If there was a play or a soccer game, you could count on John's mother being there," said another Collegiate mother. "He searched for her face and was confident he'd always find her in the crowd. What surprised us more was how many times Onassis showed up—more than quite a few of the fathers, in fact."

John and his stepfather even shared some good-natured ribbing now and then. More than once, Onassis playfully shoved John into the pool aboard the *Christina*. And when JFK Jr.'s cocker spaniel, Shannon, relieved himself on Ari's shoe, both John and Onassis doubled over laughing. Every night when John went to bed, Ari gave him a grandfatherly Greek bear hug. "Ari seemed to enjoy both children immensely," Plimpton said. "They kept him young."

Surprisingly, as much as they openly despised Jackie, Alexander and Christina Onassis treated John and his sister with affection. On board the *Christina* and on Skorpios, both Onassis children put aside their grudge against the new Mrs. Onassis to dine with their excited stepsiblings.

The mercurial Alexander, in particular, delighted in taking John crashing against the waves in his high-performance speedboat. A fledgling pilot, twenty-year-old Alexander also found John to be a kindred spirit when it came to helicopters. On several occasions over the next several years, Alexander would take the controls of Ari's private chopper and take John on a swing over Skorpios. "Jackie was thrilled to see John so happy and excited," Lee Radziwill told a friend. "She knew how much he loved flying, especially helicopters."

Wherever he was, John was never far from the one woman who was now really a second mother to both him and Caroline—their governess, Marta Sgubin. Slender and dark-haired, the self-effacing Sgubin might well have passed for a younger sister of Jackie's. She took turns walking Caroline and John to school, and according to George Plimpton, "It was plainly obvious that they both adored her."

Sgubin, a devout Roman Catholic who spoke Spanish, French, Italian, and German as well as English, made sure they did their homework, ate dinner with them, tucked them in to bed. Jackie was often up by eight to give them breakfast, but only after Sgubin, already up for an hour, had rousted them out of bed.

John knew Sgubin "cared deeply" about him, said Kiki Moutsatsos. "No one ever had to worry about the children when they were with Marta . . . There was not a moment in the children's daily lives when Marta did not know where the children were and with whom." Sgubin, observed Moutsatsos, "devoted all her life, including her personal life, to Caroline and John."

The dark side of the Kennedy legacy reared its head yet again on July 18, 1969, when Ted drove his 1967 Oldsmobile off the Dyke Bridge on Chappaquiddick Island, drowning his attractive young passenger, Mary Jo Kopechne.

The fatal accident and Ted's subsequent sloppy attempt to cover it up foreclosed any possibility of the last Kennedy brother ever reaching the White House. But John watched as his mother, who had grown close to Ted after Bobby's murder, stood shoulder to shoulder with the rest of the Kennedys at Hyannis Port. "It was another lesson in solidarity," Theodore White observed, "for John-John and all the Kennedy cousins."

Ten days after Chappaquiddick, Ari gave Jackie more than two million dollars' worth of jewelry for her fortieth birthday—almost as much as she had spent on herself during their first year of marriage.

Jackie's out-of-control spending had gotten her into deep trouble with Jack. Soon it would lead to similar tensions in her second marriage—and bitter arguments over money in front of the children. But for now Ari and Jackie squared off against what they perceived to be a common enemy—an increasingly intrusive press.

Not that John's mother didn't crave publicity. She actively sought coverage throughout her entire life, as long as it was strictly on her own terms. Jackie's secretary would phone editors and photographers to say that Mrs. Onassis would be at a certain event, and the next day her photo would be splashed across the front page of *Women's Wear Daily.* "At other times," observed *Women's Wear* publisher James Brady, "she would flee us as from the plague."

John understood his mother's frustration. Like Jackie, he was constantly shadowed by paparazzi. In Greece, one photographer—aptly nicknamed "The Shadow" by Onassis—would toss stones at John in hopes of catching the boy throwing rocks back at him.

Yet it was the indefatigable New York photographer Ron Galella who for Jackie and her children came to embody all that was wrong with the press. Galella stalked Jackie, John, and Caroline everywhere, popping out from behind shrubs and doorways, snapping hundreds of pictures while taunting his quarry and making strange grunting noises. On Mother's Day, for example, he ambushed her as she got out of a limousine and walked toward her apartment building. Quickly, she put the bouquet John had given her in front of her face, ruining the picture.

The previous Christmas, he had hired a Santa to lay in wait for her outside 1040 Fifth Avenue. When she emerged, the Santa rushed up to her and tried to position himself near Jackie so that Galella could snap a photo of them together for the cover of the *National Enquirer.* It did not work out as the photographer had planned. "She's fast," he recalled, "and Santa was slow." Later, when Galella tried to catch John sledding with Caroline and their mother in Central Park, the Secret Service shoved the photographer into a snowbank.

It was one thing for Jackie to be pursued by the press. But when it came to her children Jackie became, in the words of her onetime friend Truman Capote, "the lioness protecting her cubs."

By October 1969, Caroline had transferred from Sacred Heart to Brearley, an exclusive girls' school on Manhattan's Upper East Side. She had gone to a carnival when suddenly Galella materialized and began running around her, furiously snapping pictures and humiliating Caroline in front of her friends.

Two weeks later, Jackie and John were bicycling through Central park when Galella jumped out of the bushes, frightening her son and causing him to swerve violently. Enraged, Jackie ordered the Secret Service agent who had been following them to "smash his camera" and arrest Galella for harassment.

The criminal harassment charges were dropped for lack of evidence, and Galella sued Jackie for 1.3 million dollars, charging Jackie with false arrest, malicious prosecution, assault, and "interference with my livelihood." She, in turn, countersued for six million dollars, claiming Galella's actions were nothing short of a "nightmare"—an invasion of privacy that caused her and her children grievous mental anguish. She asked the court for an injunction keeping him at least three hundred feet away from 1040 Fifth and 150 feet away from her and her children at all times.

"Mr. Galella has dashed out at me," nine-year-old John said in a court deposition that had obviously been prepared for him, "jumped in my path, discharged flashbulbs in my face, trailed me at close distances—generally imposed himself on me." John swore under oath that he felt "threatened when Mr.Galella is present."

The case would drag on for years. In terms of the injunction, the courts would give Jackie more than she asked for. Galella was ordered not to come within 225 feet of either John or Caroline, or within 150 feet of Jackie herself. On appeal, Galella would get those distances pared down so that he could get within thirty feet of the children and twenty-five feet of her. Still, they had not heard the last from Galella.

"I'm afraid Grandpa is very sick," Jackie told John and Caroline on November 15, 1969, as she packed to leave for Hyannis Port. "He may not get better. So I want you to pray for him." By the time she got to his bedside, Joe Kennedy was already comatose. "It's Jackie, Grandpa," she said, grasping the old man's hand in hers. Then she kissed him on the forehead. Three days later at 10:30 in the morning, Joe's nurse, Rita Dallas, rang the alarm bell at the compound. Everyone knew it was tolling for the patriarch, dead at the age of eighty-one.

On November 20, 1969, John walked up the aisle toward the main altar of Hyannis's St. Francis Xavier Church and turned to face the seventy mourners—nearly all of them Kennedy family members—who had come to bid farewell to his grandfather. In a clear and unwavering voice, John recited the Twenty-third Psalm.

John returned to St. Francis Xavier two days later, this time to serve as an altar boy at a memorial mass marking the sixth anniversary of his father's assassination. Again, virtually all the Kennedys attended. But Ari, who did not attend Joe's funeral, was conspicuously absent.

By mid-1970, speculation was rampant that the marriage of Jacqueline Kennedy and Aristotle Onassis was already in serious trouble. On May 21, Ari was photographed dining with his former mistress Maria Callas at Maxim's. Jackie flew to Paris the very next day, and made a point of being photographed with Ari at the very same corner table at Maxim's. Three days later, Callas attempted to take her own life with an overdose of sleeping pills.

Asked if the rumors about Callas were true, Ari snapped, "All this is complete mythology. It is unbelievable, absurd." Nevertheless, just three weeks after toasting Jackie on her forty-first birthday, Ari was photographed kissing Callas under a beach umbrella on the Aegean island of Tragonisi. Again, Jackie, "like a Dalmatian to a fire bell," as *Time* put it, raced back to Ari's side.

Accustomed as he was to the gossip that always seemed to swirl around his mother, John had learned to simply ignore it. His world revolved around schoolwork, soccer games in Central Park, weekends at Hyannis Port, and summer idylls in Greece. "It was a wonderful time," John later said of these years. "Let's face it, I was a very, very lucky little boy. And Mr. Onassis was very nice to me. I was just this little kid, but he took the time to tell me things, to listen to what I had to say. I liked him a lot, and I like to think he liked me, too."

When John was eight, he and his sister posed for New York portraitist Aaron Shikler. To keep him company, John brought along his pet guinea pig. "John was all boy," Shikler recalled. "Restless, impatient, all elbows and knees . . . He was monumentally bored with the whole business. The sooner he could get out of the room, the better. He hates to pose." Jackie was so pleased with the results that in the fall of 1970 she selected Shikler to paint both her and her husband's official White House portraits.

After the portraits were delivered to the White House, First Lady Pat Nixon wrote Jackie asking if she was up to a public unveiling. "I really do not have the courage to go through an official ceremony," Jackie replied, "and bring the children back to the only home they both knew with their father under such traumatic conditions. With the press and everything, things I try to avoid in their little lives. I know the experience would be hard on them and not leave them with the memories of the White House I would like them to have."

Eventually, however, she did agree to bring the children on a private visit followed by dinner with the Nixons on February 3, 1971. The President sent Air Force One to pick up John, Jackie, and Caroline at New York's LaGuardia Airport and fly the former First Family members back to Washington.

When their limousine pulled up to the Executive Mansion, the First Lady walked out to greet them. Pat was, to Jackie's surprise, warm, engaging, and particularly at ease with the children. President Nixon himself showed them around the Oval Office, where, John recalled, "Daddy used to work."

While Pat chatted with Jackie, Nixon's daughters, Tricia and Julie, guided John and Caroline through the upstairs quarters they used to call home—their old bedrooms, now redecorated to suit the Nixon girls' tastes, the "High Chair Room" where Miss Shaw watched over them as they ate, even the solarium where Caroline had once attended the special White House school set up by her mother.

Although John obviously remembered almost nothing about life in the White House, he was eager to learn all he could. And Jackie watched as Caroline's face lit up when she walked into her old bedroom for the first time in seven years.

Like most ten-year-old boys, John was prone to spilling things. On the flight down from New York, Caroline bet her brother that he could not get through the White House visit without having his shirttail come untucked ("That used to happen with great frequency," he later said) or spilling his milk at dinner.

"And so I had gotten through most of the dinner and my shirttail was in and the milk was upright," John would recall. Then dessert arrived and "something caught my attention." True to form, John not only knocked over his glass of milk, but sent its contents flying into Richard Nixon's lap. The President "just didn't even blink and kind of wiped it up," John later remembered. Meanwhile, Caroline gave her brother a big-sisterly "I told you so" look from across the table.

"Thank you with all my heart," Jackie wrote Pat Nixon when she got back to New York. "A day I always dreaded turned out to be one of the most precious ones I have spent with my children." Jackie then told her son to write the Nixons a thank-you note, which he patiently penned in his fifth-grade longhand and mailed himself. It read (complete with misspellings):

February 4 1971

Dear Mr. President
Dear Mrs. Nixon

I can never thank you more for showing us the White House. I don't think I could rember much about the White House but it was really nice seeing it all again. When I sat on Lincolns bed and wished for something my wish really came true. I wished that I have good luck at school. I really really loved the dogs they were so funny as soon as I came home my dogs kept on sniffing me. Maybe they rember the White House . . .

That summer of 1971 life on Skorpios was enlivened by the arrival of Peter Beard, the dashing photographer, wildlife conservationist, and party animal. Beard's passion for adventure, his tousle-haired good looks, and his instant rapport with the children—especially John—made him a particular favorite of Jackie's.

In fact, Beard provided something Jackie felt was missing from her son's life. Try as he did to endear himself to John, the wheeling-and-dealing Ari was not really around enough to have a lasting influence on the boy. Jackie told friends that she worried John would become "a fruit" without the toughening influence of a father figure. So the athletic Beard swam, sailed, water-skied, and roughhoused with John—"the kinds of things Bobby used to do with him," she remarked.

That August, John joined his cousin Tony Radziwill at Drake's Island Adventure Center, off the rugged southwest coast of Great Britain, to spend two weeks canoeing, camping, and climbing. John found the experience so exhilarating that from then on Jackie went to considerable lengths to arrange at least one adventure for her son every year.

"John was a totally inspired person," Beard recalled, pointing out that even as a boy JFK Jr. was a talented mimic. The next spring, Beard took John and his sister snake hunting in the Florida Everglades. They were trailed by a mob of reporters who staked out the

Kennedys' hotel. When he walked through the lobby early one morning, John passed a photographer asleep on a couch, and suddenly launched into his impersonation of Mick Jagger singing "Jumpin' Jack Flash." Startled awake, the photographer grabbed for his camera—but too late. John had left the building.

In December 1971, John did actually make his theatrical debut of sorts as one of Fagin's gang in the Collegiate Christmas production of *Oliver!* Jackie and Ari showed up, flanked by a grim-faced Secret Service contingent.

Cast in the role of Big Sister, soft-spoken Caroline seemed to enjoy her brother's flamboyant, sometimes zany streak. As a Christmas present for their grandmother Rose, Caroline even wrote a poem about John:

> *He comes spitting in my room, jabbing left and right*
> *Shouting, OK, Caroline, ready for a fight?*
> *He is trying to blow us up with his chemistry set,*
> *He has killed all the plants but we've escaped as yet.*
> *He loves my mother's linen sheets and hates his own percale.*
> *He can imitate the sounds of a humpback whale.*
> *I love him not just because I oughter.*
> *But also because blood runs thicker than water.*

Partly because of their mother's influence, and partly because they had already experienced and witnessed so much emotional pain, John and Caroline were already exhibiting a remarkable degree of empathy for others. When Kiki Moutsatsos was struck in the face and robbed outside Alexander's department store in Manhattan, Jackie insisted on taking her to the emergency room. When Moutsatsos refused, Jackie brought her back to 1040 Fifth and nursed her back to health herself.

Caroline was visiting Rose Kennedy at Hyannis Port that night, but "John was home," Moutsatsos later recalled, "and was every bit as kind to me as his mother was." John decided that Moutsatsos deserved strawberries, telling her repeatedly that they would make her feel better. "He worked so hard to get me the biggest strawberries he could find in the kitchen and would cut them into small pieces for me to eat. I wasn't the least bit hungry, but I would never have refused one bite of his beautiful strawberries."

By the spring of 1972 it was obvious to everyone, including Caroline and John, that their mother's marriage was in serious trouble. Even when he was in New York, staying just down Fifth Avenue at the Pierre Hotel, Onassis was not included on the guest list for his wife's dinner parties.

Ari was now telling friends that Jackie was "cold-hearted and shallow." In addition, her spending—in a single outing Jackie spent sixty thousand dollars on two hundred pairs of shoes—was clearly out of control. To teach her a lesson, he cut her allowance from thirty thousand dollars a month to twenty thousand dollars.

"After a certain point, I never saw love on his side when it came to Jackie," said columnist Aileen Mehle, a friend of both. "Now *she* was sweet and warm and affectionate. He was aloof. He would always say, 'The Widow wants this' and 'The Widow wants that.' She tried to keep up appearances, but it was obvious he was mad at her. And I mean all the time."

With Caroline now enrolled at Concord Academy in Massachusetts, John was left in New York to witness the battle raging between his mother and his stepfather. Wanting to escape the crossfire, he begged his mother for another summer adventure like the one he'd experienced on Drake's Island the year before. Jackie agreed to send John to Androscoggin, a Maine summer camp primarily attended by Jewish boys, with his Collegiate classmate Bob Cramer.

John was getting ready to pack when, at the last minute, the FBI told Jackie that it was imperative she cancel the trip. "Lark," as John was still known to the Secret Service, was in grave personal danger. U.S., Greek, and West German authorities acting together had uncovered plots by *two* terrorist groups—a band of eight Greek leftists and four German members of the notorious 20th October Movement—to kidnap John and hold him for ransom. On July 15, 1972, Greek authorities announced the arrest of both gangs.

Ari, stunned by the news, stepped up security at Skorpios, aboard the *Christina,* and at his other residences. Jackie, meantime, instructed

John to stop playing hide-and-seek with his Secret Service detail. "It was a real wake-up call," Ari's friend Doris Lilly said. "Jackie was reminded that what she said all along was truer than ever: Her kids were the number-one targets."

Before long, however, Ari was again railing against Jackie and was thinking of ways to get her to change her behavior. He was particularly annoyed at the capricious way in which she handled the press. He knew better than anyone how much she hungered for publicity, and how irrational she became if it was not delivered on her terms. So he decided to do something about it.

In November 1972, ten photographers zipped into wet suits and lay in wait for Jackie in the waters off Skorpios. Unbeknownst to Jackie, Ari had supplied them with maps to the island and a schedule of when Jackie planned to be there. The color photographs they took—full-frontal nude shots of the former First Lady sunbathing and strolling around—were splashed across the Italian men's magazine *Playmen* under the headline THE BILLION DOLLAR BUSH. Strictly on the basis of the Jackie photos, sales of Larry Flynt's new magazine, *Hustler,* shot from a few thousand to more than two million copies.

Onassis figured that once the humiliating photos were published, there would be nothing left the press could do to offend her. She would stop complaining, learn to live with the paparazzi—and stop threatening costly lawsuits.

Instead, it had the opposite effect. Ari had failed to take into account the degree of embarrassment the pictures would cause John and Caroline. Enraged, Jackie insisted that Ari sue every publication that published the pictures here and abroad. Ari, not surprisingly, shrugged off her demands.

From John's standpoint, Ari hardly seemed like the expert his mother was when it came to manipulating the press. When paparazzi accosted Ari and Elizabeth Taylor—sans her husband Richard Burton—lunching at a café in Rome, Liz dove beneath the table and Onassis tossed a glass of champagne in the intruder's face.

The next morning, John and Caroline were in the kitchen trying to stifle their laughter when Jackie walked in and saw the *Daily News* story spread out on the breakfast table. Jackie blasted Ari over the phone. "I'm ashamed of you," she said. "The children read all about your ridiculous behavior in Rome."

In December 1972, Ari met with attorney Roy Cohn at Cohn's town house on East 68th Street and told him the marriage was over. But Onassis, Cohn said, "knew Jackie wasn't going to sit back and just accept the three million dollars he'd given her as part of the prenuptial pact." He told Cohn he intended to pay her an additional one million dollars—and no more.

A dozen blocks uptown, Jackie was unaware that Roy Cohn and her husband were plotting to end her marriage. When Ari left for Paris in January of 1973, she also had no idea that he was going to tell his son, Alexander—who had just had rhinoplasty to rid himself of the prominent Onassis nose—that he was divorcing "The Widow."

Ari also told Alexander that, after months of hearing him complain that their Piaggio amphibious plane was a "death trap," he would replace it with yet another helicopter. They would sell the amphibian, but first he wanted Alexander to check out a new pilot at the controls.

At 3:12 P.M. on January 22, 1973, Alexander was seated next to the new pilot as the Piaggio took off from Athens International airport. Fifteen seconds later, the plane veered to the right and plummeted to earth. The pilot and a passenger were seriously hurt, but only Alexander's injuries were critical.

As soon as she heard the news, Jackie phoned Caroline at Concord Academy. She told her daughter, who had been training for her pilot's license at nearby Hanscom Airfield, that there would be no more flying lessons. JFK's only daughter was grounded—literally.

John and Caroline stayed behind in the U.S. as Jackie flew to Athens. There, two of the world's top neurosurgeons Ari had had flown in from London and Boston came to the same conclusion: Alexander had suffered irreversible brain damage. With Jackie, Alexander's girlfriend, Fiona Thyssen, and an inconsolable Christina looking on, Ari made the agonizing decision to end life support. Alexander was twenty-four.

Onassis would never recover from the death of his only son. As they stood by Alexander's grave site on Skorpios, Ari turned to Christina and said, "You are my future now."

Alexander's death sent Ari into an emotional tailspin. "He became moody, short with people, and impossible to live with," said one close friend of Jackie's, society bandleader Peter Duchin. The kind surrogate father John had known was replaced by an angry, resentful old man who did little to disguise his thinly veiled contempt for their mother.

Alexander's death signaled an end to one phase of John's life. It also alerted Jackie, who had been blasé about flying in small planes, that they posed a very real threat to the safety of her own children.

John, who at the age of twelve had already witnessed more tragedy and grief than most people see in a lifetime, tried to cheer his step-father up. But Onassis, in the words of one of his Greek staff members, "was no longer interested in being a part of the Kennedys' lives. In a strange way, he blamed Jackie for what had happened to Alexander. Death and tragedy seemed to touch everyone *she* touched, and he began to wonder if he was in some way being punished for marrying her."

Several of his closest friends had always believed that. "I think ever since he married Jackie, everything went bad for him," said Stelios Papadimetriou, Ari's longtime attorney and friend. "Greeks are very superstitious. Ari called her 'The Widow.' We called her 'The Black Widow.' "

John watched as Ari lashed out at his mother, and though Onassis never spoke harshly toward the children, he left little doubt that he was no longer interested in them. There were no more extravagant gifts, no more long walks, no more appearances at John's school events with entourage in tow.

Jackie, by now so accustomed to dealing with grief, tried to ease Onassis's pain. Two days after Alexander's funeral, she invited Pierre Salinger and his wife, Nicole, to fly to Dakar, Senegal, and join them aboard the *Christina*. For the next ten days, fellow bon vivants Onassis and Salinger spent endless hours debating history and politics. "He loved Pierre," Nicole Salinger said. "They went on for hours and hours, pacing up and down the deck, talking and arguing."

There was another reason Jackie invited Salinger along. She took JFK's former press secretary aside and asked him to tell John and Caroline about their father. "I made certain to stress their father's wonderful sense of humor and his love of life—and especially of them," Salinger said. "Without going into detail about his injuries and bouts of illness, I pointed out that even though he often had reason to be sad, he was the person who cheered up all the others in the room." The image of "those two innocent, beguiling faces turned up to me and listening with rapt attention" would stay with Salinger forever.

Salinger also credited Jackie with making certain her children knew their father was, as Salinger put it, "a human being, not a myth. I wasn't sure at first if Jackie would approve, but I thought it was important they not be spoon-fed all the Camelot stuff—that would just give them a warped, unrealistic view of President Kennedy. But I still think she knew exactly what I was trying to do, and she agreed. In the end, Caroline and John had a healthy perspective on their father. All the credit goes to Jackie."

Over the next year, John stayed behind in New York and his sister at Concord Academy while their mother tried to distract Ari with trips to Spain, the Caribbean, Mexico, and Egypt. Nothing worked.

Onassis's mental state continued to deteriorate, and in time he convinced himself that his son had been the victim of an elaborate murder plot. By the summer of 1973, Onassis was offering a million-dollar reward to anyone who could prove that Alexander's plane had been sabotaged.

Several investigators were hired, but there was no evidence to support Ari's theory. He simply could not accept that his cherished only son had died in the senseless crash of a small plane. Evenings, he listened to the cockpit tapes of doomed pilots trying to regain control of their planes.

"Alexander's death really knocked him out of the box," Peter Duchin said. "He felt that fate had turned against him. He became morose, snapping, nitpicking, critical . . . Jackie got the worst of it."

The stress, meanwhile, was taking a profound physical toll on Onassis. He complained of headaches and constant fatigue. He was losing weight rapidly, and his right eyelid drooped. In December 1973, he checked into Manhattan's Lenox Hill Hospital and was diagnosed with myasthenia gravis, a relatively rare, incurable muscular disease.

At this point, Ari had so alienated Jackie that she did not bother to visit him despite the fact that the hospital was just a few blocks away from her apartment. Christina—Ari's *Chryso Mou* ("My Golden One")—stepped in to fill the void, rushing from Paris to her father's bedside the instant she heard he had been hospitalized. In early 1974 she relocated permanently to New York, where she would learn the ropes of the family business working in her father's office.

As he entered puberty, John suddenly seemed a handful. Always a ball of energy, he now seemed virtually incapable of sitting still. His concentration in class was suffering, and so were his grades. More and more often, he was trying to elude his Secret Service detail, taking off with friends down the street or on his bike through Central Park with clenched-jawed agents in hot pursuit.

Jackie wondered if John's hyperactivity was a sign of something deeper—a reaction, perhaps, to his veritable abandonment by Ari. It did not help matters that John's mother was now being publicly humiliated by Ari's old flame Maria Callas. During a *Today* show appearance in April 1974, Callas told Barbara Walters that Onassis had been "the big love of my life." She went on to observe with some conviction that "love is so much better when you are not married."

Walters then asked if Callas harbored any ill will toward John's mother. "Why should I?" she answered. "Of course, if she treats Mr. Onassis very badly, then I might be very angry."

Seeing the private lives of his mother and stepfather—and by proxy, his own—dragged through the press every day "could not," as Jackie's old friend Cleveland Amory said, "have been the most terribly healthy thing to happen to a young man."

At the same time, John seemed drawn to the very profession that had vexed his family from the beginning. Beverly Williston was spending a weekend in New Jersey's horse country when she encountered Jackie and her children. "So what do you want to be— president?" Williston asked John half in jest.

"Nah!" he answered. "I want to write about politics. Everyone wants me to be a lawyer, but I want to be a reporter."

"That's what I do," Williston told him.

"Do you get to travel a lot? Do you get to meet singers and actors?"

"Sometimes," she replied. "It's a fun job. You get to meet all kinds of people." She went on to tell him that yes, most journalists went to college—obviously something John was hoping to avoid.

There was never any doubt in Jackie's mind that John would go to an Ivy League school. But right now she was dissatisfied with his mediocre marks at Collegiate, and worried that all the headlines about her disintegrating marriage might be having a negative impact on his academic performance. She sent him to a psychiatrist, Dr. Ted Becker, to see if he couldn't help the boy overcome whatever blocks stood in the way of his getting good grades.

Jackie's boy did have a rebellious streak—the result, in part, of his constantly being shadowed by the ever-present Secret Service. In April 1974, John managed to escape his Secret Service detail and with two friends went to the Trans-Lux Theater on Broadway to see Mel Brooks's cowboy spoof *Blazing Saddles*. It took the agents nearly two hours to track John down, arriving at the theater just as John was leaving it.

Several weeks later, on the afternoon of May 15, 1974, thirteen-year-old John jumped onto his expensive Italian ten-speed and, again leaving the Secret Service behind, headed with a friend toward the Central Park tennis courts.

Jackie herself had something of a laissez-faire attitude about the dangers that lurked in Central Park. She was, after all, a regular on the jogging path around the reservoir. "Whenever she'd set out for the park at dusk on a winter's evening," Nancy Tuckerman said, "I'd warn her of all the terrible things that could happen to her, and true to form, she never paid any attention. By nature she was fearless, and I think that experience had taught her to trust her fate."

Following the example set by his mother, John was utterly oblivious to the safety issues as he sailed into the park on his bike shortly after 5 P.M. He certainly was not prepared to encounter Robert Lopez, a nineteen-year-old, strung-out addict with a pregnant wife at home and no visible means of support.

John was riding along Central Park's East Drive at 90th Street when Lopez picked a stick up off the ground and leapt out of the bushes at him. "Get the hell off the bike," he shouted at John as he waved the stick at him, "or I'll kill you! Get the hell off the bike!"

Shaken, John jumped off, but not quickly enough for Lopez, who shoved him to the ground. Lopez, still unaware of his victim's identity, then grabbed John's bike and his tennis racket and pedaled north. Lopez sold John's bike and racket and used the money to buy cocaine.

Later, Lopez and his wife, Miriam, were watching television when it was reported on the news that police were searching for a man who mugged JFK Jr. in Central Park and stole his bicycle. "Oh, my God," Lopez screamed, "that was me!"

Lopez, arrested after a robbery later that year, confessed to mugging John. "He was," Lopez told New York City Detective Richard Buggy, "an easy hit." But John's mother, fearing that any trial would be turned into a media circus, declined to press charges. Central Park police shared Jackie's concern. "Six million people in the park," one official said, "and they had to pick him."

(In yet another odd twist, Lopez would bounce in and out of jails for years until 1997, when he signed on with the Ready, Willing, and Able work program funded by the Robin Hood Foundation. By then John was on the foundation's board of directors, and knew that his organization was in fact helping the man who had mugged him as a teenager get back on his feet.)

Oddly, Jackie did not seem entirely displeased by her son's mugging. Quite the opposite. "She was pleased that this had happened to John, in that he must be allowed to experience life," Secret Service agent John Walsh reported in a confidential memo to his superiors in Washington. "He is oversheltered now with all the agents and unless he is allowed freedom he'll be a vegetable at the age of sixteen when we leave him."

"I don't want you on his heels," Jackie said. "Secret Service agents are told to follow counterfeiters all over the place without them knowing they're being followed. Why can't you do it with John?"

Clearly, John's mother had no interest in making the agents' jobs easier for them. "She does not want us to inquire of the governess when John is going or how he is getting there. We should be prepared for him to go any one of a number of ways."

Walsh went on to say that Jackie "is glad John had this experience but she is displeased about all the publicity it is receiving because people will think he isn't being accompanied by anyone and there is a danger in that."

"So can we tighten up security?" Walsh asked Jackie.

"No," she answered. "No agent is to be in John's pocket. John is not to get in an agent's car and the agents are not to walk with him. They must follow him, hiding behind cars and bushes—whatever they need to do so he never sees them. I want him followed but I don't want him to feel he's constantly being guarded. It's not healthy."

Despite her stated opinion that the Central Park mugging had actually been good for John, Jackie stressed that she would tolerate no more blunders on the part of the Secret Service. "If anything happens to John," Jackie said, alluding to the debacle at Dallas, "I will not be as easy with the Secret Service as I was the first time."

There were other, equally terrifying moments the Secret Service was never even made aware of. As Ari's mood had soured, Jackie grew more and more to rely on the support of old friends like Peter Duchin. This was never more true than the day Duchin went scuba diving with John ("by then a strapping teenager," Duchin remembered) in the Aegean. At a depth of forty feet, Duchin looked over to see John struggling with his oxygen hose. Young Kennedy showed "amazing cool," Duchin said, as the older, more experienced diver shared his mouthpiece and the two swam slowly to the surface.

"I kept thinking, 'I've got the son of the President of the United States here!' " Duchin recalled. "Jackie was very grateful, as you can imagine."

Several years later, it was John who did the rescuing, this time while diving with adventurer Barry Clifford inside a World War I freight vessel that had sunk off Martha's Vineyard. They were deep inside the bowels of the ship when one of the divers, John Beyer, suddenly couldn't breath. "Beyer's regulator broke," explained Clifford, "and Kennedy immediately gave him his regulator and they buddy-breathed."

But this time John did not merely lead Beyer slowly to the surface. The two men had to wend their way through the decaying passageways of the ship—"like going through a maze," Clifford said—to get out of the ship. "But John didn't even blink. There was no panic," Clifford recalled. "It was just cool, calm, collected, business as usual."

Jackie had just returned to 1040 Fifth from a Saturday appointment at Kenneth's hair salon when Ari's aide, Johnny Meyer, called on March 15, 1975, to say that her husband had died at the American Hospital in Paris. For three days, she had known his death was imminent; Ari's doctors called repeatedly and urged her to fly back to Paris to be with him. Instead, it was Christina who was at his bedside when he died at the age of seventy-five.

"There was an agreement that she had with Ari that she could spend part of the time with him and part of the time with her children," Nancy Tuckerman explained when asked why Jackie was not with her husband when he died. "He wanted it that way. And at the time she just felt she should be with John and Caroline." Tuckerman neglected to mention, however, that Caroline was away at Concord Academy, and while fourteen-year-old John still lived with his mother in New York, she was out on the town virtually every night.

Johnny Meyer was taken aback by Jackie's reaction to the news. He described her as sounding "almost cheerful" as she told him of her plans to fly straight to Paris aboard Onassis's Learjet. Her first call after hearing of Ari's death was to Ted Kennedy. As he had taken a leading role in hammering out the original prenuptial agreement, Ted would now be her point man in reaching a settlement with Christina over Ari's will. Then she phoned Valentino. She would be needing a new black dress. The third call was to John, who was spending the afternoon at a friend's house.

Like his mother, John reacted to the news without emotion. In the two years since the plane crash that killed Alexander, Ari had done everything he could to alienate Jackie and her children emotionally. Whatever fatherly interest he had shown John in the beginning had been all but erased by the open contempt he showed for his mother.

In Paris, Christina's reaction was quite different. Her favorite aunt, Eugenie, had died mysteriously in 1970 after marrying Ari's archenemy Stavros Niarchos. Her mother, Tina, then married Niarchos—

and in October 1974, also died under highly suspicious circumstances, at only forty-five years of age. "My aunt, my brother, now my mother," Christina cried at Tina's funeral. "What is happening to us?"

Her father's death was the final blow for the emotionally unstable Christina, who had already attempted suicide several times in the past. The same day Ari died, Christina tried to kill herself by slashing her wrists.

She blamed it all on "The Black Widow. I don't dislike her, you know," Ari's daughter said. "I *hate* her." She had come to view Jackie, and by extension her children, as pampered and undeserving.

Yet John had known almost as much tragedy in his short life—the murders of his father and his uncle, Teddy's near-fatal plane crash and the scandal of Chappaquiddick, and now the death of his stepfather. Unlike Christina, he had been taught by his mother to absorb each blow and rise above it.

While Jackie flew straight to Paris to see Ari's body lying in state in the American Hospital chapel, John, Caroline, their grandmother Janet Auchincloss, and their uncle Ted traveled ahead to Skorpios. Reporters swarmed over the Kennedy children, and at one point an exasperated John, who had been trying to lose himself in a comic book, stuck his tongue out at them.

At the funeral on Skorpios, a half-dozen pallbearers carried Ari's casket up the meandering footpath to the chapel. When Jackie took her place immediately behind the casket, Christina and Onassis's sisters literally elbowed the widow out of the procession, forcing her far to the rear. "To me it was obvious," Johnny Meyer said, "that Christina and Onassis's sisters were acting according to plan when they moved up to the coffin. It was a deliberate move to block Jackie off—to isolate her."

Shaken despite the trademark frozen smile, Jackie clung to her shaggy-maned son as they trailed behind the Onassis women. "I think he must have recognized the pain his mother was in because of the way she was treated," Salinger said. "From the very beginning, John was his mother's protector."

"In all my years in the church," said Greek Orthodox archdeacon Sylianos Prounakis, "I don't recall another funeral where the widow was pushed into the background this way. Mrs. Onassis was made to feel as if she did not really belong to the family. I find this extremely tragic."

With the battle lines drawn at Onassis's graveside, Jackie and Christina battled fiercely during the next eighteen months over what Ari's widow was entitled to. Eventually, Christina agreed to pay Jackie twenty-six million dollars in cash—a twenty-million-dollar lump-sum payment and an additional six million dollars to cover taxes. In return, Jackie waived any future claims on Ari's billion-dollar estate. "I would easily have given her even more," Christina told one of her aunts, "if it meant that I would never have to look at her again."

Christina took the reins of her father's empire and quickly proved herself to be a formidable businesswoman. Her private life, however, remained a shambles. On the morning of November 19, 1988, her body was found naked in a half-filled bathtub. She had succumbed to pulmonary edema just three weeks before her thirty-eighth birthday, the inevitable result of a lifetime spent abusing prescription drugs. Her only child, Athina, three at the time, inherited everything.

Keenly aware of the tragic mistakes Ari had made in raising his children, Jackie was now financially secure—and free to concentrate on John and Caroline. Jackie's newfound interest was not altogether welcome.

John had, in fact, capitalized on the fact that his mother had for years been consumed with trying to salvage her marriage to Onassis. At age twelve, John and a classmate named Wilson McCray were caught drinking at Madison Square Garden. Had she paid closer attention, Jackie might have noticed her son swigging Ari's favorite, Johnnie Walker Black Label scotch, straight from the bottle.

When Jackie returned several months after Ari's death for one last summer idyll on Skorpios, John wiled away the hours smoking potent Greek cigarettes and drinking wine as well as scotch—all, of course, behind his mother's back. Drinking, as it turned out, was far from John's only bad habit.

For years, John was a frequent marijuana smoker. He was still in his early teens at Collegiate when he began smoking pot, and was disciplined numerous times by school administrators. "We were always getting caught," Wilson McCray said, "for getting stoned." John would also smoke pot in the bathroom at his mother's apartment, and on the roof at 1040 Fifth. During one of their family ski vacations in Gstaad, John and McCray stole a Volkswagen van and took it for a joyride while Jackie was on the slopes.

Caroline, meantime, had some rebelling of her own to do. Her mother was constantly pressing her then-plumpish daughter to lose weight, going so far as to supply her with diet pills and badger her in restaurants. "You're not having dessert," Jackie said once over lunch at Boston's Ritz-Carlton Hotel. "You'll be so fat nobody will marry you."

Understandably, Caroline chafed under her mother's iron-willed authority. "She knows everything and I don't know anything," Jackie said of her daughter. "I can't do anything with her." One thing Jackie did not know—at least had not suspected—was that Caroline grew marijuana plants in Jackie's garden at the Hyannis Port compound. Together, John and his sister sampled the home-grown stash.

Eventually, a local policeman patrolling the area glanced over the fence and recognized the small patch of marijuana plants growing alongside the lettuce and carrots in Jackie's vegetable garden. Instead of making any arrests, he went directly to Jackie. She, in turn, confronted her children and threatened to virtually place them under house arrest if they were caught with drugs. Her trademark breathiness vanished, and her voice took on a stern, almost masculine quality. Jackie could be "absolutely terrifying," said her half brother, Jamie Auchincloss. "If she was mad at you, you knew it."

Suspecting rightly that they would probably ignore her and continue smoking pot anyway, if for no other reason than to fit in with their coddled private school peers, she instructed her staff to keep an eye on them.

Ari's death, meanwhile, had scarcely put a dent in the family's social schedule. Three days after the funeral, John and Caroline were back in Paris, representing their mother—who could not attend because she was officially in mourning—at a lunch given at the Elysée Palace by French President Valéry Giscard d'Estaing. "You

2.

Thirteen-day-old John with his parents immediately after his December 8, 1960, christening. A week later, mother and son would nearly die from the aftereffects of his difficult delivery.

Caroline turned three just two days after John was born. "Right from the very beginning," said their nanny Maud Shaw, "he loved her and she adored him."

3.

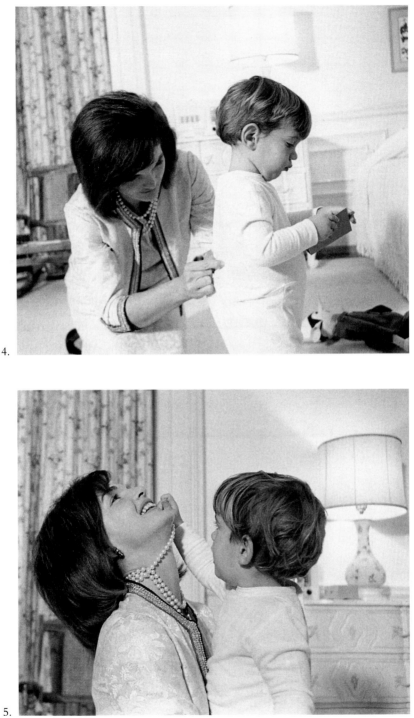

4.

5.

Bedtime at the White House. Jackie helps her son into his pajamas—
and John gets to play with a favorite toy: Mommy's pearls.

6.

John ("Lark") and his mother ("Lace") turn the tables on the Secret Service,
spying on an unsuspecting agent from behind a Rose Garden hedge.

7.

JFK seldom understood what his toddler son was saying, but he always
reacted with surprise whenever John whispered in his ear.

One of the few White House memories John would carry into adult life was of surprising Daddy by crawling through the secret panel in JFK's Oval Office desk.

8.

John clowns for his British nanny. "Miss Shaw, I'm your big boy!" he would proudly proclaim whenever he dressed himself or brushed his teeth.

9.

Nine days before JFK's assassination, the family was photographed together one last time, listening to the legendary bagpipes of the Black Watch Regiment.

11.

John delivers history's most famous salute.

12.

Uncle Bobby roughhousing with John. RFK became a surrogate father to his nephew in the years following Dallas.

13.

John bowed from the waist when he met Queen Elizabeth at the dedication of England's memorial to JFK in May 1965. The next day, he took off after an intrusive Fleet Street photographer.

14.

A Samoyed puppy nuzzles against John, five, during a ski vacation in Sun Valley, Idaho, in 1966.

15.

16.

On a visit to Honolulu's Iolani Palace in June 1966, John strikes a familiar hangdog pose as his mother scolds him for not sitting still.

Six-year-old John races into the surf on a Christmas 1966 trip to Antigua with Jackie and Caroline.

17.

John and stepdad Ari chatted as they strolled with Mom outside New York's Plaza Hotel in February 1969.

18.

Jackie and John, nine, set out on a bike ride through Central Park in 1970. He would be mugged in the park and his bike would be stolen four years later.

9.

20.

Moments before Muhammad Ali defeated Joe Frazier in 1974, John
visited his lifelong idol in his dressing room.

21.

At Ari Onassis's funeral in March 1975, his daughter Christina
and her relatives virtually shoved the widow, Jackie, and
fourteen-year-old John into the background.

22.

John and his cousin Tim Shriver took a break from helping rebuild the earthquake-ravaged Guatemalan village of Rabinal in July 1976. Next summer, he sailed to an island off the coast of Maine for survivalist training—all part of Jackie's "toughening up" campaign.

John and Caroline, strolling near Jackie's New York apartment in 1977. "They always smiled when they spoke to each other," a friend observed of them.

John, eighteen, is just another face in the crowd as he waits for his name to be called during graduation ceremonies at Phillips Academy in 1979.

Jackie pulled the plug on John's dream of becoming an actor. As a freshman at Brown, he played Bonario in Ben Jonson's *Volpone*.

John, an inveterate club-hopper in the 1980s, was surprised by photographers as he tried to leave Private Eyes in July 1984.

27.

A small army of photographers was on hand when Jackie attended her son's graduation from Brown on June 6, 1983.

28.

John took actress Christina Haag to catch Madonna's show at Madison Square Garden in 1987. Within a year he would be dating the Material Girl.

30.

John electrified the 1988 Democratic National Convention in Atlanta
when he rose to introduce his uncle Teddy.

31.

He shrugged them off after failing the bar exam a second time in 1990,
but John found "The Hunk Flunks" headlines "humiliating."

32.

During the 1992 Profile in Courage Awards ceremony at the JFK Library,
Ted, Jackie, John, and Caroline strike a Mount Rushmore pose.

After his cousin Ted Kennedy Jr.'s wedding on Block Island in 1993,
John and longtime love Daryl Hannah fled the hordes of paparazzi.

34.

Bill Clinton was sixteen when he shook hands with John's father during a White House visit. In 1993, the President joined John and Jackie on the dais during rededication ceremonies at the JFK Library.

Daryl Hannah looked like the future Mrs. JFK Jr. when he began dating Carolyn Bessette in late 1993. The first photo of John and Carolyn was of them sitting on a curb watching the New York Marathon.

35.

36.

Six weeks before her death from lymphoma at age sixty-four, Jackie
strolled through Central Park with John and her longtime
companion Maurice Tempelsman.

Following their mother's death in May 1994, John put a protective arm around
Caroline as they made their way to Jackie's apartment for her wake.

38.

John bends over to kiss his mother's coffin as Jackie
is laid to rest at Arlington alongside JFK.

39.

Familiar sights: His suit pants tucked into his socks and his backpack securely strapped on, John rides his bike to an appointment in Midtown Manhattan. During a break from one of his Central Park football games, JFK Jr. does a handstand.

40.

1.

As the clan gathered at Hyannis Port for the funeral of Rose Kennedy, John tried to lighten the mood by clowning for *(from left)* cousin Willie Smith, Caroline and Ed Schlossberg, cousin Maria Shriver, and Shriver's husband, Arnold Schwarzenegger.

42.

In August 1994, John invited Carolyn Bessette up to Martha's Vineyard for a ride aboard his aptly named boat, the *PT-109*.

"Listen, people can say a lot worse things about you," John told Barbara Walters, "than you are attractive and look good in a bathing suit."

43.

44.

John unveils his new magazine *George* on September 7, 1995. "My mother would be mildly amused to see me up here," he said, "and very proud."

5.

Three days after launching *George*, John is among spectators cheering Andre Agassi and Pete Sampras at the U.S. Open.

During their famed "Brawl in the Park," John ripped Carolyn's engagement ring off her finger, fought over their dog Friday, and sat openly weeping on a curb before making up with a passionate kiss.

46.

47.

48.

49.

John and Carolyn made no
attempt to conceal their
feelings for each other at a
charity event in June 1996.

50.

51.

On September 21, 1996, John and Carolyn pull off the
impossible: a secret wedding ceremony in a rustic
chapel on Georgia's tiny Cumberland Island.

After returning from the honeymoon in Turkey, John introduced the press to his bride outside their apartment building—and asked them to give her some breathing room.

52.

Amid reports that his marriage was unraveling, John unwound by going kayaking off Martha's Vineyard.

53.

54.

On a sweltering day in June 1997, the indefatigable jock plays Frisbee with friends in Central Park.

John was rushed to the hospital in October 1997 for emergency surgery after a nerve in his hand was mysteriously severed—the result of an unexplained "kitchen accident."

55.

Friday tagged along when John and Carolyn went shopping five days before Christmas 1997. Later that same day, John, a behind-the-scenes backer of several charities, presented gifts to dozens of needy children during a holiday party in Brooklyn.

56.

57.

58.

After labeling Michael Kennedy "a poster boy for bad behavior," John was
devastated when his cousin was killed in a skiing accident on
New Year's Eve 1997. John tightly embraced Michael's
brother Douglas at the funeral.

Jackie made him promise not to fly, but after her death John got his pilot's license. *(Right)* He checks the propeller of his first plane, a single-engine Cessna. He later traded up to a faster Piper Saratoga *(below)*. A co-pilot at his side, John takes the controls of the Piper Saratoga.

59.

60.

61.

The Bessette sisters *(from left)*—Lauren, Carolyn, and Lisa—stroll near Carolyn's building in New York's trendy TriBeCa district.

62.

63.

Days after breaking his ankle in a paragliding accident, John sticks his injured foot—cast and all—out the window of his car. A month later, he was still on crutches as he hobbled to a favorite neighborhood hangout—Bubby's—to pick up a takeout order.

64.

65.

Hours after the victims' bodies were recovered from the bottom of the sea on July 21, 1999, an ashen-faced Ted Kennedy (*far right*) watched as John's cousins helped lift his remains into a coroner's van. The next day, family members were taken aboard the Coast Guard cutter *Sanibel* to the destroyer USS *Briscoe*, where the ashes of John, Carolyn, and Lauren were scattered at sea.

67.

In the days after the crash, thousands of mourners gathered at a makeshift shrine outside 20 North Moore Street. On the Martha's Vineyard beach where debris from John's plane first washed up, one couple wept near a cross made of driftwood and grape vines.

68.

With husband Ed Schlossberg and son Jack, Caroline leaves her Park Avenue apartment for John's memorial service at St. Thomas More Church. "Caroline was crushed by his death—shattered," said a family confidant. "She was weeping constantly."

Guest

71.

have the look and smile of President John Kennedy," President Giscard told John, "and I am very pleased that his children are here."

Two weeks later, John was abroad again, this time on a tour of Russia with his aunt Eunice and uncle Sargent Shriver, and their children Maria, Timothy, and Bobby. When nineteen-year-old Maria Shriver put her left arm around her fourteen-year-old cousin John's shoulder as the family posed for pictures in Moscow, she screamed with laughter when John grabbed her hand and bit it. The next day, bored with having to wait for his uncle to finish a speech, he stood in the auditorium lobby and sailed paper airplanes over the crowd.

But what probably impressed his cousins most was John's voracious appetite—and the metabolism that kept him from gaining an ounce. John ate "everything—ice cream, caviar, anything," Timothy remembered. "He was a garbage can."

For the most part Jackie did not want John falling under the influence of the Kennedy cousins. Ethel, whose own manic mood swings made it virtually impossible for her to exert any steady control over her brood, watched as her sons wreaked havoc wherever they went. At Hyannis Port, they tossed lit firecrackers into neighbors' homes, threw water balloons, vandalized boats tied up at the pier, even fired BB guns at passing motorists. At a children's birthday party witnessed by the Kennedys' Hyannis Port neighbor Larry Newman, they pulled out a knife and robbed a young girl of her presents.

Things got more out of hand in the psychedelic sixties and seventies. Bobby Shriver and Bobby Kennedy Jr. were arrested for marijuana possession. Young Shriver learned his lesson, but Bobby Kennedy, with his brother David and cousin Chris Lawford, began dabbling in heroin.

RFK's oldest son, Joe Kennedy II, was also no stranger to drugs, and he sought help from psychiatrists as he drifted from one college to another on the strength of his name. One weekend on Nantucket, Joe got behind the wheel of a friend's Jeep and careened wildly along the narrow roads with David and David's girlfriend, Pam Kelley. Swerving to avoid an oncoming car, he plowed into a ditch—hurling all three passengers out of the vehicle. Pam Kelley was paralyzed from the waist down and would spend the rest of her life in a wheel-chair; the Kennedy boys walked away unharmed.

It was understandable, then, that when Ethel called to invite John and Caroline to Hickory Hill for two weeks, Jackie declined. "She said, 'No way,' " Ted Kennedy's aide Richard Burke recalled. "With all that stuff going on at Hickory Hill—especially with the problems the boys were having—Jackie just didn't want Caroline and John there."

"One of the big decisions Jackie made in her life," Peter Duchin said, "was to get the children the hell out of Hyannis Port and away from the Kennedys. The cousins were left to their own devices, and she knew it could only spell trouble. It was something she worried about all the time. I remember one summer Jackie sent John on a diving expedition to Micronesia just to keep him away from the Kennedy kids. She said to me, 'Do you think that's far enough away?' "

Jackie was not the only one in the family who felt that way. Pat Lawford and Eunice Shriver apparently shared her concern. Burke overheard Caroline, Sydney Lawford, and Maria Shriver talking about "what a mess [Bobby's kids] all were and how their mothers wouldn't let them go near Hickory Hill. There was definitely a hands-off attitude on the part of those three mothers—Eunice, Jackie, and Pat."

According to one friend, Pulitzer Prize–winning journalist David Halberstam, Jackie did not want John and Caroline "*inhaled* into that frenzied macho world of the Kennedys. She wanted them to be a part of their father's legacy, but she wanted them to develop the kind of self-control that many of their Kennedy cousins lacked. Jackie accomplished this very, very shrewdly, bringing them up in New York but letting them show the flag at Kennedy functions. She didn't want her children sucked in, and they weren't."

Nonetheless, when they did "show the flag" at Hyannis Port, John threw himself into the famous Kennedy family football games. He did not, however, share his relatives' win-at-all-costs blood lust. "He and Caroline were never as wild as their Kennedy cousins," Jamie Auchincloss said. "The other Kennedys would tackle hard to win

during those 'touch' football games. But John just played for fun."
Observed longtime Kennedy family friend Frank Mankiewicz: "Jackie
brought him up to be his own person, not part of the Kennedys'
tribal connection."

Because of the discipline imposed by Jackie and reinforced by
their nannies, Maud Shaw and Marta Sgubin, John and Caroline
stood apart from their Hickory Hill counterparts as well-mannered,
considerate children. When the Kennedys all got together to eat, said
Chuck Spalding, "manners pretty much went out the window. They
were a loud, rowdy bunch."

John and Caroline, on the other hand, "were sophisticated far
beyond their years—very much their mother's children," Tish
Baldrige said. Jamie Auchincloss recalled, "If there was one piece of
pie left at a picnic, neither John nor Caroline would take it. They
would always leave it for someone else. If asked they would say, 'No
thanks, you have it.' "

Predictably, none of this sat well with the more rambunctious
Kennedys. While Ethel was often accused by Jackie of being "more
Kennedy than thou," her children frequently chided John for being
more Bouvier than anything else. "You're not even a real Kennedy"
was the constant refrain from Joe, Michael, and Bobby Jr. And while
he was clearly one of the more athletically inclined members of the
family, the others often piled onto him, knowing that he would not
fight his own cousins.

"There was real resentment toward John, Jackie, and Caroline,"
said a former Hyannis Port employee. "Particularly right after Aristotle Onassis's death. JFK's children were already the stars—sort of
overshadowing everybody else—but after Ari died everyone thought
they had inherited hundreds of millions of dollars, which of course
they hadn't. But as far as John was concerned, there was always this
feeling that he was the crown prince of the family—and that somehow he didn't deserve it."

Since the Kennedy boys and not the girls were the ones who were
getting into serious trouble, nearly all of Jackie's fears centered on
John. That came to an abrupt end one crisp October morning in
1975. After graduating from Concord Academy, John's sister spent a

year interning at Sotheby's auction house in London. She was staying at the home of Conservative Member of Parliament Hugh
Fraser, an old friend of her father's and a strident foe of the IRA.
Each morning, Fraser drove his young American houseguest to her
work-study program at Sotheby's.

As Caroline got ready to leave, a huge explosion outside rattled the
windows of the Fraser townhouse and sent crockery smashing to the
floor. A bomb had gone off under Fraser's red Jaguar sedan prema-
turely, killing a neighbor who was taking his dog for a morning walk.
A shaken Jackie called and asked if her daughter wanted to return
home. John was also upset by the news, and telephoned his sister to
tell her he was concerned for her safety. But Caroline decided to stay.

The IRA, small planes, even the untamed Kennedy cousins—none
of these things worried Jackie as much as the impact celebrity would
have on John. "I never intended to let John and Caroline be subject
to the glare of publicity," she said. "I want them to lead the life of
normal youngsters. After all, those poor children have been through
so much over the past few years. I just want," Jackie added with a
sigh, "to be like any other mother with two children and lead an
uncomplicated life."

That U.S. bicentennial summer of 1976, fifteen-year-old John
mingled unrecognized among hundreds of thousands of spectators
watching an armada of tall ships and private yachts sail into New
York Harbor. John and his friends stood transfixed as foreign sailors
scrambled up and down the riggings, the yachts blared their horns in
celebration, and fireboats sprayed red, white, and blue geysers high
into the air. "You know what I want to do right now more than anything?" he asked his friends wistfully. "Just get on one of those ships
and sail away. That's all. Just—sail away . . ."

If you bungle raising your children, I don't think whatever else you do well matters very much.

—*Jackie*

Not being a Kennedy, my mother could recognize both
the perils and the positive aspects.

—*John*

I always grew up just living a fairly normal life. I thank
my mother for doing that. I always took the bus. I
always took the subways. Hotel suites and limos . . .
Whew! Forget it.

—*John*

John always had a grace and ease about him.

—*Christina Haag,
actress and John's
longtime girlfriend*

6
=

N o! I won't go! I don't want special treatment," John insisted. Ashen and sweating profusely, he clutched his stomach and prayed for the stabbing pains to stop. It was July 1976, and John and his cousin Timothy Shriver were among nine Peace Corps volunteers working to rebuild homes in earthquake-ravaged Rabinal, Guatemala. Now that he had come down with a mild form of dysentery, John's Secret Service detail wanted to drive him to Guatemala City so that he could be examined by a specialist.

John would have none of it. "I mean it—I don't want any special treatment!" he told project director Luis De Celis. Impressed by John's dedication, De Celis allowed him to stay. Once he recovered, John returned to digging trenches, hauling sand for bricks, and building outhouses, all in the midsummer tropical heat.

Determined to share the same hardships endured by their fellow workers, John and Tim bathed in a brook, slept on the rain-soaked floor of a makeshift tent barracks, and subsisted on the local diet of tortillas and black beans. "John wanted to be treated just like one of us," said fellow volunteer Tom Doyle. "He got along with everyone and tried hard to speak Spanish."

The locals were even more impressed. The Reverend Antonio

Gomez y Gomez, director of the group that sponsored the rebuilding effort, praised John and his cousin for doing "more for their country's image than many ambassadors." Rabinal mayor Gabriel Sesam said he only wished "more foreigners like John and Tim would come and help us." John's supervisor on the job, Domingo Pangan, was impressed by the boys' unassuming, down-to-earth attitude. "They worked," Pangan said, "as our brothers."

Perhaps. But the Secret Service agents were a constant reminder that "Lark" was anything but your average Peace Corps volunteer. "I felt sorry for John," said fellow volunteer Veronica Paz. "Can you imagine having two Secret Service men following you all the time?"

That, thankfully, was all about to end.

"Free at last!" John whooped as he walked onto the campus of Phillips Academy at Andover, Massachusetts, in September 1976. To be sure, he was no longer living with his mother at 1040 Fifth. And less than three months from now, when he turned sixteen, John would at long last shed the Secret Service detail that for his entire life had hounded his every step.

Founded by Samuel Phillips in 1778, Phillips Academy has the distinction of being the oldest incorporated school in the United States. Made up of 170 buildings spread across 450 acres, Andover (as Phillips Academy is more commonly called) boasted among its alumni the diverse likes of Oliver Wendell Holmes, George Bush, and Jack Lemmon.

When John arrived in the autumn of 1976 as an eleventh-grader, coeducational Andover was still regarded as the most prestigious prep school in the nation. Along with twenty-one other boys, John roomed at Stearns West Hall dormitory. John's room overlooked Rabbit Pond, into which an incorrigible Humphrey Bogart once tossed a teacher before he was booted out of school.

John had little trouble blending in. With his Pre-Raphaelite hair, ripped jeans, deck shoes worn without socks, and wrinkled Brooks Brothers shirt, he was indistinguishable from scores of other good-looking young students skateboarding across campus or tossing Frisbees. Even his dormitory room seemed calculated to prove that John was "just one of the guys," Wilson McCray said. Jutting down from a corner of the ceiling was a ship's carved wooden figurehead, a life-sized maiden with her bodice pulled down to reveal her breasts.

Still, the bare-breasted figurehead was not what impressed most students who visited John's room. A single framed photograph of John's father hung above his desk, a jarring reminder that the room's occupant was not exactly your typical American teenager.

What was typical was John's continued use of marijuana. He was not alone. Like many other prep schools filled with the sons and daughters of America's elite, Andover was coping with widespread drug and alcohol abuse on campus.

"Marijuana and cocaine were everywhere at Andover, and for that matter most prep schools—particularly in the late seventies," said one Andover graduate whose son was a classmate of John's. "I don't think 'rampant' is too strong a word. If a student was caught, administrators would talk to him and notify the parents. But that was about it."

During those first few months at Andover, two Secret Service agents were still assigned to John. It was impossible not to spot them—they wore dark suits and sunglasses—but at least the agents stayed in rooms at the Andover Inn and not on campus.

The Secret Service, in fact, knew all about John's marijuana use. But fearing a confrontation with Jackie, they looked the other way. Accordingly, John had no qualms about smoking pot at Andover parties—right under the noses, literally, of the agents assigned to guard him.

Campus police were another matter. One night an Andover security guard followed the pungent aroma of marijuana to a party where John and several of his jock friends were trading rugby stories. There was a last-minute scramble to flush the evidence, but in the end John did not deny that he had been smoking marijuana. The school, as it did in all such cases, informed Jacqueline Kennedy Onassis. "John expected his mother to go ballistic," a fellow student said. "But she was sort of evenhanded and reasonable about it. He apologized, and that was the end of it."

"John smoked grass, but it didn't appear to affect him," said Holly Owen, John's soccer coach and the head of Andover's drama department. "I think his drug escapade was part of the rite of passage.

When John experimented with drugs, it was only to be one of the boys, not because he was out of control."

Given the toll drugs had already taken on the third generation of Kennedys, it was surprising that Jackie did not "go ballistic" as John had predicted. But Jackie, so long dependent on amphetamine injections from "Dr. Feelgood" Max Jacobson, decided to dismiss this latest incident involving John as just another bit of adolescent experimentation. At least for now.

There were also other distractions in Jackie's life. With both of her children away at school, a certain ennui had set in. Two decades earlier, Jackie had been the $42-a-week "Inquiring Camera Girl" at the Washington *Times-Herald*. Now Caroline was trying journalism, just as her mother had, working as a summer intern at the *New York Daily News* (her mother's new friend, *Daily News* writer Pete Hamill, was in Hyannis Port the day Elvis died and brought Caroline along to cover the story). Caroline quickly learned that her own celebrity too often got in the way of her covering a story, so she explored other career options.

But Caroline's brief foray into journalism did reawaken something in Jackie. In September 1975, the forty-six-year-old former First Lady decided to go back to work—this time as a "consulting editor" at Viking Press. Although first dismissed as a dilettante, Jackie slowly earned the respect of her fellow editors.

"She was much more like the girl I first knew who had a sense of fun and enthusiasm," George Plimpton said. "It must have been an extraordinary thing for her to be on her own. She was always somewhat diminished by the men around her."

Yet at the time of John's marijuana bust at Andover, Jackie was dealing with a crisis of her own. Without warning her, Viking had agreed to publish Jeffrey Archer's *Shall We Tell the President?*, a suspense novel about an imaginary plot to assassinate Ted Kennedy after he took office as president in 1981. After the book was published to scathing reviews in February 1977—and she was taken to task in the press for remaining at Viking—Jackie switched to Doubleday.

Like his mother, who eagerly devoured every word written about her, John kept tabs on his mother in the daily press. There was the usual number of galas, parties, and openings—and constant speculation about Jackie's love life. One of her most highly publicized relationships during this period was with Pete Hamill, who at forty-two was five years younger than Jackie. When they began going out in mid-December 1976, it came as a shock to the woman Hamill had been living with for seven years, Shirley MacLaine.

While Jackie's high-profile romance with Hamill filled the columns for months, John had fallen in love with the lissome blond sixteen-year-old daughter of a New York surgeon. "If he had fallen out of a pickup truck, he would have still been irresistible to me," said Jenny Christian, who would remain John's steady girlfriend for the next four years. "He was extremely handsome, nice, and sweet. It was a great romance."

John was such a gentleman, in fact, that they dated for more than a year before consummating the relationship. "I lost my virginity in high school like most other people," he said. "I was kind of a late bloomer, actually."

At Andover, John forged another friendship with a young woman that would last a lifetime. Alexandra "Sasha" Chermayev, the granddaughter of noted architect Serge Chermayev, met John in 1976 and they quickly became inseparable. They went to dances and movies together, yet were never romantically involved. "John and Sasha were friends in high school," said Marta Sgubin, who became Jackie's cook after John left for prep school. "He was fond of Sasha for what she was." Over the next two decades, they would attend each other's weddings, and John would become a doting godfather to her two children, both of whom would be named in his will. Afraid of disrupting Sasha's quiet family life, John would never speak publicly about their enduring friendship.

Behind the scenes, Jackie still worked hard to keep John away from the gravitational pull of his cousins. Rose Kennedy's secretary, Barbara Gibson, remembered that John seldom visited Hyannis Port, and that when he did he was "perfectly respectful and polite—clearly the product of his mother's love and concern." But Ethel's children were spinning increasingly out of control. "The kids grew wild and undisciplined, taking what they wanted, feeling above the moral bounds that held others who were not Kennedys," Gibson said. Whenever they visited Palm Beach or Hyannis Port, she added, "It was like a horde of rampaging Huns was descending on us."

At Andover, the hours John didn't devote to partying with his friends were devoted to grueling marathon workouts at the gym. "I asked him to spend less time weight lifting and more time reading his Strunk and White book on grammar," said one of his teachers, Alexander Theroux.

John also seized the opportunity to flex his acting muscles. His interest had actually begun at home, where Marta Sgubin staged several family productions of classic plays—usually by Molière—to celebrate "Madam's" July 28 birthday. (Sgubin called Jackie "Madam" because she had always addressed her previous employer, a French diplomat's wife, as "Madame." When Jackie told her the more risqué English definition of *madam,* Sgubin was mortified. "No, no," Jackie insisted. "Keep calling me that. It's cute.")

From the time he acted in *Oliver!* back at Collegiate, John was, in the words of his cousin David, "badly bitten by the acting bug." At Andover, it was obvious that *Petticoats and Union Suits* was not just another student production when it was reviewed by the *New York Times.* The venerable newspaper's theater critic wrote that "one can't help be aware of the fifteen-year-old John Kennedy in his role, although like the others in his celebrated family, he seems to be trying painfully to avoid special attention."

A year later, John acted opposite Jenny Christian in *Comings and Goings,* and then in a 1978 production of *The Comedy of Errors.* John was nineteen when he played McMurphy—the role that earned Jack Nicholson an Academy Award—in Ken Kesey's *One Flew Over the Cuckoo's Nest.* He did such a convincing job that in the scene where his character is suffocating, Jackie, who was sitting in the audience, became visibly distressed. "She had sort of a hard time with it," said a student who was watching her. "She was gasping."

That John took obvious pleasure in acting came as no surprise to Katharine Hepburn. "Doesn't seem strange to me at all for someone who is hounded by the press to go on stage," she said. "All actors are hiding behind a mask. It's really the perfect way to cope with celebrity, because people are only seeing you play a character. They don't get to the real *you*."

His acting success aside, John was in serious trouble academically. His overall academic performance was lackluster, and he flunked math outright. A possible cause, suggested one relative: John suffered from dyslexia, which had shown up elsewhere in the family.

"One of the great myths is that he was dumb. In a kind of reverse snobbery, that's what everybody expected him to be," said Alexander Theroux, who was particularly impressed by papers John wrote on Herman Melville and Clarence Darrow. "He was intelligent, but not a genius. John was a very plucky, very quiet student."

If he was not an especially diligent student, his teacher mused, there was a reason for it: "Marcel Proust said that in every relationship there is one who kisses and one who extends the cheek. John extended the cheek. He never had to work hard because people always met him more than halfway. In that sense he was very passive—not lazy, but he just didn't have to work hard for people to come to him." Lacking incentive, John "had to work at trying harder. John Kennedy was like a salmon swimming upstream."

In the end, JFK Jr. was simply "not suited to lead the intellectual life," Theroux pointed out. "He was always outside, always in motion. He *did things*."

At the time, of course, none of that mattered. Nearly every other student who flunked a course at Andover until that time was summarily kicked out. But in John's case, school administrators would allow him to stay if he repeated the eleventh grade.

"It's highly unusual for a poor student to be allowed to repeat a year at Phillips Academy," said Thomas Wilcox, director of boarding schools for the National Association of Independent Schools. "Students who don't meet the standards are usually thrown out," said a fellow student. "John wasn't—I guess because he's the son of JFK."

News that John was being held back a year caused a minor sensation. "Are you a poor student?" a reporter asked him.

"Well, I don't know," John said. "It depends on what you call a 'poor student.' "

No one was more upset by the news than Jackie, who had long

fretted about her son's intellect. "Jackie suffered a great deal of anguish over John," recalled her friend Edward Klein. "Though Jackie never spoke of it directly, she conveyed the impression to friends, including me, that she was concerned her son might have been born with a low IQ."

Meanwhile, as part of Jackie's continuing campaign to keep her son from becoming what she called "a fruit," she signed him up in June 1977 for the Outward Bound program—a full month of survival training on Maine's rocky Hurricane Island. One phase of the program called for John to spend three days alone on an island with no food, three gallons of water, a book of matches, a tarpaulin, and a Euell Gibbons book on edible plants. What was the most important thing John took away from roughing it in the wild?

"I learned," John said, shaking his fist in the air, "I'll never allow myself to be that hungry again!"

Jackie was thrilled, but after several months at home in New York he was getting into mischief. When he was caught pouring glue down the mail chute at 1040 Fifth Avenue, Jackie decided it was time for action. In the summer of 1978 she sent him to Wyoming to work as a wrangler at John Perry Barlow's Bar Cross Ranch. A Wyoming congressman had recommended the ranch to Jackie. "She wanted John," Barlow said, "to get out and around, get in closer contact with the salt of the earth, and get his hands on something real."

When he arrived at the ranch, Barlow said, "John was like a giant Labrador puppy. Lots of energy, little focus. But he was amenable to being focused. He knew he had to measure up, and he loved the challenge."

The first assignment Barlow gave his newest hand was to dig post holes for a corral fence. "He went at it like he was killing snakes—digging through gravel and rock. He did it without complaining and with ravenous intensity."

It was the first paying job he had ever had, and while his stake in the Kennedy family fortune already amounted to five million dollars, John clearly took pride in a job well done. "This was not something his mother was paying for," Barlow said. "He was doing it on his own, and he was just delighted."

When it came to rounding up cattle, he seriously regretted the fact that he lacked his mother's equestrian skills. "You really need my mother and my sister up here," he would say as he brought up the rear, pushing along the cows and calves that lagged behind the rest of the herd. "They'd be much better at this than I am."

When Barlow told his crew that JFK Jr. would be joining them, their reaction was predictable. "They told me, 'Aw, come on. You're not going to do this to us.' Almost immediately, John won everybody over."

John's fellow ranch hands were impressed with John's physical strength as well as his lack of pretense. "I guess we expected another spoiled rich kid coming to spend a few weeks at the dude ranch," one said. "Instead, he was completely down to earth, a hard worker—just a real nice kid."

When he went home six weeks later, Jackie was ecstatic at what she perceived to be the change in John. "They kept saying I was a miracle worker," Barlow said. "But he was already a miracle when he got here." John returned to Andover and wasted no time volunteering for the school's community service program. For two days a week, he taught English to the immigrant junior high school students in economically depressed Lawrence, Massachusetts.

John more than made up for in heart what he lacked in intellect. Caroline, flourishing in her junior year at Radcliffe College, had also made her mother proud. To celebrate his eighteenth birthday and her twenty-first birthday, Jackie invited 150 people—all the Kennedys as well as friends of the birthday boy and girl—to a party at Manhattan's chic Le Club on November 26, 1978.

It was an emotion-charged evening. It had been fifteen years since JFK was murdered, and now his only surviving brother stood to toast John and Caroline for the remarkable young adults they had become. "I shouldn't be doing this tonight," Ted said, his voice shaking with emotion as it had when he gave Bobby's eulogy. "By rights, it should have been the father of these two children. Jack loved his children more than anything else. Young John and Caroline bring new life to the family."

While the polished likes of George Plimpton and Bunny Mellon sipped Dom Pérignon, John's Andover friends downed pitchers of beer and cheered loudly when two birthday cakes ablaze with sparklers were rolled out for the two guests of honor. After Jackie, Ethel, Eunice, Ted, and the rest of their generation filed out just after midnight, John and his buddies lit up joints. They remained at the club smoking and drinking tequila until dawn.

At 4 A.M., one of John's burly buddies finally staggered out onto East 55th Street, where he was confronted by photographers. "Okay, no pictures," John's beefy friend declared. "I'm giving everybody fair warning!"

Moments later, John emerged wearing dark glasses, a black jacket, and a long white silk scarf. Cameras began clicking. "The big guy starts punching and kicking," recalled *New York Daily News* photographer Richard Corkery. "Suddenly everybody's pushing."

John tried to pull his friends off a *National Enquirer* photographer—and in the process wound up sprawled on the pavement. "Stop!" John yelled, pleading for calm. Struggling to his feet, he managed to calm everyone down before leaving the scene.

The melee was splashed across the front pages of the tabloids the next day, but John was not about to deliver a repeat performance, acting career or no. When he showed up three weeks later at Studio 54 with his date, Lynn Hutter, John merely smiled politely as photographers grabbed shot after shot. Eventually, however, the commotion all proved too much for the couple. John ducked into a taxi, pulled Hutter inside, and, as they sped away, turned to make an obscene gesture with his finger.

Tempers would flare again after his Andover graduation ceremony, when reporters blocked John and his mother at every turn as they tried to make their way to the buffet table. "Look," he said impatiently, "I just want to spend some time with my mates and enjoy my graduation."

But Jackie, accustomed to the chaos, savored the moment. "Oh, Ted," she sighed to the senator. "Can you believe it? My baby, graduating!"

John Walsh, the Secret Service agent who had saved Jackie from drowning off the coast of Ireland, pulled John from a fire in Hawaii, and been a father figure to the son of the President, sat with the family. Jackie, smiling warmly, leaned over and gave Walsh's arm an affectionate squeeze.

• • •

Once again, Jackie had arranged for her son to be "far, far away," as Peter Duchin put it, "from the circus at Hyannis Port." At 1040 Fifth there had been "an awful lot of hand-wringing going on," Duchin said. "Jackie was hearing one horror story after another, and she was more determined than ever that John not be sucked into that."

This time, John and a half-dozen others trekked through the wilds of Kenya as part of a ten-week course run by the National Outdoor Leadership School. At one point, John's party became hopelessly lost. His fellow survivalists agreed that he should be the one to lead them out of the wilderness, and began to hack their way through the dense undergrowth in hopes of finding their way back to base camp. "I just hope," John kept saying, "the press doesn't get wind of this. My mother will be frantic."

Meanwhile, course officials began to panic. Masai warriors as well as search planes were dispatched in a desperate, all-out effort to find JFK Jr. It would be forty-eight tense hours before a lone Masai tracker located John and his fellow survivalists.

Fortunately, Jackie was not told that John was missing until after he had been rescued. By that time, both mother and son were immersed in plans to enroll John in college.

Although he was accepted at Harvard, John felt uncomfortable with the idea because, in the words of his friend John Perry Barlow, "he knew he hadn't earned it. John knew it was strictly because of who he was, and that he didn't have the grades, so he didn't go there." Jackie actually saw the wisdom in John's decision to attend Brown University instead of Harvard; she realized that at his father's alma mater he, unlike Caroline, would be totally submerged in the Kennedy myth. By 1979, Brown had become the school of choice for wealthy prep school graduates who craved the Ivy League experience but not the rigorous academic demands imposed by Princeton, Harvard, Yale, Columbia, or Dartmouth. Indeed, Brown had no core requirements for graduation, and each student was invited to devise his own academic program.

Founded in 1764 and the seventh-oldest college in the U.S., Brown was a cluster of red-brick and white-clapboard colonial buildings perched on a hilltop in the middle of Providence, Rhode

Island. Because of its central location, Brown, unlike the pastoral environs of Andover, offered John little protection from the prying eyes of the press. When he showed up to register for classes, photographers once again swarmed around him, causing an embarrassing scene. The flustered freshman promised to pose in front of the Brown University sign at the campus entrance if they simply left him alone long enough to register.

"Unlike his sister and the rest of the Kennedys who show entirely too many teeth, John knew how to smile for the cameras," one of the photographers said. "But half the time he was sort of saying under his breath, 'Okay, have you had enough? I feel really dumb doing this. Can we stop now, guys? Guys?' "

John was eager to be treated as just another student—and one sure pathway to acceptance was to go through the indignities required to join a fraternity. After a hazing ritual that included swallowing a live goldfish, wallowing in animal entrails, guzzling a pitcher of beer, then stripping and streaking across the campus to the howls of ogling Brown coeds, John was a proud member of Phi Psi.

No sooner did he make it through Hell Night than, on October 20, 1979, John gave his first speech at the dedication ceremony for the John F. Kennedy Library. Located outside Boston, I. M. Pei's stark white futuristic structure, with its high glass walls looking out over the sparkling waters of Dorchester Bay, reflected JFK's eternally youthful, forward-looking appeal.

Caroline, now twenty-two, sat next to John. Thanks to Jackie's unrelenting pressure for her daughter to lose weight, Caroline had turned into, in Andy Warhol's words, "a raving beauty"—all teeth and cheekbones and windblown chestnut tresses.

Yet she was painfully shy, and it was all she could do to introduce her brother to the assembled dignitaries—among them dozens of New Frontier alumni and President Jimmy Carter. Not yet nineteen and already standing a broad-shouldered six-feet-one-inch tall, the gangling boy who had tussled with photographers just the year before was now a strikingly handsome cross between the Kennedys and the Bouviers. As he stepped to the podium, he also seemed to have inherited the natural poise of both his parents. As a tribute to his father, he read Stephen Spender's poem, "I Think Continually of Those Who Were Truly Great."

During the ceremonies, wind ripped the sails of Jack's boat the *Victura,* which would remain on display outside the library. On the way out, JFK's widow and only son stopped by the boat for a moment. "You know," John whispered to his mother, "I don't even remember him. Sometimes I think I might, but . . . I don't."

For years, John had claimed that he remembered these events. And, on one or two rare occasions, a memory appeared to surface. One day Jack's friend Chuck Spalding walked in the room when John was taping one of his father's speeches—a tribute to Eleanor Roosevelt—for one of his classes at Andover.

"Listen! Right in here is where I crawl under the desk and Dad kicks me," he told Spalding. "It's coming up now. Here it is. He was talking on the radio and I crawled under the desk and grabbed him."

But as he grew to manhood, John conceded that he viewed his father "through the color of others and the perception of others and through photographs and what I've read." No matter how hard he treid to remember the moment, even the heart-tugging photo of John saluting his father's casket—one of the most famous of all time—evoked no memories.

At Brown, John made a concerted effort to understand the father he had never known. He studied his father like any other student, taking a seminar course on the Vietnam War. He prevailed on his mother, who had dated documentary filmmaker Peter Davis after Pete Hamill, to have Davis bring his controversial Academy Award–winning film *Hearts and Minds* to class.

With several classmates, John set up an informal group to debate every issue from racism to nuclear disarmament to abortion rights. "John had definite opinions about things, but he also argued on both sides of an issue," said his friend Charlie King. "He was definitely passionate about civil rights. John was very adamant about the fact that we had to have equal rights for everybody in our society."

But it was theater, not world affairs or politics, that most intrigued young John. When he appeared in March of 1980 as the soldier Bonario in Ben Jonson's *Volpone,* the critic for the *Brown Daily Herald* gave John a glowing review—then publicly retracted it in a follow-up piece.

"John doesn't move well—he's very inhibited and self-conscious on the stage," the *Daily Herald* reviewer wrote. "And his voice is off-putting. He sounds like a rich New York preppie." Why, then, had he gushed over John's performance in the first place? "I didn't think John was as good as I made him out to be," he tried to explain. "But I was sitting next to his mother on opening night and I guess I was dazzled."

Badly bruised but not defeated, John continued to hone his acting skills. As an undergraduate, he would have major roles in plays ranging from *The Tempest* and David Rabe's *In the Boom Boom Room* (where his new crew cut caused a bigger stir than the student actress who went topless to play his go-go dancer girlfriend) to J. M. Synge's classic *Playboy of the Western World* to Miguel Pinero's gritty prison drama *Short Eyes*.

Rick Moody, who played John's sidekick in *In the Boom Boom Room,* was impressed by Kennedy's natural acting style—"a little Brando, a little De Niro, a healthy dollop of Nicholson, maybe a dash of his dad's inaugural pluck." Later, Moody wondered why he had been surprised when John delivered his lines "with uncanny reserves of charisma. What's the surprise in this? He'd been acting his entire life."

On opening night, John and Moody were backstage waiting to go on when suddenly they heard a hearty laugh from the audience. "That's my sister," John said with a smile. "That's Caroline."

Jackie also dutifully attended most of his college productions, but she did not approve. "His mother laid down the law," said a Brown classmate. "She told John in no uncertain terms that acting was beneath him, that he was his father's son and that he had a tradition of public service to uphold."

Mother and son "really had terrible fights over this. John is really pretty good at controlling his temper, but there were times when he talked about his mother when he just lost it. What he wanted from her was respect, and for a while there he just didn't feel as if he had it."

John had not yet turned twenty when *Saturday Night Fever* producer Robert Stigwood offered him the chance to play his father in a feature film based on JFK's early years. He begged his mother to let him take the role, but Jackie put her foot down. She wanted him to finish college.

"And then can I do anything I want?" he asked.

"Anything," she answered, "but act."

Increasingly, John chafed under his mother's iron-fisted authority. "His mother would come up and visit and it was obvious they had a very close relationship," said another classmate who became a well-known journalist. "It was obvious she ran the show and he was not always happy about that. There was a lot of friction under the surface that people just don't know about. He wanted her to take him seriously, to treat him like an adult, the way she treated Caroline. But she didn't. Jackie was a stern taskmaster."

With good reason, apparently. Throughout his college career, John, whose approach to study was decidedly lackadaisical, would teeter precariously on the edge of outright expulsion. In one letter to Jackie, Associate Dean Bruce Donovan pointedly stated that John's grades would have to improve or he "may become liable to dismissal." Pointing out that by his junior year he had yet to pass four courses in any given semester, Professor Edward Beiser warned John, "Even with our modest graduation requirements, you are skating on very thin ice."

Jackie took the warnings seriously even if her son did not. "Living up to academic responsibilities has always been of first importance in our house," Jackie wrote back on her trademark blue stationery, "so neither John nor I will fail to be galvanized by your message." Responding to news that John was on academic probation, Jackie wrote that the shock "should teach John the vital lesson of how to allot every second of his time. I am sure it will sink in as he frantically tries to make up his work."

On another occasion, she wrote from Hyannis Port, "I look forward to hearing that he is off probation—and to never getting another notice that he is on it."

There were times when John did rise to the occasion—particularly when the subject hit close to home. "I had heard that John was a dummy, that he was more interested in sex than in school," said Steve Gillon, a teaching assistant for an American history course that covered the Kennedy administration. "But he was very articulate and intelligent. He contributed things to the discussion that went beyond the textbook. In fact, he dominated discussions in certain areas, such as civil rights and the role of the Supreme Court." In class, John always referred to his father as "The President." John received a B+ in the class, but it was not enough to offset a report sprinkled with D's and F's.

While his mother cracked the whip, John kept whatever feelings of frustration he might have had concealed from his friends on campus. Jackie did visit periodically, and relations between mother and son always seemed "very warm," said John's fraternity brother Richard Wiese. One afternoon, while John and Wiese were sitting on top of a brick wall outside the fraternity, John suddenly remembered he'd forgotten to turn in a paper and jumped down.

"Can you wait here for my mom?" John asked his friend. "You know what she looks like—dark hair, big sunglasses."

"Yes, John," Wiese said, "I think I'll recognize her."

When Jackie did arrive a few minutes later, she asked Wiese ("I was a wreck") to show her to John's room so she could use the phone. John's room looked "as if someone had tossed a grenade in there." Clothes were strewn everywhere ("John never hung anything up—just dropped it on the floor where he took it off"), and books, papers, sports equipment, bottles, cans, and food wrappers littered the floor. All surfaces—floors, beds, furniture—were buried under a thick layer of junk.

Jackie spotted a black phone cord on the floor and, Wiese recalled, "got down on all fours and followed it," burrowing through soiled laundry and discarded pizza boxes. When she got to the end, the former First Lady discovered that it led to a stereo. "But where," she demanded, "is the *phone*?" Wiese invited her next door to use his.

There were other, unexpected reminders of John's place in history. Perhaps as part of his continuing effort to be accepted as just another student, John continued to smoke pot. For a time, he sampled stronger substances. At one party, John was present when his friends allegedly passed around a silver straw and an ashtray filled with cocaine. Each time someone took a hit, a little more of the design on the bottom of the ashtray was revealed.

As it was handed to John, everyone shuddered at what they saw on the bottom of the ashtray—the face of John F. Kennedy staring up at them, with the dates 1917–1963 printed below. There was a tense moment. Then John, according to one witness, "saw what was on the ashtray and took it anyway."

"Despite those experiences and the reckless seam that ran deep through the Kennedy nature," said Kennedy biographer Wendy Leigh, "he had a powerful inner compass that ultimately steered him away from excess."

The occasional bizarre incident notwithstanding, John largely succeeded in his campaign to be treated like any other Brown student. Said Wiese: "He was a pretty upbeat guy. People gravitated toward him." More often than not, it was John who broke the ice. "He'd come up to you and stick out his hand and say, 'Hi, I'm John,' " recalled Rick Guy, a fellow history major and a player on Brown's lacrosse team. "It was never John Kennedy, always just John . . . He joined me for dinner several times and at first I was just incredibly flattered. But he would totally disarm you by asking questions—and not in that artificial way people have of pretending to be interested in you. He really wanted to know about other people's lives. Everyone walked away from John thinking one thing above all else—that he was just a tremendously decent, regular guy."

In keeping with his "regular guy" image at Brown, John drove a beat-up gray Honda Civic littered with beer cans, shot hoops on the patio into the wee hours, and to "earn some extra cash" raised a pig in Phi Psi's basement to sell for slaughter (he eventually gave it to someone else to keep as a pet).

A group of coeds planned to kidnap the pig and replace it with a pile of bacon, but scrapped the plan at the last minute. Yet John was not above being the target of his friends' pranks. Once when he was in full Shakespearean costume and makeup and leaving for opening night at the theater, John was bombarded with water balloons fired from a makeshift cannon across the quad as soon as he stepped outside. "He kind of gasped," recalled Rick Guy, whose fraternity brothers pulled the prank. "And then he looked exasperated. But he didn't yell or scream like a lot of other people would have. He just turned around and went back in and cleaned up. John took everything in stride because he wanted more than anything to be treated like an ordinary guy." Toward that end, John was himself a willing combatant in cafeteria food fights.

And while there was an unspoken rule that they would never mention his father's name to him, his frat brothers were not above capitalizing on John's celebrity to attract women. When they hung a sign outside the frat house saying he was in residence, the line of attractive young coeds waiting to get in stretched around the corner.

John ignored the hundreds of calls he received from women—complete strangers—asking for a date, and complained that it felt uncomfortable to be the object of so much female attention. It didn't help that John stripped off his shirt at every available opportunity. He was, in fact, already garnering a reputation as something of an exhibitionist. Like his father, who swam naked in the White House pool and sunbathed nude in Palm Beach, JFK Jr. had no qualms about displaying his body in public. John, who weighed 175 pounds at the time but could bench-press an impressive 250 pounds, was "proud of the fact that he was in great shape," Guy said. "As far as the girls were concerned, nobody was paying attention to you if John was in the vicinity."

By his junior year John had broken up with Jenny Christian, who was away at Harvard studying psychology, and begun a long-term relationship with a chestnut-haired history and literature major named Sally Munro. It was significant that John would remain friends not only with Christian, but with all of his former lovers. Even more remarkable—given the fact that many if not most relationships end on a sour note—not a single former love of John's would ever make even a mildly negative statement about him.

Born and raised in a harborfront estate in picturesque Marblehead, Massachusetts, toothy, Boston Irish Munro was a dead ringer for John's sister; frequently photographers would identify Munro as Caroline in captions. She had even graduated from the same prep school Caroline had attended, Concord Academy. More wholesomely attractive than stunning, John's new girlfriend made no attempt to conceal the fact that she was smitten.

Jackie had approved of Jenny Christian, and Sally Munro also won her stamp of approval. Their on-again, off-again romance would stretch over five years, a period during which John also explored relationships with a number of other women. "John was not a womanizer like his father," said one of his fraternity brothers, "but his thing with Sally wasn't exclusive. When she wasn't around, he did date a couple of other girls. You've got to remember, his phone was ringing off the hook with calls from girls he knew—and some he didn't know. Women were mailing him their panties and hanging around outside claiming to be his fiancée. We all thought John showed remarkable restraint, considering."

John's mother, meantime, had quietly settled into a serious relationship of her own. Jackie and wealthy diamond merchant Maurice Tempelsman had actually had their first date on August 20, 1975. Born into an Orthodox Jewish family in Antwerp, Belgium, he fled the Nazis for New York in 1940. Forgoing college, Maurice joined his father's diamond-importing business, Leon Tempelsman & Son. Using his attorney, two-time Democratic presidential nominee Adlai Stevenson, to forge links with the powerful Oppenheimer diamond-mining family, he soon became a "Sightholder"—one of only 160 people in the world allowed to purchase diamonds directly from the De Beers cartel ten times a year.

Hefty contributors to the Democrats, Maurice and his wife, Lily, became casual friends of the Kennedys when Jack was still a senator, and later frequent guests at the Kennedy White House. Although he was still very much married to the devoutly Orthodox Lily—not to mention the father of three children—Jackie made no effort to conceal her growing affection for Tempelsman.

Eventually Tempelsman would obtain a divorce, of sorts. After Maurice moved into Jackie's apartment in 1982, Lily granted him a "get," an Orthodox Jewish divorce. But, legally, Maurice and Lily remained husband and wife.

On the face of it, the balding, pudgy, self-effacing diamond mogul seemed an unlikely choice for Jackie. "Husbands did not always treat her the way she deserved," Jackie's friend Vivian Crespi observed. "Maurice, however, worshiped the ground she walked on. He did not dominate her, she did not dominate him. They were equals." Aileen Mehle was one of those who felt Tempelsman was "perfect for Jackie. A teddy bear. A very smart teddy bear." Indeed, beginning in the late 1970s, Tempelsman oversaw all of Jackie's financial affairs, and would wind up parlaying her twenty-six million dollars from Onassis into a $100 million–plus fortune.

At about the same time, Caroline was also falling in love. After graduating from Radcliffe with honors in 1980, she went to work in the Metropolitan Museum of Art's Film and Television Department. It was there that she met Edwin Arthur Schlossberg, a self-styled cultural historian–artist–author and founder of a small company that produced multimedia video projects for museums and businesses. Thirteen years Caroline's senior and Jewish, Schlossberg was the son of a wealthy textile manufacturer.

After a party in Aspen, Andy Warhol noted in his diary, "Saw Caroline and the Schlossberg boy. They're madly in love." Soon she had moved into his million-dollar loft. At her Christmas party that year, Jackie welcomed Ed warmly and led him around the room. "I want you all," she said in her little-girl whisper, "to meet my daughter's new friend, Ed Schlossberg."

Jackie's boyfriend, meanwhile, had quietly arranged for John to spend the summer of 1980 in South Africa learning the ropes of the diamond business, just in case he might someday be interested in entering the Tempelsman family trade.

Instead, John returned to Brown with an insight into the evils of apartheid and a determination to do something about it. With financial backing from Tempelsman, John set up the South African Group for Education, a campus lecture series designed to spread the word about the political situation in South Africa. The first person John invited to speak: Andrew Young, who at various times was a civil rights leader, mayor of Atlanta, and U.S. ambassador to the United Nations.

It was a side of John the American public had not seen. Over the years, there had been a growing perception that JFK's only son was turning out to be something of a disappointment. Most of the newspaper stories about John—from his mugging in Central Park to his being held back a grade at Andover to the eighteenth-birthday brawl that left him spread-eagle on the sidewalk—had not shown him in an altogether favorable light. And recent photographs of longhaired John, looking foppish in a fake mustache and period costume for his role in the campus production of *Volpone,* only served to raise more eyebrows.

Aware of John's public image as a lightweight, Ted begged Jackie to let John give a press conference at the Center for Democratic Policy, where he was earning a hundred dollars a week interning during the summer of 1981. "People should see," Ted reasoned, "that there is a lot more to John than what they've been reading in the papers."

At the conference, John instantly disarmed reporters. When one pointed out that there was an ink stain on his white shirt, John looked down and said, "I would wear one of those plastic pocket protectors, but they make you look like a Republican." Asked if he was contemplating a political career, John shrugged, "I'm not really thinking about careers at the moment. I'm not a big planner."

In truth, John still yearned to be an actor, and had already elicited help from his actor uncle Peter Lawford. "Peter encouraged John to pursue acting if that was his dream," Lawford's widow, Patricia Seton Lawford, later said. "When she found out, Jackie wrote Peter and told him not to interfere—and that, of course, made Peter even more determined to support John in whatever it was *he* wanted to do."

What John wanted to do in his junior year was move off campus into a house at 155 Benefit Street. His new housemates were tennis team captain John Hare, lacrosse player Rob Littell, aspiring actress Christina Haag, and Christiane Amanpour, who would go on to be a star correspondent for CNN and CBS.

Acting may have been his passion, but John also felt a family obligation to public service. Six years earlier, John and his cousin Timothy Shriver had worked side by side to rebuild a Guatemalan town destroyed by earthquakes. Now, in the summer of his junior year, John was spending six weeks with Shriver at the University of Connecticut teaching English to the children of immigrants.

Not that John was devoting himself entirely to good works. He showed up frequently at Xenon, one of a handful of discos that dominated New York nightlife in the early 1980s and, like Studio 54 before it, a hedonistic blend of drugs, sex, spectacle, and brain-rattling music.

After weekends spent club-hopping in Manhattan, he would drive

back to Connecticut in his gray Honda Civic. Like his father and the
rest of the Kennedy clan, John was notoriously lead-footed. By the
end of his senior year, he had amassed a small bushel of speeding tickets in four different states—Massachusetts, Rhode Island, Connecticut, and New York. He ignored the summonses, and in early 1983
his Massachusetts license was suspended. Not that it mattered. "John
drove anyway," said a Brown classmate. "When it came to speeding
and parking tickets, he just didn't take it seriously. He grew up in
New York City, where a lot of people just thought it was one big
game."

As he headed into the final stretch at Brown, John was more convinced than ever that his true calling was the theater. His role that
April in *Short Eyes,* which dealt with the prison murder of a child
molester, earned him glowing reviews. "John played his part to per-
fection," wrote campus theater critic Peter DeChiara. "The gum-
chewing, tattooed Kennedy throws his bulk around the set with
infinite self-assurance and an air of stubborn defiance."

Glowing reviews or no, Jackie vetoed John's plan to apply to Yale
Drama School. "Jackie just felt," Letitia Baldrige said, "that a career
in show business was not necessarily the best thing for her son."
Jackie did not, as was later reported, threaten to disinherit John if he
didn't go to law school as she wished. She didn't have to. "The single most important person in John's life," Peter Duchin said, "was his
mother. He was very protective of her and wouldn't do anything to
disappoint her, even if it meant giving up something that was important to him."

Acting was not the only thing John was pressured by his mother to
forgo. In February 1988, John decided to pursue his lifelong dream
of becoming a pilot. He secretly began taking flying lessons from
Arthur Marx at the Martha's Vineyard Airport. "I was impressed by
him immediately," Marx recalled, "because he rode his bike to the
airport from his mother's house at the other end of the island and it
was freezing. That's how much he wanted to fly."

Marx remembered John the student pilot as "full of enthusiasm.
He really, really dug it. And he took flying seriously." Over the next
decade, Marx would take several flights with John at the controls.
"He was always focused in the airplane," said Marx, who would

make his last flight with John in 1998. "I never saw him as a pilot act in an impulsive way. In fact, John was probably better than he thought he was."

After several months, John worked up the courage to tell his mother that he was taking flying lessons. He even brought Jackie to meet Marx. "He said, 'This is my mother, Jacqueline Onassis'—as if I wouldn't know who she was," Marx said. "If she had any problem with John's flying, I didn't see it. She was perfectly charming."

As she had learned to do so deftly over the course of her life, Jackie was concealing her true feelings from Marx. In spite of the fact that Jackie had encouraged him to embark on adventures in such far-flung locales as India and Africa, there was, Maurice Tempelsman told a friend, "something about John piloting a plane that frightened her."

Jackie, who had relived her husband's assassination in her dreams for years, was having nightmares about her son. She demanded that John drop the flying lessons. "Please don't do it," Jackie begged her son when he initially refused. "There have been too many deaths in the family already." Out of deference to his mother and a desire to spare her any further anxiety, John relented.

On June 5, 1983, Jackie and John applauded as Senator Ted Kennedy was introduced at a Brown forum on nuclear disarmament. The next day John was to graduate, and Ted veered from his script to invoke his slain brother's name once again. "I know how much my brother Jack cherished John's future," Ted said, pausing to clear his throat. "And how proud he would be if he could be here today." That night, at a dinner at Providence's elegant Biltmore Plaza Hotel, John appeared moved when Ted presented him with a graduation gift: a framed copy of notes his father had scrawled during the Cuban Missile Crisis.

The next day, John, wearing white jeans, a black T-shirt, and cowboy boots beneath his cap and gown, filed onto the green with the rest of the graduating class of 1983. Spotting Jackie in the crowd of family members, John waved and loudly shouted, "Hi, Mom!"

Then a cheer went up from the Kennedys, and Jackie motioned for John to look skyward. He and his classmates shielded their eyes and looked up to see a skywritten message—a variation of the botched inscription on a cake that once had them convulsed with laughter: GOOD GLUCK JOHN.

Caught between his abiding passion for acting and his mother's insistence that he enroll in law school, John needed time to sort things out. That July of 1983 John, clearly no longer in need of further "toughening up," embarked on another summer adventure.

This time John signed on with his old diving buddy Barry Clifford in Clifford's quest to raise the wreck of the fabled pirate ship *Whydah,* which sank off Cape Cod in 1717 in a fierce storm. When it sank, the *Whydah* was reportedly loaded down with $200 million of loot amassed by the buccaneer known as Black Sam Bellamy.

With his eye on sunken treasure, Clifford set out for the site aboard his seventy-foot research ship, the *Vast Explorer.* When John asked to join the crew, Clifford vouched for his friend's expertise. "Look, I've been diving with this guy for years, and he's good," he told Richard "Stretch" Gray, the *Vast Explorer*'s six-foot-ten, 325-pound captain. "He's a good diver, and a helluva athlete, and you can depend on him, believe me."

But first Stretch was determined to make the rich preppie prove himself. His first job was to clean out the lazarette, part of the rudder mechanism. "It's just filthy," Clifford said. "The bilge makes a cesspool smell." As was his habit, John did the job without once complaining. "And when John came out of the bilge, in Stretch's mind he had made the team."

Unassuming, disarmingly friendly John quickly became one of the most valuable members of the salvage operation—diving six hours a day, unwinding with his shipmates at Vineyard pubs, then bunking down with them belowdecks. Constantly trading barbs with the others, he quickly became the ship's resident joker. "Who left personal belongings in the dive room?" he bellowed when he caught Clifford breaking a ship's rule. "Let's throw them overboard."

Clifford did actually locate the *Whydah*—the only pirate ship ever found—but not until two years later. But the experience had left an indelible mark on John ("How often do you get to do something like dive a shipwreck?")—and vice versa. "John was someone," Clifford said, "we all liked and appreciated . . . I had the highest respect for him."

While he was still on board the *Vast Explorer,* John was studying for his next big voyage of self-discovery. Both he and Jackie dreaded the approaching twentieth anniversary of JFK's assassination and the media frenzy that would inevitably accompany it. Jackie feared more attention than ever would be focused on JFK's son and namesake, at a delicate time when he was still trying to sort out just what it was he wanted to do with his life.

In October 1983, John flew to India, where he would spend nine months studying public health and education at the University of New Delhi. "It was great gallantry on Jackie's part to send him to India for nine months during the twentieth anniversary of his father's assassination," Jackie's friend the writer Gita Mehta told Ed Klein. "I mean, he could have grown up terrified, with a state-of-siege mentality, but she has given him the courage to address a place as alien as India without any sense of fear. That is an example of how subtle and intelligent a parent she has been."

It was precisely because of the twentieth anniversary that she wanted him out of the country. Ever since millions of Indians jammed the streets to cheer her as First Lady, shouting *"Jackie Ki Jai! Ameriki Rani!"* ("Hail Jackie! Queen of America!"), Jackie had felt a spiritual bond with the subcontinent. Oddly, perhaps, it seemed to her that he would be safer there.

On his return to New York in June 1984, John moved into a small apartment on West 86th Street and went to work for a group his mother founded, the nonprofit 42nd Street Development Corporation. His salary was twenty thousand dollars a year.

Still, Jackie was stunned to learn that John had not abandoned his dream of becoming an actor. Within Jackie's tight-knit New York circle of friends, only Rudolf Nureyev showed the courage to stand up to the intimidating Mrs. Onassis—or at least press her son to do so. "Show some balls!" Nureyev told John. "Do what *you* want."

While Jackie kept a tight rein on John, she could not have guessed that dependable, solid Caroline would come closest to becoming embroiled in the dangerous antics of Bobby's tribe. David, son of Bobby and Ethel, made regular trips to Harlem to feed his heroin addiction. On August 25, 1984, his body was found in Palm Beach's Brazilian Court Hotel. He had died after injecting himself with cocaine, the tranquilizer Mellaril, and the painkiller Demerol. But no illegal drugs were found in the room, leading police to believe someone may have cleaned up the death scene.

In depositions, the bell captain was asked if anyone could have gotten into the room before he discovered the body.

"Could have been Caroline Kennedy," he replied. Caroline had shown up that morning looking for him. "She called the room; there was no answer. She walked back toward the room, knocked on the door; this is what I heard. This is when I saw her coming out from the south wing area."

Caroline insisted she was never even in the vicinity of David's room, and the police dropped the matter. It was the only time she came close to being dragged into a Kennedy family scandal.

On Christmas Eve 1984, John lost his strongest ally in the ongoing dispute with his mother when Peter Lawford died at age sixty-one after years of alcohol and drug abuse. John spent Christmas with his mother and sister at 1040 Fifth, then flew to Los Angeles the next day to attend his uncle's funeral. After attending the memorial dinner that night at La Scala, he hopped a flight back to New York and ever more uncertain future. "When Peter died," Pat Seton Lawford said, "Jackie was grief-stricken. She and Peter had been very close, and when she called me the day he died she was very emotional, and very kind and understanding to me. John was so sweet, and a little lost— Peter was one hundred percent behind his wish to become an actor if that was what he really wanted, and John counted on him for advice. With Peter gone, there was really no one else in the family who would back him. All the other Kennedys apparently agreed with Jackie that John should go to law school."

Undecided, John indulged his love of sports—running, tennis, roller-skating (later in-line skating), biking, hiking, swimming, rowing, sailing, water-skiing, playing football in the park, working out at the gym—while weighing his options. He also spent Monday nights at sports bars watching football with his friends, and regularly attended Knicks games at Madison Square Garden.

He explored other interests as well. Wearing shorts and a backpack as he strolled through Times Square unnoticed in the middle of the day, John would closely study the photos of nude women posted out-side sex clubs. Then, having decided which women most appealed to him, he went inside to watch LIVE SEX LIVE. For a brief time, he also seemed fascinated by pornography. At one point, a video store owner accused him of running up more than a thousand dollars in fines for dozens of X-rated videos he had failed to return.

Meanwhile John, whose chiseled physique was regularly displayed in newspapers and magazines around the globe, was himself garner-ing a reputation as something of an exhibitionist. At Edgartown on Martha's Vineyard, locals accused him of walking around town wear-ing only a towel around his waist and coyly letting it slip. "He loves to walk around in the nude," said Couri Hay, who worked out at the Aspen Club in Colorado when John was there. "He walks around in the gym with his bathrobe open, and when he takes a shower he leaves the curtain open." According to Hay, John skinny-dipped at a Hyannis Port pool party, then strolled around nude while waiters served guests drinks. Hay wound up thinking JFK Jr. "could have been a porno star."

The exhibitionist streak would persist. Years later, in 1990, John vacationed on St. Bart's, in the French West Indies. Once again, he swam and walked around on the beach nude—only this time he was captured on film by New York travel agent Shelley Shusteroff. The photographs, for which Shusteroff was allegedly offered a six-figure sum, were not published.

But John was not yet twenty-five, and could not let go of his act-ing dream without first, he told his mother, "testing myself on the professional stage to see if I even have any real talent." In March of 1985, he agreed to play the male lead in *Winners* by Brian Friel, the Irish playwright who would go on to write *Dancing at Lughnasa*. In a case of art foreshadowing life, John played opposite his former Brown housemate Christina Haag in the story of star-crossed lovers who drown in a boating mishap.

During rehearsals, Haag, who had been studying drama at Julliard for a year, was surprised to learn that John had "a tremendous ear for accents." At one point, they argued over the correct Irish pronuncia-tion of the word God. The director, who was Irish, determined that

John was right. "After that," Haag said, "I took my pointers from John."

But before anyone could say "break a leg," John did—or at least his right ankle, while working out in the gym that April. At first John thought he had merely suffered a sprain, but Jackie insisted on taking him to nearby Lenox Hill Hospital herself. There, X rays revealed a small fracture. The mishap, one of many to befall the accident-prone Kennedy, forced the company to postpone the play's opening by one month.

On August 15, 1985, JFK Jr. made his professional acting debut at Manhattan's tiny Irish Arts Theater. Jackie and Caroline, both adamant that he not pursue a show business career, pointedly refused to attend. Moreover, Jackie insisted there be no reviews or reviewers. "Jackie was terrified," her cousin John Davis said, "that the critics would come and see John in *Winners,* since rave reviews might encourage him to continue a career in acting."

The play's director, Nye Heron, called John "the best young actor I've seen in twelve years." Agreed the Irish Arts Center's Sandy Boyen, "John is an extraordinary and very talented young actor. He could have a very successful stage and film career if he wanted it." Added Heron, "Evidently, that's not going to happen." (Years later, John would make his film debut delivering two lines as a "guitar-playing Romeo" in *A Matter of Degrees.*)

John was the first to deny that his role in *Winners* was anything more than a lark. Several producers offered to take the play to Broadway if he remained in the cast, but John demurred. "This is definitely not a professional acting debut by any means," he insisted. "It's just a hobby."

He did seem serious, however, about Christina Haag. "We fell in love," Haag later said succinctly. "We began a romance that lasted until 1991." The daughter of a wealthy marketing executive and a graduate of Manhattan's exclusive Brearley School, which Caroline had also attended, the lushly beautiful Haag had actually known John since they were both fifteen. Their friendship had deepened at Brown. "In many ways," she said, "we grew up together."

The relationship with Haag, as with several of his serious loves, was a stormy one—due in part to the fact that on occasion he dated other women when the opportunity availed itself. Given who he was and what he looked like, the opportunity availed itself with some degree of frequency.

"John was a passionate person. He had a temper, no doubt about it," John Perry Barlow said. And while he felt free to play the field—though by no means to the unfettered extent his father had—John also had "a jealous streak," a classmate said. "He might blow up and yell, or pound his fist against something—I even saw him stamp his feet like a little kid—but he would never, ever harm anyone. And if he did blow up he regretted it three minutes later and apologized."

A mounting source of frustration was Jackie's determination to manipulate her children's love lives, especially John's. At 1040 Fifth Avenue, she made a point of screening all of John's calls. If someone tried to reach him, the routine was always the same.

"Who's calling? What is this for?" And, in the nine out of ten instances when she did not approve, "He's not available."

In coming years, several very public contretemps between John and his lover of the moment would be captured on film. But, as frustrated as he often became with his mother's ongoing efforts to control his life, John never showed a hint of displeasure in public. "He was too well brought up for that," Baldrige said, "and he respected her far too much."

When it came to Jackie, John allowed his Vesuvian temper to erupt only behind closed doors. Thwarted by his mother at every turn in his efforts to become an actor, John exploded in a rage, punching a hole in the wall of his apartment on West 86th Street. (It was not the only damage done to the apartment. "It looked," a friend of John's told writer Michael Gross, "like a herd of yaks had lived there." John left the apartment in such a shambles—the carpets were burned, "like they'd had cookouts on it," said a neighbor; the floors were so damaged that "every surface had to be sanded, spackled, and patched"; mildew covered the shower stall; and there was the pesky matter of the fist-sized hole in the wall—that the landlord sued John for damages when he moved out in 1986. The case was settled out of court.)

Not long before John broke his ankle, Jackie held the hand of her half sister, Janet, as the thirty-nine-year-old mother of three died of lung cancer. Devastated, Jackie journeyed to the place she had come to regard as her spiritual wellspring: India. John joined her that fall, staying with his mother in the glittering palaces of Jaipur, Hyderabad, Delhi, and Jodhpur.

Back from India, John took part in a roller-skating party to celebrate the twentieth anniversary of the Bedford Stuyvesant Restoration Project set up by his uncle Bobby. (Cousin Rory Kennedy, who had been born after her father's assassination, was also on hand.) JFK Jr. strapped on a pair of skates and, grasping the hands of two neighborhood children, went for a spin.

Noticing that the press was there to cover John's every move, one boy looked up at him and said, "I didn't know you were so famous. What's your name?"

"John Kennedy."

"John Kennedy!" the child said. "He was one of our presidents."

"Yeah, I know," John replied. "He was my dad."

Choking back happy tears as she clung to John, Jackie watched her daughter marry Ed Schlossberg on July 19, 1986, at Cape Cod's Church of Our Lady of Victory. In insisting on the wedding date— it was the seventeenth anniversary of Chappaquiddick—the bride and groom showed little regard for the possible political fallout.

John was best man and his cousin Maria Shriver maid of honor. At the bridal dinner the night before the wedding, John stood up and gave a toast in which he talked about how close he, his sister, and their mother had been. "All our lives, it's just been the three of us. Now," he said, turning to Schlossberg, "there are four."

Later, author Doris Kearns Goodwin talked to Jackie about that touching moment. "I want that kind of closeness for my sons," Goodwin said.

"It's the best thing," Jackie said, looking Goodwin straight in the eye, "I've ever done."

Caroline had already enrolled at Columbia Law School when, in the fall of 1986, John delighted his mother by starting classes at New York University Law School. With both her children taking their first tentative steps toward respectable careers in the legal profession, Jackie felt she had fulfilled her unspoken promise to Jack. John was now launched. "Now," Jackie joked, "I can die a happy woman."

You, especially, have a place in history.

—*Jackie, in her final*
note to John

A person never really becomes a grown-up until he loses both his parents.

—*John, after*
the death of
his mother

He grew up with the notion that life has to be lived to the fullest. He didn't shrink or hang back from experience.

—*Frank Mankiewicz,*
Kennedy family friend

7

J FK's son, now fully mature and handsome in a way that transcended even Hollywood's exacting standards, stepped to the podium at the 1988 Democratic National Convention in Atlanta to introduce his uncle Ted. A collective sigh went up from the delegates, and *Time* magazine's Walter Isaacson worried that the roof of the Omni auditorium might collapse "from the sudden drop in air pressure caused by the simultaneous sharp intake of so many thousands of breaths."

"Over a quarter of a century ago," John intoned, "my father stood before you to accept the nomination of the presidency of the United States. So many of you came into public service because of him and in a very real sense it is because of you that he is with us today."

Watching John's polished performance on television, his mother was overjoyed. She had waged a war of attrition to force him to abandon his dream of becoming an actor, and now it looked as if he was about to enter the family business—politics. The remarkably poised twenty-seven-year-old, who had spent the previous summer clerking at the Justice Department in Washington for $353 a week, was now spending the summer at the Los Angeles law firm of Manatt, Phelps, Rothenberg, and Phillips at eleven hundred dollars a week. This fall he was entering his last year at New York University Law School. The timing could not have been better.

But, in what Jackie saw as a devastating setback, *People* magazine proclaimed John the "Sexiest Man Alive" on the cover of its September 12, 1988, issue (two years earlier, on the eve of Caroline's wedding, *People* had dubbed him "America's Most Eligible Bachelor;" *US* accorded him the same honor in 1987).

People's "Sexiest Man" story began: "Okay, ladies, this one's for you. But first some ground rules. GET YOUR EYES OFF THAT MAN'S CHEST! He's a serious fellow. Third-year law student. Active with charities. Scion of the most charismatic family in American politics and heir to its most famous name."

"Listen," John would later tell Barbara Walters, "people can say a lot worse things about you than you are attractive and you look good in a bathing suit." As flattering as the *People* story was, however, it effectively defused any immediate political aspirations John might have entertained. Overnight, he was transformed from Camelot's last best hope to the power elite's equivalent of Hollywood hunk.

Even those who had known him for years conceded that John's looks were exceptional. "I am a heterosexual male," said John's longtime friend John Perry Barlow, "and there are times when he was sitting across from me at the table and I would sort of be taken aback by how handsome he was. You'd sort of say to yourself, 'God, this guy looks *perfect.*'"

No matter. The Sexiest Man was subjected to merciless ribbing from his friends, which he endured graciously. "Gee, John," Richard Wiese would tease his buddy, "so you're the sexiest man on the planet? Is that *this* planet? Ever?"

"That's right," John shot back. "Jealous?" Eager to poke fun at himself, John went to one Halloween party as "The Golden Boy" clad only in a loincloth and gold glitter. He attended another bash as Michelangelo's David, wearing something akin to a fig leaf.

Now that his once-unruly locks were cropped short, his friends teased him about his perfect hair, too. "We used to call him 'Helmet Head,'" said his friend Hilary Shepard-Turner. Once Shepard-Turner had him paged at the airport: "Mr. Head. Mr. Helmet Head." John answered the page.

"He thought it was hysterical," Shepard-Turner said. From then on, he signed his letters to Shepard-Turner and other close friends "H. Head."

Jackie, however, found John's Sexiest Man Alive image not at all amusing. She saw the story as a crass commercial attempt to cash in on the Kennedy name, and fretted over the damage it had done to her son's nascent public-service career.

John had spent the rest of the summer of 1988 with Christina Haag in Venice, California, where she was appearing in a play at L.A.'s Tiffany Theater. But in the wake of the *People* cover, there was more speculation than ever about John's private life.

Comparisons with his father were inevitable. Ever since stories of JFK's affairs with Marilyn Monroe, Judith Campbell Exner, and others began to surface in the late 1970s, Jackie had managed to convince John that they were to be discounted as fiction.

An unwelcome reminder of JFK's affair with Marilyn manifested itself in the person of Madonna Louise Ciccone. "I'm tough, ambitious, and I know exactly what I want," she was fond of saying. "If that makes me a bitch, okay."

Already a global pop icon, Madonna was perhaps best known at the time for her "Material Girl" persona—a video homage to Marilyn's "Diamonds Are a Girl's Best Friend" number from the 1953 film *Gentlemen Prefer Blondes*. As a result, she was constantly being compared to the other blond bombshell.

John met the Material Girl after a 1985 concert at Madison Square Garden and dated her briefly—and secretly—before she married actor Sean Penn in August of that year. By 1988, following the breakup of her violent marriage to Penn, she made the conscious decision to pursue the Sexiest Man Alive. Beyond the obvious reasons—her voracious sexual appetites were legendary—Madonna described her motivation for wanting to become involved with John as "cosmic."

Madonna had read every Monroe biography ever written, and knew all the details of her steamy affair with JFK. As undisputed heir to Monroe's persona, she confided to friends that she felt fated to consummate her relationship with the President's only son.

For his part John, who was not above being starstruck, was daz-

zled by the notion of dating Madonna, the most glamorous, celebrated, and, by all accounts, exciting woman of her generation. "You
could see it in his eyes that first time they met," said dancer Erika
Belle, then one of Madonna's closest friends. "John was totally in
awe."

They decided to keep their relationship as private as possible.
Since they both worked out rigorously at the same health club, it
provided a convenient locale for their rendezvous. They jogged
together in Central Park, and later John took Madonna to meet his
mother.

At 1040 Fifth, Madonna was greeted somewhat frostily by Jackie.
She stepped off Jackie's private elevator into the entry hall and signed
the guest register "Mrs. Sean Penn."

Jackie was not amused, according to a friend of John's. Kennedy
told him that after meeting Madonna, his mother "hit the roof. She
warned him to stay away from Madonna. She felt Madonna would
exploit the Kennedy name for publicity, and basically that she was a
crass social climber, a tramp—and still married to Sean Penn."

Madonna was a Roman Catholic, but her habit of publicly thumb-
ing her nose at church rituals and symbols disturbed Jackie. "Jackie
thought Madonna's use of crucifixes and other Catholic images was
incredibly sacrilegious," another family acquaintance said. "Jackie
didn't want her son becoming involved with a woman who was
being widely condemned as a heretic."

Jackie's objection to Madonna may have had as much to do, sug-
gested John's friend, with the woman Madonna sought to emulate.
"Jackie was shocked when she picked up *Life* magazine and saw
Madonna looking exactly like Marilyn."

Had Madonna not ridden to fame on a shock wave, Jackie would
probably have found her less onerous. The exponent of blond
ambition was well read, articulate, and knowledgeable about fashion, dance, and art. She was also a brilliant businesswoman. According to *Forbes,* which put Madonna on its cover, at the time she was
pursuing John she was worth in the neighborhood of thirty-nine
million dollars.

John and Madonna managed to conceal their affair from the press in New York, going so far as to attend plays and parties separately, only to get together afterward. They let their guard down on Cape Cod, where, bundled in sweaters and jackets, they jogged along the beach near the Kennedy compound at Hyannis Port.

Sean Penn was not oblivious to what had transpired between his wife and JFK Jr. After a tribute to Robert De Niro at New York's American Museum of the Moving Image, John joined Penn, Liza Minnelli, Jeremy Irons, Matt Dillon, and other celebrities at a party in De Niro's honor at the TriBeCa Grill.

John spotted the ex–Mr. Madonna chatting with a friend. He went up to Penn, extended his hand and introduced himself.

"I know who you are," Penn replied stonily. "You owe me an apology." John said nothing, and walked away. Apparently, Penn was still seething over reports linking John to Madonna during their marriage. The next morning, John received a funeral wreath of white roses with a black-and-gold ribbon bearing the inscription MY DEEP-EST SYMPATHY. The card read simply, "Johnny, I heard about last night." It was signed "m."

The JFK Jr.–Sean Penn incident coincided with yet another *Vanity Fair* Madonna cover story. Again, she conjured up the ghost of Jack's legendary paramour. To illustrate a story titled "The Misfit," Madonna struck two nude poses as part of her "Homage to Norma Jean" pinup portfolio.

No sooner had he been upbraided by Sean Penn over his affair with Madonna than John moved on to another dazzling blond star, albeit one better known for her on-screen performances than her private peccadilloes. John and Daryl Hannah had actually met when they were both eighteen and vacationing with their families at La Samanna, on St. Martin. John, who brought along his then-girlfriend Christina Haag, could not help but be impressed with Hannah at the time. Stepdaughter of billionaire Chicago financier Jerry Wexler (whose brother was famed Hollywood cinematographer Haskell Wexler), Daryl carried a teddy bear with her wherever she went.

By the time they met again at Aunt Lee Radzwill's wedding to director Herb Ross in September 1988, Daryl had already rocketed to stardom in such films as *Splash, Wall Street, Roxanne,* and Ross's

Steel Magnolias. She was living with rocker Jackson Browne, and John had returned to Jackie's favorite potential daughter-in-law, Christina Haag (Jackie and Christina remained such good friends that she paid a condolence call on Haag when her father died in 1992).

But that October, JFK Jr. and Daryl were spotted dining in a West Village restaurant and then shooting pool until 3 A.M. at a TriBeCa bar called S.T.P. And while Haag beamed proudly alongside Jackie and Caroline at John's NYU Law School graduation in May 1989, a week later it was Daryl who went cruising with John on Virginia's Smith Mountain Lake aboard a forty-six-foot yacht.

Still, Daryl was not yet willing to sever her ties with Browne. "She kept playing both ends," said Daryl's former assistant, Natalie Crosse. "She knew John was seeing other girls, and until she was the only woman in his life, she wasn't about to give Jackson up."

The Kennedy–Hannah Affair unraveled for the first time in July 1989, when Hannah finally made her choice and returned to Browne only one week before John took the brutal twelve-hour-long New York State bar exam for the first time. John failed—along with 2,187 others—in part, Caroline theorized, because Daryl's abrupt departure had left her brother "heartbroken." John offered no excuses. "Now I have to suck it up," he said, "and give it all I have next time—so I won't have to do this again."

The setback did not keep John from joining Manhattan District Attorney Robert Morgenthau's office as one of sixty-four rookie assistant prosecutors. Ostensibly, John would be paid an annual salary of thirty thousand dollars to interview defendants, do legal research, and, once he had passed the bar, prosecute low-level cases in court.

Before he could start, however, he had to clear up some minor legal problems of his own. Just five days after being sworn in as an assistant district attorney, John dispatched his lawyer to a Queens court to settle several outstanding traffic violations ranging from speeding to driving an unregistered vehicle. He also had to clear up twenty-three hundred dollars in parking tickets that he had ignored for years.

John would don a meticulously tailored Versace suit, climb onto his bike outside his Upper West Side apartment, and then wend his way through clogged Manhattan streets to the DA's office on Hogan Place. The first day he arrived, more than one hundred reporters were there to greet him. Inside, things weren't much better. In the elevator, uniformed officers would ask for his autograph. A paralegal was offered ten thousand dollars by a tabloid just to snap his picture at his desk. Unlike others in his office, he did require a secretary of his own. Recalled Jill Konviser, whose office adjoined John's, "There were love letters, invitations to parties, lots of pictures of naked girls. The other idiots in my office would fight over them."

As a rookie, John was assigned to the complaint room, where prosecutors meet with defendants twice a week. "It's three o'clock in the morning and you haven't eaten and you are exhausted," recalled Konviser. "You're wrecked... Here it was disgusting, it was filthy... And it stinks, and people scream at you. We *all* complained; he never did."

"In ways that are most meaningful, he was just one of us," said another officemate, Owen Carragher. "Except with better girl-friends."

John took the bar exam a second time in February of 1990, and failed again—this time prompting a media frenzy. THE HUNK FLUNKS, blared the *New York Post*'s now-famous front-page headline when the results were released on April 30. "Obviously, I'm very disappointed," he told the pack of reporters who waited for him outside the district attorney's office. "But you know, God willing, I'll go back there in July and I'll pass it then. Or I'll pass it the next time, or I'll pass it when I'm ninety-five. I'm clearly not a major legal genius." He pointed out that he had fallen eleven points short of a passing grade of 660, but added, "Close is only good for horse-shoes—not for the bar exam."

He was not alone. "It's not uncommon for someone to fail the bar exam once or twice," said Michael Cherkasky, his boss in the district attorney's office. "John went to NYU—a national law school that doesn't concentrate on preparing for the bar exam of a specific state the way other law schools do. He was very smart, very committed, and a good lawyer."

John Perry Barlow was among those who believed that the HUNK

FLUNKS characterization of John was "a myth. John was very, very intelligent. A little scattered, but *really smart*. I don't think people knew that. The people who came in contact with him tended to be surprised by his dignity and his quiet goodness."

There was the occasional word of encouragement: "I failed the bar exam, too," former New York City Mayor Ed Koch wrote John. "It didn't stop me, and it won't stop you." But John was, said a friend, "shocked and distressed" not only by the fact that he had failed, but by the beating he was taking in the press.

So, too, was Jackie, who publicly shrugged off the news but privately flew into a fury. "Compared to his sister, John was a more open personality," said a friend. "In that regard, John was more a person after Jackie's own heart, more a loose cannon, unpredictable."

By contrast, Caroline had passed the bar exam her first time out and had begun writing a book with her classmate Ellen Alderman— all in addition to being a full-time mom. Caroline gave birth to her second child, Tatiana Celia Kennedy Schlossberg, on May 5, 1990. (Caroline's first child, Rose, named after the Kennedy matriarch, was born on June 25, 1988.)

Less than a year after Tatiana's birth, William Morrow and Company marked the bicentennial of the Bill of Rights by publishing the Alderman–Kennedy co-authored *In Our Defense: The Bill of Rights in Action*. The book was critically well received, and, largely on the strength of the Kennedy name (Caroline did not add the "Schlossberg"), became a *New York Times* bestseller.

If John failed the bar a third time, it would not only brand JFK's son as an intellectual lightweight, but force him to give up his job in the DA's office. At his mother's insistence, John hired a tutor for $1,075 this time to help him pass.

It was evident to one fellow test taker that the same wellspring of nervous energy that led John to pump iron daily at one of three private gyms he belonged to made it difficult for him to concentrate on his studies. "What really struck me was his restlessness," said a corporate lawyer who took a bar-review course with John. "He couldn't sit still for more than ten minutes at a time. The classroom had a door that opened up onto a little deck, and every day he'd get up and open the door three or four times for really no reason."

To be sure, there were more than the usual number of distractions that summer. First, there was the thousand-dollar-a-plate Kennedy Foundation dinner at the JFK Library on June 1, followed by the wedding of his cousin Kerry Kennedy to New York Governor Mario Cuomo's son Andrew at St. Matthew's Cathedral in Washington. It was at the Kennedy–Cuomo nuptials that he was again reminded of just how thoughtless some of his male cousins could be.

A marble marker on the center aisle near the cathedral's main altar denotes the spot where JFK's coffin had been placed during his funeral mass. To spare the feelings of JFK's children, the bride had thoughtfully placed a round Oriental rug over the marker.

The other Kennedy cousins were not all so considerate. "Hey, John," one yelled out. "Come over here, we want to show you something."

John walked up and stood where his cousin asked him to. Then the cousin yanked off the rug, revealing the marker commemorating his father's funeral.

"Look at that, John," the cousin laughed. "How about that?"

John reeled back in shock while other cousins tittered that the exam-flunking John "doesn't even know where his father's funeral was."

"Put it back," ordered another wedding usher, James Hairston. "Put the rug back!"

But the damage had been done. "John was aghast," an eyewitness said. "It was stunning and stupid."

Hurt feelings aside, John joined his cousins in celebrating Grandmother Rose Kennedy's one hundredth birthday on July 22, 1990. Just two days later, John took the bar exam—and passed. "I'm very relieved," he said when he was told the results months later. "It tastes very sweet at the moment."

The day after he got the news that he had finally passed the bar exam, family friend Ted Van Dyk called him at the district attorney's office. "How do you like it there?" Van Dyk asked.

"Oh, it stinks," John answered frankly. "I'm just going to do this for a while to meet my family's expectations, and then I'm going to do something else."

But something about the job appealed to John, and he would

wind up spending four years of his life there. "When you're in the prosecutor's office, you are definitely wearing the white hat, and he clearly liked that," Michael Cherkasky said. "You're putting away the bad guys—people who have swindled elderly widows out of the their life savings, or sell drugs to schoolchildren. John wanted more than anything else to help people, and in the end his time in the DA's office was a terrific experience for him."

John would go on to win all six of the cases he actually prosecuted in court. "He was a natural competitor," Cherkasky said, "and trying a case in court is definitely a one-on-one sport." In the process, Kennedy even earned the respect of some of the people he sent to jail. "Even though his job was to put me away, I liked the guy," said Venard Garvin, who was sentenced to two to six years in prison for drug possession. "At the recess, I spoke to him. I remember I said, 'It's the job—it's not you.' Even though he was a DA, he didn't have the killing instinct."

That summer of 1990, Daryl Hannah, growing ever more unsure about her relationship with the mercurial Jackson Browne, trysted with John at a Boston hotel. Over the next two years, they would have several such furtive rendezvous while publicly denying there was ever anything between them.

Meantime, Christina Haag was among those toasting John at a lavish thirtieth birthday party Jackie threw for him at Manhattan's Tower Gallery. If it had not been obvious before, it seemed painfully so now. After five years, they were officially *finis* romantically but would remain, as he would with all his former lovers, close friends.

By this time John had moved into a TriBeCa loft and Daryl Hannah purchased a spacious Upper West Side apartment. But Santa Monica, where she shared a house with Jackson Browne, remained home base for the dazzlingly beautiful actress.

While Hannah vacillated between the rock star and the president's son, young Kennedy played the field with a vengeance. He showed a taste for long-limbed models, and in early 1992 began dating Wilhelmina model Julie Baker. A doe-eyed, whispery-voiced brunette, "Jules" bore an uncanny resemblance to Jackie. Although he and Baker would remain close for the rest of his life, that did not keep

John from dating Clic model Audra Aviznienis and six-foot-tall *Sports Illustrated* swimsuit cover model Ashley Richardson. "Is he sexy? Oh, yes," allowed Aviznienis. "He has this quiet sadness. There's something pensive and sad about him . . ."

He also connected with theatrical director Toni Kotite and with actress Sarah Jessica Parker. "The body's beautiful," Parker acknowledged, but added that she could not handle being upstaged by him. "What you have is wrong," she joked with him. "It's not right. It's unfair, as a woman, to have to stand next to you."

One woman who had no qualms about standing next to John was the Brazilian blond bombshell known as Xuxa (pronounced "*Shoo-sha*"), one of South America's biggest television stars and reputedly worth more than two hundred million dollars. She pursued John, and when he took her out to lunch and for a stroll through his TriBeCa neighborhood, a television camera just happened to record the whole thing.

Through it all, John still carried a torch for Daryl. While filming *At Play in the Fields of the Lord* in the Brazilian rain forest, she was hospitalized with a mysterious jungle fever. She was delirious for days, and when she came to, her room was filled with one thousand long-stemmed American Beauty roses—with love from a concerned John.

John was also concerned about the welfare of William Kennedy Smith, who among the Kennedy cousins was closest to John. Family loyalty was tested once again when Willie, Jean Kennedy Smith's son and a fourth-year medical student at Georgetown University, was charged with raping Patricia Bowman, twenty-nine, on the lawn of the Kennedy estate in Palm Beach. The incident, which occurred in the early morning hours of March 30, 1991, followed a night of drunken revelry with Uncle Ted and Ted's son Patrick at Palm Beach's trendy Au Bar.

Out of loyalty to Jean, who had always been the closest to her of all the Kennedy sisters, Jackie did bring her children to play touch football with all the Kennedy cousins, including Willie, at the clan's annual Labor Day picnic on the Cape. The photo opportunity conveyed the message that all the Kennedys were standing firm.

That December, the rest of the family—Eunice and Sargent Shriver, Ethel, Pat, and their respective broods—put up a unified front, appearing at Willie's trial and declaring their unshakable belief in his innocence to any reporter who would listen.

While Caroline followed her mother's lead and resisted family pressure to attend, John yielded to incessant pleas from his cousins and spent five days in the courtroom. He was also spotted having lunch with Willie's high-powered defense team. Asked by reporters why he had risked besmirching his own reputation by standing by Smith, John replied, "He's helped me out in the past and I was glad to come and be of assistance. Willie is my cousin. We grew up together. I thought I could at least be with him at this difficult time." Ultimately, Smith was acquitted.

At around the same time, Oliver Stone's controversial new film *JFK* was released. Refusing to see the film or to publicly comment on its speculations concerning the assassination of his father, John was upset by the media frenzy that accompanied it. Understandably, the subject of his father's violent death—now Topic A across the country—was still a painful one for his son. "Maybe," he told a *Time* writer, "I'll just have to leave town."

In early 1992, Daryl flew into New York to promote her new film, *Memoirs of an Invisible Man*. On February 13, she and John were standing on the street outside his loft. Their ensuing quarrel, which was captured on film, presaged a similar battle that would erupt four years later between John and his bride-to-be, Carolyn Bessette.

This time, John was shouting the same question over and over again. "So why did you come back, Daryl?" he asked. "Why did you come back?"

Hannah hemmed and hawed and pleaded for understanding, but finally told him point-blank, "John, I want to make it work with Jackson. I can't see you anymore."

The next day, Valentine's Day, the television tabloid show *A Current Affair* ran its report on John's date with Xuxa. Although she claimed not to have been aware that a video crew was covering their every move, John, convinced it had all been a publicity ploy, was furious.

For all his liaisons—both real and imagined—with beautiful young women, John also sought comfort and advice from women his mother's age or older. While his mother was a glamorous, larger-than-life figure ("Queen Jackie" was what her half brother, Jamie Auchincloss, called her), John had actually been raised by the more nurturing likes of Maud Shaw and Marta Sgubin.

Over the years, John went out of his way to form friendships with waitresses, maids, secretaries, and mothers of friends in the sixties and seventies. At the DA's office, he became fast friends with cleaning lady Carolyn Neal. "When he came into work in the morning," she recalled, "he'd Rollerblade down the hallway to his office. I'd tell him not to because it left track marks." Soon he was bringing her Valentine's candy and sharing his thoughts with her.

In October 1991 John, a blues aficionado, made a secret pilgrim-age to the Helena, Arkansas, Bluesfest and stayed at a bona fide "blues hotel"—the Riverside in Clarksdale, Mississippi. It was at the River-side that Bessie Smith died in 1937. There he befriended Mrs. Z. L. Hill, the Riverside's eighty-three-year-old owner. "John did not want anybody to know he was here," said Hill's son, Frank "Rat" Ratcliff. "*Nobody.* I hate to admit it, but I talked to him every day for four days before I finally realized who he was. John was such a regu-lar guy—no putting on airs or anything like that, he'd sit in the lobby and talk with folks for hours. He knew a lot about the blues, but he wanted to learn more. To us, he was just John."

But Rat's mother knew who he was from the very beginning. "John was staying in one of the hotel's cabins, and every night he'd come to my mother's room and knock on her door. Then he'd sit on the edge of her bed and they'd talk until dawn. They talked about the blues, about life."

John called the African-American woman "Mother." The feeling was mutual. John quickly got in the habit of bringing a breakfast tray to Mrs. Hill. One morning when Rat asked if he could bring her something to eat, his mother replied, " 'Don't worry about it, my son is bringing something for me.' That's how she thought of John, as her boy.

"Funny thing is, John had brought a young lady with him. I never saw her. He would leave this girl behind in his room while he stayed up all night talking to Mother Hill."

That summer, after dutifully teaming up with Caroline to promote the John F. Kennedy Profile in Courage Awards on ABC's *Prime Time Live,* John once again escaped into the wilderness—this time kayaking with three friends to the Aland Archipelago between Sweden and Finland. At one point, a friend capsized and John rescued him, à la JFK's PT-109 experience in the South Pacific. The man's legs were so numb he couldn't walk; John carried him to shore and wrapped him in a sleeping bag.

John was paid six hundred dollars to write about the trip for the Travel section of the *New York Times.* In his piece, titled "Four Desk Jockeys in Search of Manageable Danger," John waxed poetic about "the extravagance of a sky where sunrise, sunset, and moonrise occur almost simultaneously."

There was sharp disagreement about John's ability to handle danger—manageable or otherwise—even among his closest friends. Expert kayaker Ralph Diaz, who knew John, said his friend "showed an overly casual approach" to the sport. Watching John take a kayak out onto the Hudson River one Saturday without a life jacket or any other safety equipment, Diaz thought to himself, "this guy is going to get hurt one day."

In September 1992, Daryl Hannah decided to leave Jackson Browne for John and told Browne so. A fight ensued and she ended up in the hospital. John rushed to Daryl's side, brought her to New York, and nursed her back to health.

It hardly mattered to the producers of television's *Seinfeld* that John was, for the time being at least, apparently out of circulation. The October 26 episode, entitled "The Contest," had Elaine (Julia Louis-Dreyfus) shamelessly pursing an unseen John—only to have him wind up deflowering a virgin played by *Frasier's* Jane Leeves. A *Seinfeld* fan, John missed the show when it aired, but watched it the next day on tape after friends deluged him with calls.

Two months later, John was still providing a shoulder for Daryl to cry on—this time over the death on November 7th of her stepfather, Jerry Wexler. Two weeks later, he flew with her to Chicago for a celebrity-packed memorial tribute to Wexler at the Drake Hotel. Wearing knee socks and glasses, her hair a mousy brown, Daryl looked, said her friend Sugar Rautbord, "about fourteen years old." Throughout the ceremony, which featured a gospel group singing a raucous version of the Mary Wells hit "My Guy" in praise of the flamboyant Wexler, John behaved, said one observer, as if he were "Mr. Daryl Hannah—one of the family—and believe me, they were happy to have him."

As far as John's mother would know, Daryl was the last serious woman in his life. He moved into Hannah's West Side apartment and, until August 1994, they appeared to be a couple. There were countless newspaper and magazine articles chronicling the Kennedy–Hannah romance.

They were photographed necking on a stoop, in the park, against a parked car, on an Amtrak train bound for Providence and his ten-year Brown reunion; in-line skating down Fifth Avenue; on the L.A. set of her HBO movie, *Attack of the Fifty-Foot Woman,* and vacationing everywhere from Switzerland and Hong Kong to Vietnam and the Philippines.

IT'S LOVE, trumpeted the cover of *People* magazine, which went on to proclaim them "two of a kind—JFK Jr. and Daryl Hannah have fame, fortune, fabulous bone structure—and each other." Typical was the story of the New Yorker who looked out her window to see a shirtless six-foot-one-inch John and a lingerie-clad five-foot-ten-inch Daryl dancing dreamily on a rooftop.

Just as John made a concerted effort to fit in with Daryl's family in Chicago, Daryl insinuated herself into John's life in New York. Even before the birth of Caroline's third child, John Bouvier Kennedy Schlossberg, on January 19, 1993, John was a doting uncle. Now Daryl joined in when he tagged along with Caroline and the kids on weekend outings in Central Park, or when "Grand Jackie" took her grandchildren to Serendipity on Third Avenue for ice cream sundaes.

For Daryl, the road to acceptance by John's family was a little more uncertain. On Memorial Day 1993, while his mother was vacationing with Maurice in Provence, John and Daryl threw a party for their friends at Red Gate Farm, Jackie's estate on Martha's Vineyard. They left the place a shambles. It was not the first time. When his mother wasn't there, John would invite as many as sixteen people at a time, drinking beer and, apparently, smoking pot.

John's former governess Marta Sgubin, who remained with the family as Jackie's cook and majordomo, had scolded John once before. "You should have more respect for your mother's house!" she insisted. A convincingly contrite John promised that it would never happen again—but it did.

When Marion Ronan, who worked as a maid at Red Gate Farm, walked inside she was taken aback—to put it mildly. "I couldn't believe my eyes," she told reporter David Duffy. "The house was strewn all over with wet towels and empty champagne, beer, and wine bottles. The carpets were stained, there were half-eaten plates of food discarded in every room, and food had even been splashed onto the walls." Ronan claimed she also found half-smoked joints in the bedrooms and bathrooms. Enraged, Jackie exiled John permanently to "the Barn," the guest house he shared with Daryl.

After four years in the district attorney's office, John left his $41,500-a-year job in July of 1993. By way of saying goodbye, he gave a party for six of his co-workers at New York's Old Homestead steak house, ordering up hundred-dollar Kobe beefsteaks for each of his friends. Free-spirited Daryl later joined the awestruck prosecutors for brandy and cigars.

"Daryl really liked him," said her friend Sugar Rautbord. "She was *desperate* to marry him." Her purchase of an antique wedding dress at the Rose Bowl Flea Market in Pasadena fueled speculation that nuptials were imminent. The couple did, in fact, take out a California marriage license in late July of 1993 but did not go ahead with plans to get married in Santa Monica. Months later, friends were given only two days' notice for a top-secret wedding ceremony on Martha's Vineyard, and within hours were told that the nuptials were off.

Not the least of Daryl's problems was John's family. Jackie was genuinely fond of Daryl, and certainly appreciated the fact that Hannah's family had money—considerably more than the hundred million–plus in net assets Jackie had managed to accumulate with guidance from Maurice Tempelsman. Daryl told friends Jackie was "very warm and supportive" after her alleged battering at the hands of Jackson Browne. But Jackie also made it clear to John that a movie star—particularly a sexy blond movie star—was not an appropriate choice for the only son of John Fitzgerald Kennedy. According to Ed Klein, "She felt Daryl was not the most stable person for John."

"There was a lot of tension between John and Jackie," a friend observed. "There was something in him where he just resisted any authority. He liked to play with fire. He was a pretty explosive guy. He went out and slammed doors."

If John expected a warmer reception from Caroline, whom he now affectionately called "Old Married Lady," he was mistaken. While she was usually not inclined to interfere, Caroline showed no reluctance when John asked her point-blank what she thought of marriage to the famously flaky star. "Kiddo," she said, using her current nickname for her little brother, "she's nice—but she's not the one."

Jackie and Caroline reinforced this message when, after learning Daryl would be accompanying John to Ted Kennedy Jr.'s wedding on Block Island in October 1993, they abruptly canceled their plans to attend. Without Jackie or Caroline there to distract at least some of the paparazzi, a dour-faced John grabbed Daryl by the hand and literally dragged her into the church.

Daryl's stock suffered another blow when newspaper and magazine ads began running for *Attack of the Fifty-Foot Woman,* showing the star as a skimpily clad Amazon. Jackie cringed. By the fall of 1993, Jackie made little effort to conceal the fact that she was avoiding John's girlfriend. When they visited 1040 Fifth, Jackie ate dinner alone on a tray in her room while John and Daryl were eating in the dining room.

On November 22, 1993, the thirtieth anniversary of JFK's assassination, John and Caroline kept a low profile. Jackie, meanwhile, was spending the day jumping horses at the Piedmont Hunt Club in Virginia when the horse ahead of her knocked some stones off a fence.

Jackie's gelding, Clown, cleared the fence but stumbled on the stones, throwing his rider to the muddy ground.

Jackie was unconscious for an alarming thirty minutes and was rushed to a nearby hospital. There, doctors discovered a swelling in her abdomen—possibly a slight injury that had become infected. Antibiotics were administered and the swelling subsided.

During the Christmas holidays, Jackie and Maurice were sailing in the Caribbean aboard the *Relemar* when she became ill. She was rushed back to New York Hospital–Cornell Medical Center. A biopsy of lymph nodes in her neck revealed she was suffering from a particularly aggressive form of non-Hodgkin's lymphoma. If there was any hope for survival, she would have to begin chemotherapy immediately.

Jackie summoned John and Caroline to 1040 Fifth and in her living room, with Maurice holding her hand, told them the grim news. Stunned, John and Caroline embraced their mother. All three broke down crying.

Within moments, Jackie regained her composure; she was determined to remain resolutely upbeat. John's mother joked with Arthur Schlesinger Jr. about her disease being "a kind of hubris." She had always been, Jackie said with mock indignation, "proud at being so fit. I swim, and I jog . . . and walk around the reservoir—and now this suddenly happens . . . Why in the world did I do all those push-ups?"

Along with Maurice, John and Caroline conspired to keep Jackie's life-and-death struggle a secret. But it soon became obvious that would not be possible. The side effects of chemotherapy—bloating, nausea, blotchy skin, and hair loss—could not be hidden for long under floppy coats, wigs, and scarves. On February 11, 1994, Nancy Tuckerman confirmed to the *New York Times* that Jackie was being treated for non-Hodgkin's lymphoma and added that "there is an excellent prognosis."

Anxiety over his mother's worsening condition took its toll on John's already shaky relationship with Daryl. So, too, did the appearance of a rival for his affections. John first encountered Carolyn Bessette while jogging in Central Park in the fall of 1993. A personal shopper to the stars at Calvin Klein, Bessette, then twenty-seven, out-fitted the likes of Diane Sawyer and Annette Bening. When John arranged for someone to help him buy a suit at Calvin Klein, he walked away with three, as well as several shirts and ties—and Bessette's phone number.

Svelte (five feet eleven inches tall and 135 pounds), blond, and ethereally beautiful, Bessette bore an uncanny resemblance to Daryl. Yet there were important differences. Hannah, who in her off-hours favored the unkempt grunge look popular at the time, also shared John's decidedly casual approach to her surroundings. The apartment they shared was strewn with clothes and, said a friend, "did not look much better than a dorm room." Daryl was also charmingly flaky in the manner of Annie Hall, fragile, even needy.

In contrast, Bessette impressed John as intelligent, poised, chic, and very much in control. "I think," said Jamie Auchincloss, "she may have reminded him more of his mother."

That November, John and Carolyn were spotted holding hands and cuddling on a bench in Central Park. Days later, they sat on the curb with thousands of other spectators and watched as participants in the New York Marathon raced by. Photos of John and his stunning new friend were soon splashed across the pages of newspapers around the world, and a distraught Daryl began demanding answers.

Shortly before noon on January 13, 1994, the couple was walking down a street just a few blocks from Jackie's apartment when suddenly John, oblivious to passersby, flew into a rage.

"Make up your mind!" he shouted at Daryl, who was crying. "Where do you want to go?" John was clutching a wrapped package for his mother and Daryl carried a bag from the Madison Avenue gourmet store E.A.T.

Daryl pleaded softly, but John interrupted her, waving his arms and shouting, "So what do you want me to do?" With his thumb, he gestured for her to leave, and then stormed off toward his mother's apartment.

But she did not leave. "She kept dabbing at her eyes as she followed him inside the apartment house, walking about three steps behind," a witness said. They emerged shortly afterward, walked to a nearby restaurant for lunch, and when they left forty minutes later "John seemed even more upset than before. As Daryl tried to talk to him, John kept moving away from her."

Finally, John hailed a cab, hopped in, and left Daryl standing on the sidewalk—shocked, alone, and shivering. A cameraman had been filming the whole episode. It would not be the last time John vented his anger at his lover in public, nor would it be the last time such an incident was captured on film.

Whether they were arguing about their future together or Carolyn Bessette or merely where to go for lunch, the incident spoke volumes about John's penchant for letting off steam publicly.

As for John's growing interest in Carolyn, John Perry Barlow recalled the night at Tramps, the Manhattan disco, when John confided in him about this woman who was having "a major effect on him. Out of loyalty to Daryl, he was not pursuing it romantically. But he was really struggling. He just couldn't get his mind off this girl."

"Well, who is she?" Barlow asked John.

"Well, she's not really anybody. She's some functionary of Calvin Klein's. She's an ordinary person." According to Barlow, John's relationship with Carolyn stayed platonic while he remained with Daryl. "For a man in John's position, he was just terribly decent in the way he treated women. He always tried to do the honorable thing. That's one of the reasons you will never hear anything bad about him from his former girlfriends. To one extent or another, they never stop loving him."

That March, as snowstorms bore down on the Northeast, Caroline brought Rose, Tatiana, and Jack to Grand Jackie's apartment every afternoon. The frigid temperatures notwithstanding, Jackie insisted on her daily walks through Central Park.

Most of the time she was accompanied by Maurice. Occasionally John, who had taken a suite at the nearby Surrey Hotel to be closer to Jackie, would don his parka, pull a knit cap over his head, and stroll over to 1040 Fifth. Taking his mother's arm, John would escort her up Fifth Avenue and then across the street and into the park. Clouds of vapor billowing from their lips, they talked hopefully about the future.

As much as she worried about her son's future—especially his private life, given the public squabbles with Daryl—Jackie was proud of all he had already accomplished and told him so. Jackie, whose own passion for preserving New York landmarks led her to spearhead a campaign that saved Grand Central Station, was particularly impressed with the way John worked quietly behind the scenes to make a difference in the lives of ordinary people.

Seven years earlier, Aunt Eunice Shriver had challenged the Kennedy cousins to invent projects aimed at aiding people with mental disabilities in the way the Kennedy-founded Special Olympics had already done for decades. The kids would vote on the best ideas, and a family foundation would award fifty thousand dollars to the most innovative proposals.

John attacked the problem head on, and after months of research had come up with a winning concept. To begin with, he identified a previously ignored problem—the dismal pay and inadequate education of front-line mental-health-care workers like the ones who cared for his own aunt Rosemary, left severely retarded by a lobotomy.

John set out to change that, starting a program called Reaching Up to persuade local officials to fund training programs for health-care workers. He also lent the prestige of the family name to the Kennedy Fellows, a group of seventy-five health-care workers selected each year to receive one-thousand-dollar scholarships.

In 1991, John had joined the board of the Robin Hood Foundation, a group of movers and shakers who raised money for projects in New York's most blighted neighborhoods. Both Reaching Up and the Robin Hood Foundation differed radically from other charities in that they closely studied where the money was going, how it was being spent, and whether it was delivering results. "It's easy to throw money at a problem and walk away," John said. "Your conscience is clear—but is your money getting to the people it's supposed to get to, or is it being wasted? Results—that's what really matters."

John made good his promise to keep close tabs on both programs. He frequently visited Kennedy fellows to ask what courses they were taking, if they were learning what they had to learn to better their lives as health-care workers, what their career plans were. As a Robin Hood Foundation board member, he took the subway to Harlem and the South Bronx to check up on how the money of corporate donors and wealthy individuals was being spent there.

What made John's brand of philanthropy even more special was the fact that so much of it was done without fanfare. "He didn't need to be congratulated all the time," said a Reaching Up staffer. "He thought that was kind of cheesy."

He went very public in March 1994, however, as host of *Heart of the City,* a six-part public television series profiling local volunteers in New York. Predictably, John's participation in the PBS project triggered a flood of television offers. But John had a different and wholly unexpected career path in mind. Weeks before the first *Heart of the City* aired, he confirmed that he was putting together a plan for a provocative, irreverent monthly magazine that would apply the rules of personality journalism to politics.

Jackie and Caroline were, like the rest of the Kennedys, aghast. From a purely business standpoint, launching a magazine in an already crowded field would be risky at best. Ninety percent of all magazine start-ups, Maurice Tempelsman pointed out, fail in the first year. With Jackie's blessing, Maurice urged John not to proceed.

Then there was the profession itself. Although she was still trying to make it into the office at Doubleday in spite of her illness, Jackie drew a distinction between book editing and publishing a magazine—especially a magazine that intended to pry into the private lives of politicians and at times make light of weighty political issues. "Are you sure," Jackie asked her son, "you want to become one of *them?*" John later told Toronto businessman Keith Stein, "My family kept asking why I wanted to join the 'Other Side.' "

In a sense, John was only following in both his parents' footsteps. Had Jack's older brother, Joe Jr., not been killed in World War II—leaving Jack next in line to carry the Kennedy banner to the White House—Pulitzer Prize–winner JFK would, according to those closest to him, probably have pursued a career in journalism. And Jackie, of course, had been a working photojournalist for the *Washington Times-Herald.*

Undeterred, John told his mother during one of their strolls that he and his partner, Michael Berman, an old Brown buddy, had even come up with a name. "We're thinking of calling it *George.*"

"*George?*" Jackie replied quizzically.

"Yeah, *George*—you know, as in the Father of Our Country? *George.*"

They walked a few more steps in silence. "John," Jackie said calmly, "I think it would be a good idea if you talk to Maurice again. And this time, listen to what he has to say."

Jackie spent her last Easter in New Jersey, making fanciful bonnets for her grandchildren to wear in the local Easter Parade. But on April 14, she collapsed at her apartment and was rushed by ambulance to New York Hospital. There she was operated on for a perforated ulcer, a not-uncommon side effect of chemotherapy.

Once out of the hospital and while she could still think clearly, Jackie sat down and wrote notes to her children, who now filled her with pride. To Caroline, she wrote, "The children have been a wonderful gift to me and I'm thankful to have once again seen our world through their eyes. They restore my faith in the family's future. You and Ed have been so wonderful to share them with me so unselfishly."

Jackie's note to John was decidedly different in tone. In it, she made it clear that JFK Jr. was to be Camelot's standard bearer. "I understand the pressures you'll forever have to endure as a Kennedy, even though we brought you into this world as an innocent," she wrote. "You, especially, have a place in history.

"No matter what course in life you choose, all I can do is ask that you and Caroline continue to make me, the Kennedy family, and yourself proud.

"Stay loyal to those who love you. Especially Maurice. He's a decent man with an abundance of common sense. You will do well to seek his advice."

John continued to drop in on his mother daily, and occasionally substituted for Maurice as Jackie's escort on her walks through the park. The two strolled arm in arm across Fifth Avenue, each sporting a knit cap. For John, the cap was symbolic. "John loved hats," Marta

Sgubin recalled, "so it became a family tradition to give him a new one every year on his birthday. He became very sentimental about them." (It was also a family tradition for Marta to prepare John's favorite dessert, floating island, to be served along with her home-made chocolate birthday cake.)

As Jackie's condition deteriorated, the walks through Central Park became more and more difficult for her. By May, the pain was unbearable. According to John's friend Steven Styles, "she telephoned John and, sobbing, told him, 'I don't think I can take it anymore.' "

Jackie was determined that her death, as her life, would be carried out on her own terms. On Wednesday, May 18—just six days after she last ventured outside with Maurice—family members and a few close friends were summoned to Jackie's bedside at 1040 Fifth. That night and throughout the next day, John, Caroline, and Maurice seldom left Jackie's bedside. Daryl was on hand to lend John moral support, but tried to keep in the background.

Jackie had asked that several books by her favorite authors be placed at her bedside, including the works of Colette, Jean Rhys, and Isak Dinesen. As their mother, her head wrapped in a print scarf, slipped in and out of consciousness, John and Caroline shared treasured memories with one another and read aloud passages from her most cherished books of poetry.

Shortly after noon on Thursday, May 19, Monsignor Georges Bardes of St. Thomas More Church administered the last rites of the Roman Catholic Church. That evening, several family members stood in the living room, murmuring to one another and occasionally wiping away a tear. In her bedroom, bathed in the glow of three antique lamps, Jackie lay with her lips gently parted in a morphine-induced sleep. John and Maurice took turns keeping vigil in a chair beside her bed.

Maurice, emotionally and physically drained, left for just a moment to speak with John. When they returned, Jackie had slipped into a final coma. An hour later, at 10:15 P.M. on May 19, 1994, Jackie's heart stopped. John was at his mother's bedside, along with Caroline and Maurice.

The next morning, John stepped before the small army of cameramen and reporters encamped outside the building where he had been raised. "Last night, at around ten-fifteen, my mother passed on," he said. "She was surrounded by her friends and family and her books and the people and things that she loved. And she did it in her own way, and we all feel lucky for that, and now she's in God's hands.

"There's been an enormous outpouring of good wishes from everyone in both New York and beyond," he continued. "And I speak for all our family when we say we're extremely grateful. And I hope now that you know, we can just have these next couple of days in relative peace."

That was not about to happen, of course. A few hours later, onlookers jostled to catch a glimpse of John, Caroline, and Maurice as they climbed into a limousine that would take them the short distance to the Frank E. Campbell Funeral Chapel. There they picked out Jackie's mahogany coffin and discussed funeral arrangements.

Once back at 1040 Fifth, Jackie's children argued with Uncle Ted about the size of the funeral. Ted argued passionately for a large public funeral, but Caroline insisted—as she would when another tragedy befell the family just five years later—that it be a private affair. John remained neutral, but in the end his strong-minded sister prevailed. With one concession: Speakers would be set up outside Manhattan's St. Ignatius Loyola Church—the church where Jackie had been baptized and confirmed—so that people gathered on the street could hear the service.

John, who had shown such grace and self-composure in announcing his mother's death to the world, was now given the job of compiling the guest list and making the arrangements. "It's fine," he told Daryl. "I want to keep busy."

That Sunday John and Daryl, both clad in T-shirts and shorts, Rollerbladed up Park Avenue on their way to Jackie's hastily arranged wake at 1040 Fifth, nearly knocking over several photographers in the process. Jackie's death had come as such a shock—it was only four months earlier that her illness had been made public—that many Americans were troubled by the sight of her son Rollerblading about town with his movie star girlfriend.

But for John, such strenuous physical activity served several purposes: It distracted him from his deep feelings of grief. It helped burn up his vast stores of nervous energy, which made it impossible for him to sit still for more than ten minutes. And, perhaps most significantly, it reaffirmed what had been the guiding principle of his life: No matter what happens, life goes on. "The Kennedys had these raucous Irish wakes when John was growing up," a longtime friend said. "That's how they coped—by celebrating the life of the person who had died. John felt he was honoring his mother by doing what he loved because he knew that's what *she* would have wanted. It was an act of celebration. Besides, all the Kennedys run out and do something physical at times like these. It's a family trait."

More than one hundred people came to the apartment that Sunday for Jackie's wake. Hundreds of others—well-wishers and the just plain curious—gathered on the sidewalk outside. When John appeared on the fourteenth-floor balcony with Daryl to wave to the crowd below, the throng burst into a spontaneous rendition of "The Battle Hymn of the Republic."

The next morning Hillary Clinton and Lady Bird Johnson were among the hundreds of writers, politicians, business leaders, social lions, and entertainment figures who gathered inside St. Ignatius Loyola to pay their last respects to John's mother. Jackie's friend Frederick Papert called the whole event "one of those logistical miracles. It's sad but true that the Kennedys know how to do this. They've had too much practice."

The service had been planned around Scripture and readings that John hoped would "capture my mother's essence. Three things come to mind over and over again and ultimately dictated our selections. They were her love of words, the bonds of home and family, and her spirit of adventure."

Jackie's friend the film director Mike Nichols read a brief passage from the Bible. Jessye Norman sang "Ave Maria." Caroline read one of her mother's favorite poems, Edna St. Vincent Millay's "Memory of Cape Cod."

Once again, it fell to Uncle Ted to deliver the eulogy. "During those four endless days in 1963, she held us together as a family and a country," he said. "In large part because of her, we could grieve and then go on.

"Jackie's love for Caroline and John was deep and unqualified," he went on. "She reveled in their accomplishments, she hurt with their sorrows, and she felt sheer joy and delight in spending time with them. At the mere mention of their names, Jackie's eyes would shine and her smile would grow bigger."

That afternoon, Jackie's body was brought to Arlington for burial beside JFK. On either side lay John's stillborn sister and his brother, Patrick, whose death had brought Jack and Jackie closer than they had ever been in the months before Dallas.

"In the end," President Clinton said, "she cared most about being a good mother to her children, and the lives of Caroline and John leave no doubt that she was that, and more."

John and Caroline each gave brief readings, then, as sixty-four bells—one for each year of her remarkable life—rang out from Washington's National Cathedral, they knelt down and kissed their mother's coffin. Then John walked the few steps over to where JFK lay and, leaning forward, touched his father's gravestone.

The pain had been etched in Caroline's face for days, but John had revealed nothing of his feelings. Now it finally hit him. It had always been the three of them against the world, and now she was gone. With the right hand that had saluted his father thirty years earlier, John reached up and brushed a tear from his cheek.

"He was devastated, naturally," Pierre Salinger said of John's stoicism. "He and his mother were extremely close. But the family doesn't go in for public displays of emotion. John inherited that great sense of personal dignity from both his parents."

To the public, it appeared that Daryl Hannah was likely to soon become Mrs. John F. Kennedy Jr. Indeed, over the month prior to Jackie's death, John and Daryl seemed closer than ever. On a typical—and very public—outing at high noon in Central Park, they hugged, kissed passionately, wrestled on the grass, and basically wrapped themselves around each other with abandon.

Less than two weeks after Jackie's death, Daryl looked every inch the Kennedy as she and John roughhoused on the lawn at Hyannis Port. The flag flew at half staff over the compound out of respect for

Jackie, but the mood was festive as John, Daryl, and the Kennedy cousins engaged in their annual Memorial Day touch football game.

At one point during the game, John tackled Daryl, wrestled her to the ground, and then playfully spanked her. "You'll regret this!" she screamed in mock indignation. "I'll get even." Then she pounced on him, and they rolled around the grass laughing hysterically.

Not for long. With Jackie gone, Daryl now no longer saw any obstacles to her becoming Mrs. John F. Kennedy Jr. They had canceled wedding plans at the last minute once before, and now, according to friends, Daryl literally got down on bended knee and proposed to John a second time.

But John now balked at the idea of marriage, particularly since he and Caroline faced the formidable task of untangling their mother's $150 million estate—the bulk of which was to be divided between her two children. John was also now heavily involved with business partner Michael Berman in plans to find a backer for *George.*

"Don't push me," he told Daryl. "I don't respond to ultimatums."

After six years, it was over. In late July, Daryl returned to Los Angeles and, incredibly, picked up where she left off with the man who had allegedly abused her, Jackson Browne.

Just as quickly, John was back with his old flame Jules Baker, the sable-haired Wilhelmina model and Jackie look-alike. That September, John was best man at Tony Radziwill's wedding and brought the head-turning Baker along as his date—knowing full well that Daryl, a friend of Tony's stepfather Herb Ross, would also be there. At the reception, John kissed Daryl on the cheek, then walked across the room and passionately embraced Baker.

Off and on for the rest of 1994, John would continue to see the willowy Jules. "I was always there for him," said Baker. "And he was always there for me." Yet, increasingly, it was the woman who was *not* always there for him who most intrigued John.

At about the same time he rekindled his romance with Baker, John cruised the waters off Hyannis in his powerboat *PT-109* with a thong-clad Carolyn Bessette poised at the bow like the voluptuous figurehead that had decorated his room at Brown. Local fisherman watched as John helped his passenger wriggle into a skirt, then swept her off her feet and carried her to shore so she wouldn't get wet.

"She managed John really well," said a friend of Bessette's. "She knew how to disappear, she knew how to drive him nuts." Carolyn, observed John Perry Barlow, was "one of those mysterious creatures that understands, on some deep level, mystical femininity. She knows how to handle men like practically nobody I've ever met. She knows where all the levers are, and she is very deft in her operation of them."

Carolyn Bessette never met Jackie. But nearly everyone who knew them both would draw the same conclusion: "Carolyn is a lot," Barlow later mused, "like the woman who would have been her mother-in-law."

I'm hoping he'll grow up to be as smart about it as John Kennedy Jr. I want William to be able to handle things as well as John does.

> —*Princess Diana,*
> *on Prince William and*
> *the media*

Carolyn has her own sense of mystery, doesn't she?

> —*Letitia Baldrige*

8

She had never met Jackie. But similarities between the two women abounded. Both were tall, slender, and elegant, with wide-set eyes, broad shoulders, full lips, long necks, and patrician profiles. Each had an aristocratic bearing that bordered on the aloof, a unique sense of style, and a carefully cultivated aura of mystery. Both were closet smokers (in contrast to John, who smoked a single cigarette every day as a sign of his self-control)—and both were self-conscious about their size 11 feet. Each wielded a rapier wit in the company of friends, but kept it discreetly sheathed in the presence of strangers.

Most important, Carolyn Bessette and Jackie Bouvier Kennedy Onassis were determined to wed powerful men. When she was eighteen, Jackie said what she wanted most was to be "part of a great man's life." Toward that end, she gave her undivided attention to any man who was lucky enough to be in her presence. "Jackie was a skillful listener," family friend Chuck Spalding said. "She had this way of focusing on you with those enormous brown eyes and hanging on your every word so that the rest of the world just sort of fell away. Men, needless to say, tended to find this irresistible."

By the same token, Carolyn was a "very strong one-on-one person," John's pal Richard Wiese said. John "always found her provocative." Another close friend, John Perry Barlow, added that she had "a genuine appreciation of men. Carolyn is extremely female, and I think it is only appropriate there would be a lot of voltage across that gap. She is hardwired to relate to people who are male."

Although she also bore a striking physical resemblance to the equally leggy and blond Daryl Hannah, Carolyn was Daryl's diametric opposite when it came to her approach toward men. Where the movie star was always there for him, Bessette made it clear from the outset of their affair that she had no intention of being at John's beck and call. Hannah pressed for marriage, but Bessette would turn out to be the one with commitment problems. "She is certainly a challenge," said a onetime co-worker of Carolyn's. "It would be hard for any woman to stay mysterious for this guy, who basically can order it up. If there is anything she is up to, it is that task: never seeming easy."

Just as Jacqueline Bouvier pursued and won JFK, it was no accident that Carolyn Bessette became the fairy tale bride of Camelot's crown prince. Born in White Plains, New York, Carolyn was six and her older twin sisters, Lisa and Lauren, eight when their parents—kitchen designer William Bessette and public school administrator Ann Marie—broke up. In 1973, Ann married wealthy orthopedic surgeon Dr. Richard Freeman, and moved with her daughters to the tony Connecticut suburb of Greenwich. Aside from the few times they phoned William Bessette or sent him a birthday card, the girls rarely had contact with their father.

When she graduated ten years later from St. Mary's Catholic high school, where she dated a school jock named Eugene Carlin ("hot and heavy" was the way he described their relationship), Carolyn was voted "Ultimate Beautiful Person." Carlin, who became a stockbroker, would later describe Bessette as someone who "would make you jealous and if you tried to do it back she'd ignore you. Then you go completely crazy.

"She's sexy. She wears sexy clothes. She's passionately sexy," Carlin added. "Use your imagination . . . Beautiful. Sophisticated. Tough. Driven. She can drive you nuts."

At Boston University, Carolyn dated hockey star John Cullen, a John Kennedy look-alike who would go on to play professionally with the Tampa Bay Lightning. At the same time, she was reportedly carrying on a simultaneous affair with his friend and teammate Chris Matchett. "Cullen was crazy about her," a Boston University class-mate said. "He would have done anything for her. But Carolyn was sort of known as the campus maneater—she dumped him, broke his heart, and moved on to the next victim."

Wasting no time, Bessette posed for a "Girls of BU" Calendar while she dated fashion empire scion Alessandro Benetton. When her parents cut her off for a time because of her excessive spending, Carolyn went to work waitressing at a local Chi-Chi's.

Graduating in 1988 with a degree in elementary education, Car-olyn went to work for the Lyons Group, doing promotion for Boston area nightclubs. In 1990, Carolyn tried her hand at modeling, posing for a series of jeans ads that never ran. The pictures showed a volup-tuous, frizzy-haired Carolyn in torn jeans and leather, arching her back, pouting seductively, and snuggling up to a variety of question-able characters. In one, she is leaning dangerously forward, nearly falling out of a low-cut negligee. In another she reclines back on a haystack wearing a black dress that is hiked up nearly to her waist, bare legs apart, her hands lingering between her thighs. "I could tell," said Bobby Di Marzo, who took the photos, "she had great expectations for her future."

That year Bessette went to work as a salesgirl in Calvin Klein's Boston store. Spotted by Susan Sokol, then president of Klein's women's collections, Bessette was transferred to New York for the purpose of catering to the demands of celebrity clients. "She wasn't intimidated," Sokol recalled. "She had a wonderful ease about her. She was comfortable with anyone, and she has a lot of self-confidence, aside from looking great."

Bessette, who befriended Klein's wife Kelly and his daughter Mar-cie, was soon promoted to publicist for the company's pricey "col-lection" line. In that capacity, she became known for clashing loudly and often with models and other staffers. "What set Carolyn apart from the rest," said one co-worker, "was that she wasn't afraid to speak her mind. If she thought something didn't work, she'd tell Calvin—and he appreciated her honesty." Sciascia Gambaccini, fash-ion director of *Marie Claire* and a friend of Klein's, believed Carolyn "intrigued Calvin a lot, and inspired a lot of his campaigns . . . She's a healthy, beautiful American, and that is what Calvin likes most in a woman."

It was equally clear to all who knew Carolyn the publicist that she was her own most important client. A regular at such trendy Manhattan clubs as Rex, the Buddha Bar, the Merc Bar, and MK, Bessette, like so many of her young colleagues in the fashion industry, developed a taste for cocaine. It did not, her friends would later insist, develop into a full-blown addiction. "She'd come in a lot," said MK's Eric Goode. "But she wasn't wild and crazy or anything."

When she first met John in the fall of 1993, Carolyn was heavily involved with Calvin Klein model Michael Bergin, who at twenty-five was nearly a decade younger than JFK Jr. At the time, Bergin, clad only in briefs, loomed over Times Square on a billboard advertising Calvin Klein underwear; Bergin's physique would later help him land a major role on the television series *Baywatch*.

For the next three years, Bergin would serve as Carolyn's most important bargaining chip in her attempt to win John. "Kennedy has a reputation for keeping the best-looking women on the side," a friend of Bergin's pointed out. "Carolyn wanted to hang on to the best-looking man. Michael was her ammunition to remain equal to John."

No one else believed she would trade JFK Jr. for the Calvin Klein underwear model, but that did not matter so long as John believed it. If John canceled at the last minute or spent time in the company of another woman, Bessette's response was predictable. "Fuck you!" she screamed at him more than once within earshot of their friends. "I'm going off with Michael."

"Most women sort of became tongue-tied around John," Wiese said. "But that wasn't Carolyn's problem. She was very strong-minded and knew what she wanted and had absolutely no difficulty speaking her mind."

"She would tell people, 'I'm not going to wait around for him,' knowing it would get back to John," a member of their inner circle said. "But in fact she would stay home and wait for him to call."

In fairness to John, other women accounted for only some of the distractions in his life. Since his mother's apartment at 1040 Fifth

Avenue was filled with too many memories, John paid $700,000 for a twenty-six-hundred-square-foot, tenth-floor penthouse co-op at 20 North Moore Street in TriBeCa. In January 1995, Jackie's apartment was sold for $9.5 million to oil magnate David Koch. As movers emptied the Fifth Avenue apartment of his mother's belongings, John sat unnoticed on the curb across the street and watched in silence.

That same month, another chapter in the Kennedy saga closed when Rose Fitzgerald Kennedy died at the age of 104. On January 25, 1995, John and Caroline were among the hundreds of mourners who crammed into St. Stephen's Church in Boston for the matriarch's funeral. Rose, the eldest daughter of Boston's legendary Mayor John Francis "Honey Fitz" Fitzgerald, had been baptized at St. Stephen's. Until disabled by a stroke in 1984, John's grandmother had showed up for mass every Sunday and placed a single dollar bill in the collection plate.

Of John's twenty-six cousins, Ethel's son Michael Kennedy was the only one not in attendance. Michael—whose own turbulent private life and sudden, tragic death would later make headlines—had checked into an alcohol rehabilitation program outside Baltimore and was "too ill" to make the trip to Massachusetts.

In April 1995, Carolyn moved in with John. But she had to accept his new mistress: *George.* Over a six-month period, Random Ventures co-founders JFK Jr. and Berman had managed to raise three million dollars to launch their magazine—reportedly less than a third of what was needed. In March, Hachette-Filipacchi, publishers of twenty-two magazines from *Premiere* and *Elle* to *Woman's Day* and *Road & Track,* agreed to spend twenty million dollars on *George* over a five-year period or until it began turning a profit.

Hachette was banking heavily on John's celebrity to lure not only subscribers and advertisers, but interview subjects and sources as well. "Having John Kennedy as editor in chief," explained Hachette's U.S. chief, David Pecker, "is going to be a big benefit to the magazine. He has access to almost everyone."

For the first time in his life, John was telling friends, he had found something he could call his own. There had been repeated offers to run for office in New York and Massachusetts, but he was not yet ready to make the commitment. "You'd better be damned sure it's what you want to do, and that the rest of your life is set up to accommodate that," he said. "It takes a certain toll on your personality and on your family life. I've seen it personally. So if I were to do it, I would make sure it was what I wanted to do and that I didn't do it because people thought I should."

To be sure, the founding of a political magazine—albeit one that was nonpartisan and decidedly pop culture friendly—could be considered a tentative first step toward a political career. Pointing to the fact that his father had covered the founding of the United Nations in 1945 as a working reporter and his mother's background as a photojournalist and editor, starting a magazine seemed only logical. "For me," John explained, "the marriage of publishing and politics simply weaves together the two family businesses."

As he approached his thirty-fifth birthday, Kennedy was also "desperate to be taken seriously. People were only focusing on his girlfriends, whether he's going to get married," Pierre Salinger said. "That annoyed him."

One week before the scheduled launch of *George,* a front-page tabloid story not only had eyes focused on John's sex life, but triggered a real crisis in his relationship with Bessette. On August 22, 1995, the *National Enquirer* reported a "sizzling secret romance" between John and Sharon Stone on Martha's Vineyard.

In late July, John and Carolyn had joined the actress for dinner at Tashmoo Farm, the Martha's Vineyard estate Stone had rented for the season. But according to the tabloid, Stone invited John back a week later, and this time he came alone.

Carolyn immediately checked the story out with friends. While she could not find solid proof of an affair, she quickly determined that Stone had invited John to a dinner party and that they had been seen together on the island. After an angry confrontation with John, she told him she was moving out.

John was also linked to Melanie Griffith prior to Griffith's marriage to Antonio Banderas. Kennedy confided to one business colleague that Griffith was particularly zealous in her pursuit of a relationship. "I had to bolt the door," he said with a wink.

On September 1, John slipped a small diamond-and-emerald ring on Bessette's finger and asked her to marry him. "I'll think about it," she replied.

"I wish John the best," said Jackie's stepbrother, Yusha Auchincloss, when news of the proposal hit the papers. "I'm sure Jackie would be ecstatic seeing that her son did not pick another Hollywood actress."

In what some would see as a genuine reluctance to spend the rest of her life in the spotlight and others as a calculated move to keep him off balance, Bessette would keep John hanging for months. "She'll drag it out," said a mutual friend, "just to make him sweat. That's her specialty."

John also faced some unexpected health concerns that summer. Suffering from extreme fatigue and unexplained weight loss (fifteen pounds in three weeks), John underwent tests at New York Hospital. In view of his mother's battle against lymphoma and his father's history of Addison's disease—a potentially fatal illness—John was understandably nervous. His fears were allayed by noted New York endocrinologist James Hurley, who diagnosed John as suffering not from Addison's disease but from a hyperactive thyroid.

If John was feeling any strain, it did not show at the unveiling of *George*. On September 8, 1995, more than 160 reporters jammed into New York's landmark downtown Federal Building for the much-hyped event. "I feel a little bit like Barry Manilow right before introducing Bruce Springsteen," Michael Berman cracked. "Being John Kennedy's partner," he went on, "is a lot like being Dolly Parton's feet. It's nice, but you tend to get overshadowed."

With that, John stepped to the podium and announced, "I don't think I've seen as many of you in one place since they announced the results of my first bar exam." With an easy grace and disarming self-deprecation, John proclaimed, "I hope eventually to end up as president . . . of a very successful publishing venture." Then he volunteered answers to all personal questions before anyone could ask them: "Yes. No. We're merely good friends. None of your business. Honest, she's my cousin from Rhode Island. I've worn both. Maybe someday, but not in New Jersey."

His audience effectively won over, John explained the rationale behind *George*: "Politics isn't dull—why should a magazine covering it be? Politics is about triumph and loss. Politics is about the pursuit of power and the price of ambition."

Still, he stressed that the magazine would not play favorites: "Uncle Ted said, 'John, if I'm still talking to you by Thanksgiving, you're not doing your job.' "

What would his mother have thought? someone asked. John allowed that he was glad she wasn't at the press conference, but added, "My mother would be mildly amused to see me up here, and very proud."

The debut issue of *George* featured supermodel Cindy Crawford on the cover as a bewigged, bare-midriffed George Washington, and contained, among other things, a piece by John's friend Madonna ("What I Would Do If I Were President") as well as John's own interview with former Alabama Governor George Wallace. With a huge initial circulation of five hundred thousand copies and a record-breaking 175 pages of advertising, the glossy bimonthly hit news-stands on September 26, 1995. Hachette-Filipacchi's faith in the marquee value of John's name appeared to be justified: *George* was, for the time being at least, a huge commercial success.

Unfazed by the inevitable public perception that he was little more than a dilettante, John took a hands-on approach to his new job. Riding his bicycle or taking the subway to work each morning, he worked into the night and often on weekends. He came up with story ideas, persuaded established names to contribute articles, edited copy, and wrote headlines as well as the editor's note that bore his name.

Over the next four years, John would also polish his own tech-nique as a journalist, interviewing the wildly varied likes of Muham-mad Ali (whom John often described as one of his personal heroes), Billy Graham, Nation of Islam leader Louis Farrakhan, Garth Brooks, Secretary of State Madeleine Albright, and Fidel Castro.

But it was as front man that John made his most valuable contri-bution to *George.* The week of the magazine's launch, *Newsweek, Esquire,* and *New York* magazines all seized the opportunity to put John on their respective covers. To promote the magazine, the once camera-shy Kennedy now submitted to scores of newspaper, maga-zine, and radio interviews. "I have a slightly contrarian impulse I can't seem to shake," John said of his decision to join the press that had hounded him all of his life. "Sometimes the weight of expectations, of doing anything, can be a little bit heavy. For me, it's always sort of fun to try and play with the blocks and see what you can come up with that's a little different."

To hype his magazine, he would also agree to television interviews with Barbara Walters, Rosie O'Donnell, and Oprah Winfrey, among others. John even seized the opportunity to make his television acting debut, playing himself on the hit prime-time sitcom *Murphy Brown*. The ninety-second cameo featured John offering Brown (played by Candice Bergen) a copy of *George* with her face on the cover. He offers her a subscription as a wedding gift and she makes it clear she is underwhelmed. "Don't come crying to me," John warns her as he storms out, "when you have to pay full newsstand price."

Kennedy approached it all with a benign smirk. "It's kind of drenched in irony, right?" he cracked. "Me in a media conglomerate." But he was confident he had made the right choice. "It's pretty cool," he said. "It was important to me to go outside the arena for a number of reasons. I think everyone needs to feel that they've created something that was their own, on their own terms."

John and Carolyn decided to spend Thanksgiving 1995 with a dozen friends at a secluded resort in Guanaja, Honduras. One of the group, writer Peter Alson, was having breakfast with JFK Jr. when he asked, "So, if you weren't spending Thanksgiving here, where would you be right now?"

John stared at him, tears welling in his eyes. It was only then that Alson realized that it was November 22, the thirty-second anniversary of his father's assassination—and only the second Thanksgiving since Jackie's death. Alson felt bad, "but moved, too, that he could, even for a moment, be so vulnerable."

At the beginning, *George* appeared to be a raging success. But things were not going so smoothly behind the scenes, as Bessette became more and more miffed at the amount of time John was spending away from her. Nor was she accustomed to the inevitable media stampede when they did venture out in public. "Carolyn became a 'thing' in the eyes of the public," said the Kennedys' friend John Perry Barlow, "and she was treated accordingly. She had no concept of what it was going to be like—people camped out on your doorstep day and night. She felt like a refugee."

Things came to a head on the morning of February 25, 1996, when John and Carolyn were walking their dog Friday through Washington Square Park. Their Sunday stroll suddenly turned violent, with the two lovers screaming and shoving each other. "What's your problem?" Bessette shouted at John, who slammed his hand down on her wrist and ripped the diamond ring he had given her off her finger.

Bessette burst into tears, but John grabbed the dog's leash out of her hand and began walking away. She stood still for a moment, then charged after John, screaming as she grasped him by the throat.

The brawl continued as they left the park and finally John, emotionally spent, sat on the curb, put his head down on his folded arms and began sobbing openly. She walked up to him and demanded the ring. "Give it to me!" she yelled. He took it out of his pocket and handed it to her.

Her ring in hand, she knelt down next to him, their heads touching, and began crying. At that point, he pushed her away—and the fighting began again. Bessette tried to wrest the leash from John.

"You've got your ring!" John yelled. "You're not getting my dog!"

"It's *our* dog!" she shouted back. A tug-of-war ensued, but after several yanks John let her have the leash. They walked in opposite directions, but after a few minutes Bessette returned, led John to a bench and the couple quietly began talking. They got up to leave, walked down the street, stopped in the middle of the sidewalk, and in full view of passersby passionately embraced. Tears were streaming down both their faces.

For someone who was trying to be taken seriously as a magazine executive, it would have been embarrassing enough if the "Brawl in the Park," as it came to be known, had only been witnessed by the scores of pedestrians who happened to walk by. But a photographer who had staked out the couple's apartment captured the shocking lovers' quarrel on videotape.

The pitched battle was reminiscent of John's frequent public spats with Daryl Hannah. It also underscored the volatility—and the passionate intensity—of the Kennedy–Bessette relationship. Asked for the Kennedy family's reaction to the highly publicized fight between her brother and his girlfriend, Caroline Kennedy Schlossberg said tersely, "It's private. I don't want to talk about it. John's doing fine."

For his part, John was mortified. "He was profoundly embarrassed by the whole thing," John Perry Barlow said. "It was very undignified—and so unlike John." Still, he managed to handle the highly public airing of his private affairs with characteristic humor. Only a few days after airing of the videotape, John made a surprise appearance on shock-jock Howard Stern's radio show. Had he seen the controversial videotape? Stern asked.

"I didn't have to see it." John shrugged. "I was in it."

Scarcely six weeks after their celebrated donnybrook, a beret-clad John and Carolyn were spending a romantic April weekend strolling along the banks of the Seine and window-shopping in Paris. Arm in arm, stopping on the street to cuddle or wrestle playfully—at one point she pretended to bite his arm—they seemed "utterly besotted with each other. To me," sighed a friend, "when I look at this couple, it's a very simple guy; it's a very complicated girl."

In the spring of 1996, John's mother was about to take center stage yet again—this time nearly two years after her death. The city of New York had already paid tribute to its most famous citizen by naming the Central Park Reservoir after her.

Now, over a four-day period in April 1996, a tribute of a very different sort was being paid as some 1,195 lots from the estate of Jacqueline Kennedy Onassis went under the gavel at Sotheby's in New York. The historic auction brought another $34,461,495 into John's and Caroline's coffers. The sale, which Jackie had approved prior to her death as a means of raising extra cash to pay the huge taxes on her estate, also had the backing of the children's chief financial advisor, Maurice Tempelsman.

In defending the sale, Nancy Tuckerman pointed out that before anything went on the auction block, John and Caroline culled through their mother's possessions for themselves and the Kennedy Library. In the end, they donated thirty-eight thousand pages of documents, more than forty-five hundred photographs, and two hundred works of art and artifacts, including the dress Jackie wore when she married JFK in 1953.

Nevertheless, many viewed the sale of such personal items as John-John's high chair, Jackie's jewelry, and JFK's golf clubs, humidor, and rocking chair as an appallingly tasteless public spectacle. Others felt John and his sister were only following Jackie's orders—and that she would not have been disappointed by the outcome. "I'm sure Jackie," said her friend Dina Merrill, "would have been *thrilled*."

No more so than John, who suddenly found himself collecting fifteen million dollars—more than enough to offset his share of the taxes on Jackie's estate. But while he continued on his year-long promotional tour for *George,* questions began to arise concerning Carolyn's whereabouts. Bessette quit her job at Calvin Klein in July and all but vanished, fueling speculation that their rocky love affair was finally over.

In reality, she was at last ready to wed—and to sign the prenuptial agreement that would give her three million dollars in the event they divorced. The terms of the prenuptial contract were not as important to Carolyn as her inevitable loss of privacy. "What will it be like with the children?" she asked her friend Dana Gallo Strayton. " 'We'll always be hounded.' She was excited but she wanted to make sure it was the right decision. She knew the limelight would be there."

Limelight that, as a magazine editor, John now sometimes sought out. The young editor had no illusions about the market value of his name. "Any time you have a lot of hype, people want to kind of see you take it on the chin," he said. "But we've managed to reach people who probably wouldn't have been reached if my name was Joe Smith."

Knowing that it would raise eyebrows—and boost newsstand sales—he put Drew Barrymore on the cover of *George*'s September 1996 issue, reenacting Marilyn Monroe's famous "Happy Birthday, Mr. *Pres-i-dent*" song to JFK. "It's reprising a song sung to my father in 1962," he said disingenuously. "I don't see what possible taste questions could be involved. If I don't find it tasteless, I don't know why anyone would. It's part of the iconography of American politics—an enduring image. I wouldn't be doing my job if I didn't come up with interesting, engaging ideas." Albeit an idea that would have, observed his uncle Jamie Auchincloss, "horrified and angered Jackie."

It was carried out with all the stealth and precision of a commando operation. After six months of meticulous planning, secrecy, and sub-terfuge, John and Carolyn pulled off the impossible on September 21, 1996—a private wedding that caught press and public completely off guard. John even managed to fool his colleagues at *George,* taking great pains to be seen hoisting a golf bag over his shoulder as he announced he was escaping for a weekend of golf.

The surprise nuptials, Letitia Baldrige said, "required the skill of a James Bond and the whole CIA. Jackie must be smiling in heaven." (The strain of keeping the event under wraps apparently took a toll on John. Just two weeks earlier, the characteristically courteous JFK Jr. flew into a rage at a photographer shooting him on the beach in Hyannis Port. John shouted obscenities at hapless video cameraman John Paparo and then dumped a bucket of water over his head. Cooling off just as quickly, John apologized.)

Over the course of several days starting on September 18, some forty guests—nearly all family—began arriving by boat and private plane at tiny Cumberland Island, a four-by-seventeen-mile strip of sand off the coast of Georgia inhabited by wild horses, armadillos, bobcats, and just twenty-one people.

The rehearsal dinner was held at Greyfield Inn, a stately mansion that had been built as a retreat for the Carnegie family and the only inn on the island. Carolyn wiped away a tear as John stood and toasted her. "I am," he declared in a sly reference to the "Sexiest Man Alive" sobriquet, "the *luckiest* man alive."

The next evening, guests crammed into the tiny, white-clapboard Brack Chapel of the First African Baptists Church, built in 1893 by former slaves. It was very much a family affair. Tony Radziwill, John's favorite cousin and closest friend, was best man. Caroline Kennedy Schlossberg was maid of honor. Her daughters, Rose and Tatiana, were flower girls; John's nephew Jack, just three at the time, was ring bearer. Jackie's sister Lee Radziwill Ross was there, as were Uncle Ted and the last love of Jackie's life, Maurice Tempelsman. On hand representing the bride's family: her mother, stepfather, and sister Lisa.

John wore a midnight-blue wool suit and white vest, one of his father's shirts, his father's watch and, with the other men in the wedding party—a blue cornflower, JFK's favorite, as a boutonniere. As the bride appeared wearing a sleek size-six pearl-colored silk crepe floor-length gown, a veil of silk tulle, and long gloves—all designed by her friend Narciso Rodriguez for Nino Cerruti at a cost of forty thousand dollars—little Jack's eyes widened. "Why," John's nephew blurted loudly, "is Carolyn dressed like *that*?"

Several of the guests brushed away a tear when they realized Carolyn was clutching a bouquet of lilies of the valley, Jackie's favorite flower. The bride wore her hair pulled back and held in place with a comb that had belonged to Jackie, a gift from Caroline. The bride, observed John Perry Barlow, "came in the church looking like some beautiful ghost."

The brief candlelight ceremony—the chapel was without electricity—was conducted by the Reverend Charles J. O'Byrne, a Jesuit deacon from Manhattan's St. Ignatius Loyola Church; it was so dark inside that O'Byrne used a flashlight to read the service. Behind them was a rustic cross made of sticks tied together with twine.

"I shed tears of absolute joy as John and his bride exchanged vows," Marta Sgubin said. "He has always been a very, very sensitive boy, and as I watched him I could read in his eyes how much he wished his mother could have been there to see him married."

No one threw rice when they left the church, but the couple lingered outside and savored the moment in a gently falling rain. As they walked past a fence, Carolyn felt a tug—one of the island's wild horses had wandered over and nibbled at her bouquet.

At the dinner that night, complete with a three-tiered vanilla butter-cream wedding cake, Ted once again evoked Camelot in his toast to the bride and groom. "I know," he said, "that Jack and Jackie would be very proud of them and full of love for them as they begin their future together."

"It was particularly touching and poignant," the senator's spokeswoman Melody Miller said, "and it moved everyone to tears." After

Ted's toast, the couple took to the floor for the first dance to their song, Prince's "Forever in My Life."

Carolyn was promptly hailed as "The New Queen of Camelot" in headline after headline. But only on her terms. Before the ceremony, while Carolyn and John were getting blood tests and filling out the necessary paperwork, Camden County Court Clerk Shirley Wise asked if Carolyn was taking John's surname. "I still want to be known as Bessette—Bessette-Kennedy," she insisted. "I want the name with a hyphen." Said Wise: "You could have knocked me over with a feather. After all this, she didn't want to take the world's most famous name!"

Incredibly, John and Carolyn had been married for two days before the press reported the story. By then they had already sneaked off on their honeymoon—first to Turkey for three days, then a ten-day Aegean cruise aboard the 123-foot double-masted schooner *Althea*.

Carolyn got a taste of what life as Mrs. John Kennedy would be like as they sat on the terrace of a rooftop cafe in Turkey. At the next table, ten vacationing magazine editors from New York, oblivious to the newlyweds' presence, chatted about having spotted the couple in the bazaar earlier that day.

"He was gorgeous," one of the women at the table gushed. "She was with him, and let me tell you, that woman is no beauty queen." When someone else in the group described her as "cute," the woman replied, "Nah, *Julie Nixon* is better looking than she is."

It was only then that they realized the honeymooners were sitting immediately behind them. "His back was to us and sort of hunched down—clearly they heard every word," recalled one of the editors. Carolyn "stared at us the entire time they were there. She looked like she wanted to come over and stab us with a fork."

It was clear that the honeymoon was indeed over when they emerged from 20 North Moore Street for the first time as man and wife and were greeted by a barrage of flashing cameras. Well-mannered to the core and smiling warmly, John asked his fellow members of the press to give his stern-faced bride some breathing room. "This is a big change for anyone," he told the throng of reporters, "and for a private citizen even more so. I ask that you give Carolyn all the privacy and room you can."

That, of course, was not to be. Only days later, as she arrived at the post-wedding party thrown for her at Caroline Kennedy Schlossberg's sprawling apartment at Park Avenue and East 78th Street, Bessette shielded her eyes from the blinding flashbulbs and pleaded with photographers, "Please! I can't see."

"My wife went from being a private citizen to a public one overnight and she really bore up very well," John later said of this period. "I'm really proud of her." But the glare of the spotlight had in fact sent the mercurial Mrs. Bessette-Kennedy into an emotional tailspin. "The curiosity the first year was taxing," he cautiously conceded. "I have a thick skin about it, but I think people sort of forget how hard that can be. Carolyn is a very private woman. It's like you go from having a life you've built on your own terms and all of a sudden it's being snatched away from you. It's hard."

At first Carolyn viewed the constant presence of the paparazzi as "kind of a joke. But then it just got bizarre," she later recalled. "I realized that a lot of the photographers really didn't like me. They wanted me to do something wrong, so they could photograph it."

One day she stumbled on the steps coming out of her apartment building, and the pack of photographers "just went crazy. Nobody helped me up," Carolyn said. "They just kept snapping."

One refuge was Bubby's, a funky, brick-walled restaurant just up the street from their apartment. With its white ceiling fans, balloons for the kiddies, copper-topped bar, framed vintage photographs of African-American families adorning the walls, and the words HOME-MADE PIES printed on the windows, Bubby's seemed an unlikely hangout for America's most glamorous couple. But it was here that John and Carolyn came to escape the prying eye of the press.

John, usually dressed down in khakis, T-shirt, and a beret, would scan the papers as he wolfed down breakfast. Invariably, he would also forget to carry cash (since prep school days his friends had complained that he always stuck them with the bill) and have to make a quick trip to an ATM across the street before settling the bill.

Once while having lunch at Bubby's, John looked out the window to see two men unchain his bike and start to pedal away. He jumped up, ran outside and chased them down the street. The thieves finally decided to abandon the bike and make their getaway on foot. Afterward, recalled another Bubby's patron, Jaimie Collins, "he came back, sat down and finished his coffee."

Another hangout was Socrates on Hudson Street, where waitress Bia Ayiotis regularly served John breakfast. Ayiotis was surprised when he first spoke a few words to her in Greek. "My stepfather," he explained, "was Greek."

"He'd sit at the counter or at a booth with his baseball cap on and read his paper in peace," she said. "For his power and his money, he was a very plain person. That's what I liked about him. He was a sweetheart."

While he took the staring and murmured comments from other patrons in stride, Carolyn felt, as she often said, "like a hunted animal." Said Bubby's co-owner Seth Price, "She would have to hide in here. She'd go out the back door to get out. It was just horrible. She just wanted to spend time with her husband."

To further complicate matters, John was chasing yet another dream. With his mother no longer around to object, he was now determined to fly. He purchased his first ultralight, a Buckeye powered parachute, and took to the skies for the first time in August 1996—after just two hours of instruction. The Buckeye powered parachute did not require a pilot's license.

Over the next two years John forged a friendship with Buckeye Industries' design engineer Lloyd Howard, traveling to Buckeye headquarters in Argos, Indiana, to spend time with Howard's family and check out the company's latest models. "He said his mother was always afraid for him," Howard recalled, "that she did not want him flying. If anything, he was more cautious than most people *because* of his mother—that was ingrained in him."

John also alluded to the fact that Jackie had ambitions for her son. "He made it pretty clear that he was under pressure from his mother to enter politics—that she expected him to follow in his dad's footsteps. He was going to, but he didn't feel the time was quite right."

On his visits to Argos, John once again found himself cast in the role of surrogate uncle, this time to Howard's grandchildren. On the thirty-fourth anniversary of his father's assassination, John decided to escape Manhattan with Carolyn and spend a quiet weekend in Indiana with the Howards.

As outgoing as John was, Howard was surprised that Carolyn "was even more so. The first time I saw her, she gave me a big bear hug. Like everybody else, I'd seen those pictures of her looking sort of aloof, but she was very open, very warm, very friendly."

According to Howard, John's wife was also unexpectedly chatty. "Carolyn talked your ear off," he said. "John just listened while she went on and on." Her pet peeve, not surprisingly, was the press. "She said some of the photographers made their life hell—that no one understood what it was like to not be able to walk out your front door without somebody shoving a camera in your face. Carolyn admired John for the way he handled it, and she said she was learning from him. But it was hard."

Howard also observed that Carolyn "babied John. She treated him like he was her child—always asking him how he felt, reminding him to wear a scarf, that sort of thing." After dining at Argos's Loghouse Inn one evening, they were walking to Howard's sport-utility vehicle when they realized John had vanished. "We all went back inside the restaurant and there was John frantically searching for his black knit cap."

"Can you believe it?" John said. "Somebody stole my cap."

"He really seemed upset about it," Howard recalled. "But when we got back to the car, we realized that John had accidentally dropped the cap behind the backseat. He was just so delighted to find it." Later, Carolyn took Howard aside and explained why. "That black cap," she whispered to him, "was the last present his mother gave him before she died."

According to Howard, Carolyn did not share Jackie's concern for John's safety in the skies. After an instructor took her up in one of Buckeye's flying machines, she told Howard that she wanted to learn to fly an ultralight. "She was very excited by the idea of soloing," he said. As for John's flying, "I don't know how she felt about planes, but Carolyn seemed to get a kick out of watching John fly the powered parachutes."

Something else had been gnawing at the grandfatherly Howard, who in addition to being a design engineer was an ordained minister. The Kennedys' Indiana host had seen the tabloid stories about trouble brewing in the young couple's marriage, and he felt compelled to ask them if there was any truth to the rumors.

"Now, John and Carolyn," Howard said point-blank, "I want to know if you've been having problems."

John and Carolyn shook their heads and smiled. "They told me in no uncertain terms that it wasn't true, that their marriage was stronger than ever and that I shouldn't worry."

As soon as they returned to New York, however, they were once again under siege. The quiet days spent out of the limelight in Indiana had reminded Carolyn of what it was like to actually have a private life, and that left her feeling only more depressed.

By Thanksgiving, Carolyn was, in the words of one friend, "crumbling under the stress." When she and John did not show up at a Metropolitan Museum of Art gala honoring the late designer Christian Dior, none of the other guests was more bitterly disappointed than Princess Diana. To be sure, in tapes made public by the Duchess of York's "spiritual advisor," Madame Vasso Kortesis, "Fergie" had predicted that she and Diana would battle for the man they had both met and now lusted after—John F. Kennedy Jr.

In December, John's wife fled to Germany, ostensibly to visit her sister Lisa, who was studying there. No sooner had Carolyn returned than she and John were accosted outside their apartment while walking their dog, Friday.

This time, John snapped. He had been told that the woman sitting at the wheel of the parked Jeep, celebrity photographer Angie Coqueran, was the very same photographer responsible for the infamous video of their battle in the park. John climbed up onto the hood, pressed his face to the windshield and began shouting, "I know who you are. I know who you are, and I'm going to get you."

A stunned Carolyn tried to calm him down, but John kept it up. When Coqueran rolled down her car window a few inches and asked him to back away so she could leave, John, still shouting, lunged inside the vehicle and grabbed her by the collar. Carolyn tugged on her husband's arm, trying to get him to stop, but he pulled away.

Then he spotted Coqueran's partner riding up on a bicycle. John ran toward the man, and, fists clenched, screamed into his face. "Leave us the hell ALONE!" Kennedy repeated as Carolyn, now frantic, tried to pull him off.

Finally, John stormed off alone—leaving Carolyn and Friday to try and catch up with him. When they did, Carolyn broke down crying. "Look," John later said, "I put myself out there, but she never did. She never called a press conference, never gave a speech."

"I didn't blame him one bit for getting angry," Coqueran later said. "Before he got married, he was gentle as a bunny with us—even when he was pissed off. He had spent his whole life being hounded by the press and he knew how to handle it. But when your wife is upset and the paparazzi are making her cry, your first instinct is to protect her. I don't blame him at all for coming after me. In a way, I think it shows what a great guy he was. He tried to strangle me and I *still* love the guy—that's how great he was."

Coqueran, who had witnessed their comings and goings for years, also sympathized with Carolyn's plight and noted how the transition from being John's girlfriend to being Mrs. JFK Jr. had left Carolyn "a changed woman. She went from a sweatclothes-and-sneakers, let's-go-play-in-the-park, tomboyish kind of gal to this drop-dead crea-ture in high heels and Versace dresses. I think she was trying to live up to something when she would have been happier just staying the sort of fun-loving person that she was."

It had become increasingly difficult for the couple to maintain their emotional equilibrium given the ceaseless swirl of media spec-ulation linking John to Daryl Hannah and Carolyn to several men, including her old flame Michael Bergin. Especially painful were reports that persisted throughout their marriage that Carolyn was pregnant, that she had suffered one or more miscarriages, and ulti-mately, that they suffered fertility problems.

Although John had already picked out the name Flynn for a son, their decision not to embark on a family immediately was a con-scious one. "They were holding back," their friend Christa D'Souza said, "because neither of them could bear the idea of all the media attention."

Carolyn, in particular, could not countenance subjecting a child to such scrutiny. "It would be totally unfair, just too cruel," she said. "Just another form of child abuse."

In the meantime, John and Carolyn reveled in time spent with the children of their friends. "My three daughters all loved John," John Perry Barlow recalled. "But when Carolyn came along, she was all they wanted to talk about. They saw her as this enchanted fairy godmother.

"Children were definitely on the agenda for John and Carolyn," Barlow continued. "But they wanted things to kind of settle down first. They were already in this unremitting klieg glare, and they couldn't imagine what it would be like with a child. They didn't see any rush to have children. They thought they'd be around a while . . ."

There were stresses on John's office marriage, as well. Much like his relationship with Carolyn, John's partnership with *George* co-founder Michael Berman was at times tempestuous. Even before their first issue hit the stands, the two college pals had battled over what would go into the magazine.

By February 1997, their simmering feud boiled over after John dispatched Carolyn to Europe to persuade top designers to advertise in *George*. Soon she was offering her ideas on what direction the magazine should take, and John was listening. When Berman offered his opinion—"She doesn't know what she's talking about"—John hit the roof. At one point, the two men reportedly scuffled in a hall-way at the *George* offices and had to be pulled apart by security guards. John was left with a torn shirt. Three months later, their part-nership—and their seventeen-year friendship—was *finis*.

The burst of immaturity that led to John's showdown with Berman was not atypical. That March, police rushed to the scene when Hyannis Port residents reported seeing a man at the controls of a flimsy motorized parachute being blown farther and farther out over the icy Atlantic. By the time they arrived, John had somehow managed to steer the contraption back toward shore and land it on the beach. When police warned him that he could easily have been killed, John merely shrugged. "I wasn't worried."

But his friend Richard Wiese was. Before John founded *George* he had actually considered going into business with Wiese selling ultralight aircraft. "Once, I was telling him about accidents with ultra-lights—common ones," Wiese said. "He didn't want to hear about it. He said, 'You're trying to discourage me.' " That bothered his old college buddy. "A good pilot always assesses risks," he said, "and decides how to avoid them."

What most disturbed Wiese and others who knew John well was his occasional lack of focus. "He was very intelligent," Wiese said, "but he would space out on things. He would constantly lose things. He always had his keys attached to his pants. I don't know how many dozens of bicycles he lost."

That June, John took Carolyn to Milan for a romantic second honeymoon. As on their first honeymoon, they seldom left their room. The break seemed to have worked: When they returned to New York, the couple were photographed arm in arm around town. But Carolyn was plunged back into depression when she returned to Milan only weeks later—this time for the July 22 funeral of her friend Gianni Versace, who had been gunned down on a Miami street by serial killer Andrew Cunanan.

At the service, Princess Diana was so busy chatting with rock star Sting and comforting a distraught Elton John that she failed to recognize Carolyn sitting directly behind her. When Diana died only five weeks later in a Paris car crash, Carolyn and John were, like the rest of the world, stunned. "Those poor boys," Carolyn said, shaking her head as she scanned the newspaper at Bubby's.

When it was revealed that she had wanted her sons to grow up being able to handle the media the way JFK Jr. had, he reacted with characteristic modesty. "That's very nice," he said. "But it's really not the same situation. I was really able to lead a normal life from about the age of five. I went to boarding school and then to college. Diana's sons will have to constantly deal with the media starting now."

Whether John ever led a truly "normal life" was open to debate. But he had learned the art of hiding in plain sight. "John was a magician," John Perry Barlow recalled. "He could just flat out disappear."

Once, following a Bruce Springsteen concert at Madison Square Garden, John and Barlow made their way toward an exit when suddenly they were mobbed by photographers. "John had been standing right beside me," Barlow remembered, "and when I turned to talk to him, he had vanished. A few moments later, when the crowd had sort of dispersed, I heard this sound. 'Psst. Psst, over here.' Then John popped out from behind a pillar. He'd been standing there, right in the middle of everything, the whole time. He knew how not to be seen if he didn't want to be seen, and he did it often."

That summer, as the clan reeled from two headline-making scandals, several Kennedys may well have envied John's knack for making himself disappear. Massachusetts Congressman Joe Kennedy, in the midst of a gubernatorial campaign, was being widely criticized for finagling an annulment of his twelve-year marriage to Sheila Rauch. Another of Bobby's sons, Michael Kennedy, had an even bigger problem: He was accused of sleeping with his family's underage babysitter.

Carolyn had been one factor in the breakup of John's partnership with Michael Berman. Now, with Carolyn's encouragement—and an eye on reviving slumping magazine sales—John also broke ranks with his Kennedy cousins. Branding Michael and Joe "poster boys for bad behavior," John used the editor's letter in the September 1997 issue of *George* to fire a broadside on the branch of the Kennedy family that his mother had successfully shielded him from. "One left behind an embittered wife," he wrote of Joe. "Another, in what looked to be a hedge against mortality, fell in love with youth and surrendered his judgment in the process."

As for the public drubbing both Joe and Michael had already received, John wrote, "Perhaps they deserved it. Perhaps they should have known better. To whom much is given, much is expected, right?" To further fuel the flames of controversy, the photo accompanying John's damning letter showed him nude—though in shadow—gazing up at the forbidden apple under the heading "Don't Sit Under the Apple Tree."

Joe Kennedy, who would quit his campaign for Massachusetts governor as a result of the brouhaha, waxed philosophical about John's attack in *George.* "I guess my first reaction was," Joe said, " 'Ask not what you can do for your cousin, but what you can do for his magazine.' " Michael also tried to shrug off the ambush from one of his own, and stressed that he still regarded John as "not just my cousin but my friend."

"He cheapened his image," said pollster John Zogby, echoing the sentiments of many who felt John had betrayed his family. "It was a stupid thing to do." But John's defenders argued that he was wholly justified in speaking out against his scandal-plagued cousins. "John F. Kennedy has taken hold of the leadership of the Kennedy family within his generation," Jackie's cousin John Davis declared. JFK Jr.'s magazine piece was, Davis added, "an initial attempt to clear the family name in the face of this alarming criticism that's been going on. I think it's a good sign."

To John Perry Barlow, the editorial was part of John's own voyage of self-discovery. "He was always thinking, how do I define myself as a person and not simply as a Kennedy? He had a strong sense of Irish loyalty, but he felt that he was different and he *was* different. John was far more Bouvier than Kennedy."

As much as Jackie wanted her son to ultimately embark on his own quest for the White House, she wanted him to do it on his terms. "Jackie had a profound sense of responsibility—*not* obligation— and she managed to impart that to her son. She was one of the great human beings."

It is doubtful she would have approved of John's controversial *George* editorial criticizing his cousins, however. Despite Jackie's dislike for Ethel and her successful campaign to keep the Hickory Hill gang away from John, Jackie remained steadfastly loyal to the Kennedy name. Through Chappaquiddick, David Kennedy's heroin overdose, Willie Smith's rape trial and numerous scandals and controversies in between, Jackie never wavered in her support of the Kennedys. "Whatever her personal feelings," Pierre Salinger said, "showing a unified front to the outside world was always very important to Jackie."

No matter. Copies of *George* flew off the newsstands that week, and John rewarded himself with an eight-day kayaking trip to Iceland in the company of three buddies. Carolyn stayed behind in New

York. "The poor lady didn't know what to do with herself," a neighbor said. "We'd see her walking the dog and picking up groceries, but for the most part, she hid inside her apartment."

When he returned from his latest adventure roughing it with the boys, John flew with Carolyn to Martha's Vineyard, where they joined John's sister at a dinner party for Bill and Hillary Clinton on August 20. The following day, Carolyn returned to New York to keep an appointment with her hairdresser, leaving John behind.

Enter Daryl Hannah, who arrived on Martha's Vineyard just as Carolyn was leaving and checked into room 201 at Edgartown's Harbor View Hotel. Daryl hid behind scarves, hats, and dark glasses, and no one reported seeing John and Daryl together that weekend.

Two days later, Carolyn joined John at Hyannis Port for a family get-together arranged by Uncle Ted. The weekend of touch football was specifically designed to mend fences between John and his cousins and to show the outside world that the clan remained united. Privately, Ted fumed over John's scathing editorial. But publicly, he blithely dismissed any talk of a family feud.

It was not until they returned to New York that Carolyn learned of Daryl Hannah's presence on Martha's Vineyard the week before—on the very day John was there alone. Understandably, Carolyn was eager to go along with her husband when he returned to Martha's Vineyard on Labor Day weekend. While they waited to take off from Newark Airport aboard a small Continental Express plane, the couple bickered loudly, mindless of the other ten people on the plane who heard every cruel word.

"Maybe we should get divorced," John shouted at Carolyn. "We fucking talk about it enough."

"Oh, no," she fired back. "We waited for your mother to die to get married. We're waiting for my mother to die to get a divorce." The argument continued on throughout most of the one-hour flight. Carolyn returned to New York by private charter the following day, leaving John behind to let off steam bicycling aimlessly around the island for hours.

That fall, as he dealt with the fallout from his editorial slamming Joe and Michael Kennedy, John tried to get his marriage back on track. He turned one of his business trips to California into a romantic second-anniversary getaway. After two nights in San Francisco, where they nuzzled in the lobby bar of the Huntington Hotel before heading up to their suite, the couple drove 150 miles south to the Ventana Inn at Big Sur.

When they returned to New York, John was determined to keep Carolyn from sinking back into a state of depression. "He set aside two lunch dates per week for Carolyn, and instructed the staff to interrupt him whenever she called. "I don't care if I'm in a meeting or on the phone to the White House," he said, "put Carolyn straight through."

But Carolyn, still forced to run the gauntlet of photographers every time she left their apartment, again became bored and withdrawn. When they did venture out, her demeanor was chilly. "John was a real gentleman," photographer David McGough said. "He was very polite to photographers at events, and would stop and smile for them. He knew how to give—but she never did. Carolyn seldom smiled. She could be cold as ice. It was clear there was resentment there. She certainly didn't try to hide it."

The anger, fueled by Carolyn's growing sense of isolation, spilled over at home. One evening, John was rushed to the hospital to have emergency surgery after a nerve in his right hand had been mysteriously severed in what was described by *George*'s spokesmen as a "kitchen accident."

The mysterious mishap, which left his hand and forearm bandaged and in a brace, did not prevent John from flying to Havana on October 23, 1997, for a historic meeting with Cuban dictator Fidel Castro. There, thirty years after the Cuban Missile Crisis, John interviewed his father's bearded nemesis over a five-hour dinner of grapefruit, shrimp, chicken, and ice cream. John was surprised when Castro professed to be a great admirer of JFK, and when he seemed to apologize for refusing Lee Harvey Oswald an entry visa into Cuba in October 1963—an act that almost certainly would have prevented Oswald from being in Dallas one month later.

Back in New York that December, there was yet another confrontation with the paparazzi. One day John surprised photographers waiting outside his apartment by videotaping them—evidence, he explained, for the harassment suit he intended to file against them.

More than ever, John felt the need to escape from it all. He secretly began taking flying lessons at the Flight Safety Academy in Vero Beach, Florida. But Carolyn was against the idea. She had not objected to the Buckeye powered parachute because she viewed the ultralight not as a full-blown aircraft, but as more of a toy for grown-ups; John pointed out repeatedly that the Buckeye was so safe it did not even require a license to operate.

But piloting a plane struck Carolyn as something with a decidedly greater potential for disaster. John had told Carolyn about his mother's concerns, and now that she had married into the star-crossed Kennedy clan, Carolyn harbored similar doubts. On their way back from Florida the day after Christmas, the couple was about to board a flight in Atlanta when, in front of other passengers, they began arguing about John's flying lessons. "I mean it, John," she said. "I have a bad feeling about this. I don't want you taking flying lessons."

Five days later, on New Year's Eve, Michael Kennedy was killed in Aspen, Colorado, after colliding with a fir tree during a typically reckless Kennedy game of night football on skis. Michael's sister Rory cradled his head and cried, "Stay with us, Michael!" as she attempted to revive him while his children sobbed by his side. Michael was thirty-nine. It was not the last Kennedy family tragedy that would touch Rory.

Despite their reconciliation at Hyannis Port the previous summer, Michael's shockingly sudden death stirred up resentment among the cousins over John's public skewering of Michael and Joe. At the funeral in Centerville, Massachusetts, Joe whispered comforting words to mourners, but greeted John with stony silence. "It was difficult," a family member recalled. "Everyone was still in shock . . . It didn't help that John's attack on Michael came so close to his death."

As they waited to board a flight at the Hyannis airport, John and Carolyn were cornered by two photographers. "Why can't you just leave us alone?" John said, then pulled out a camera of his own and began shooting back. The two paparazzi turned to leave, but Carolyn grabbed the camera out of John's hand and ran after them. Once she caught up to photographer Laura Cavanaugh, Carolyn walked up to her and spit in her face.

Carolyn was clearly at the breaking point for several reasons, not the least of which was the fear that her daredevil husband might wind up like Michael. "With this family's history, John is the last person on earth who should be piloting his own plane," Carolyn told a friend from her Calvin Klein days. "I can't stop thinking John could be the next to go."

She confronted him with her fears. "Walk away now, while you still can—please, for my sake," she pleaded.

John laughed off his wife's concerns. "You're just being paranoid and superstitious," he told her. "Don't worry. I won't take any chances."

But Carolyn would not stop there. She enlisted Ted Kennedy's help in persuading John to call a halt to the flying lessons. Uncle Ted pointed out that John's bride was under considerable strain already. To allay Carolyn's fears—and out of respect for his mother's wishes—John should put his flying career on hold. Reluctantly, John agreed. He informed his flight instructors that he would not be returning due to "personal and family conflicts."

Four days after Michael Kennedy's funeral, on January 7, 1998, Carolyn Bessette-Kennedy celebrated her thirty-second birthday. Before she blew out the candles on her cake, Carolyn told John her wish: "All I want for my birthday is to know you'll always be around."

She started calling him "Mouse." He called her "Kitty Cat." And for the next several months John and Carolyn seemed to achieve, as he told his sister, a certain "equilibrium" in their lives.

In February, they attended a state dinner for British prime minister Tony Blair at the White House. As they stood in the receiving line, Joseph Nye, dean of the Kennedy School at Harvard, turned to John and asked, "Do you remember this place?"

"Only vaguely," John replied.

"Do you want to come back?"

John looked at Nye with a smile. "Only vaguely," he repeated.

President Bill Clinton, incorrectly believing it was Kennedy's first homecoming, then took John and Carolyn aside for a special tour, making sure it was captured by a White House photographer. In truth, it had been almost twenty-seven years to the day since John had lost the bet with his sister and spilled his drink in Richard Nixon's lap.

From there they jetted off for a ski trip in Utah, then returned to New York for a celebrity-packed sixty-sixth birthday party at the St. Regis Hotel for Uncle Ted. In April, they clung to each other at a black-tie Municipal Arts Society dinner.

At gala after gala, John and Carolyn seemed happier and more comfortable than they had at any time during their marriage. Much to his obvious delight, Carolyn would walk over to him at a party and plop down on his lap. "She'd whisper something in his ear and he'd throw back his head and laugh," said New York photographer David McGough. "It sort of seemed for public consumption, but who knows? He seemed genuinely happy—maybe by this stage she was, too."

Not entirely. Only weeks after promising to Carolyn and his uncle Ted that he would give up flying lessons, John persuaded his wife to let him return to the Flight Safety Academy in Vero Beach, Florida. Carolyn accompanied him to Florida on at least two separate occasions, but spent most of her time at the gym and by the pool at their hotel.

As he had done many times before, John found a "Mom" he could confide in—Lois Cappelen, a fifty-six-year-old waitress at C. J. Cannon's, a coffee shop near the flight school. "That first morning I thought someone I knew came in—a young guy, a model we all thought looked exactly like John Kennedy Jr. But when I went up to him I realized he wasn't my friend," Cappelen said. "So I introduced myself and he said, 'Please, just call me John.'" It wasn't until the younger waitresses took her aside and squealed "That's JFK! That's JFK!" that she realized this was the genuine article.

Every morning for several weeks, John walked into C. J. Cannon's, sat at Lois's table with his back to the rest of the customers, and ordered a breakfast of oatmeal, eggs, fruit, and juice. She was instantly struck by "how open and unaffected he was. Strangers would come up to him, and he would get up, shake their hands, and talk to them." She was also impressed by "how funny he could be."

When Cappelen informed him that she had twin grandsons, John pointed out how odd it was that in his huge extended family there was not a single set of twins. "Hmmm, come to think of my cousins," John added, "one of each is plenty!"

"When I got to know him a little better, I asked him why he'd waited so long to get flight training," Cappelen said. "Most cadets are young kids. He told me he had wanted to fly since he was a boy—that when he was little he thought Air Force One was *his* plane—and that nothing gave him so much pleasure. But his mother just hated everything about flying, and she told him to put any idea of flying out of his mind. But after she was gone, he decided to start."

One Saturday in April, John met Richard Wiese in Central Park for a game of football. "You can now call me 'Aviator John Kennedy, licensed pilot!' " he announced. Wiese presented his friend with a poster from the movie *Top Gun* with John's picture pasted over the face of star Tom Cruise. "The skies," Wiese inscribed the poster, "will never be the same."

Despite John's repeated invitations, Wiese refused to fly with him. So did every other friend, not to mention every member of his family. "John may have pushed his limitations getting his pilot's license," said his cousin Willie Smith, "but he hasn't overcome them yet. He's yet to persuade any of his relatives to fly with him."

Not that he didn't try. At the family's Hyannis Port Fourth of July weekend, John tried to cajole anyone and everyone into coming aloft with him. Still, there were no takers.

That did not dampen the festivities, however. A barefoot John wrestled with his nephews and nieces, joked with his cousins, and got into a tickle fight with Carolyn. For her part Carolyn, her long blond hair flowing down her back, fit in perfectly with the Kennedys. She was warmly embraced by virtually every member of the clan, and at one point decided to do some showing off of her own by turning cartwheels on the lawn. "A perfect day," John told his cousins. "Just a perfect, perfect day." Uncle Ted, taking it all in from his perch by the buffet table, was impressed. "God, those kids really are in love, aren't they?" he said to no one in particular. "God, how his parents would have loved to see this . . ."

The next month, Carolyn and John traveled to Italy to attend the wedding of Christiane Amanpour. His old Brown University house-mate, now a star CNN war correspondent, was marrying State Department spokesman James Rubin in the medieval chapel of Santo Stefano. The Kennedys held hands throughout the wedding ceremony, and when the priest told the groom to kiss the bride, John leaned over and kissed Carolyn tenderly.

No one was happier for the couple than John's sister. "Caroline knew they had had problems," a friend observed. "John never said a negative word about his wife to Caroline, but she knew all about their fights. So when it looked like Carolyn had finally come to terms with being in the spotlight, Caroline was thrilled."

John's sister was not thrilled, however, with John's new status as a licensed pilot. "She reminded him whenever she could that their mother did not want him flying, that it would break her heart to know he was going against her wishes. But after a while, when it became obvious that he didn't want to hear it, Caroline just gave up trying."

Mrs. JFK Jr. gave up as well. In the autumn of 1998, Carolyn was spending more and more time with her sister Lauren, who had returned after a year in Hong Kong and was just settling into her own penthouse apartment two blocks from 20 North Moore Street. The two women often shopped at upscale stores like Barneys or Prada, and made a point of meeting for lunch at least once or twice a week, sometimes more. Periodically, Carolyn spent the night at her sister's. When she wasn't with Lauren, Carolyn usually spent time with her fashion-industry friends—several of whom were gay and nearly all of whom kept a discreet distance from John. Donatella Ver-sace observed that John had "a completely open mind about her friends, who were different from his friends. He adored her person-ality, her outlook on life."

John, meantime, had his hands full with *George*. Thanks in large part to the unfolding Monica Lewinsky scandal that threatened to topple the Clinton administration, *George* posted record advertising sales of $1 million in April 1999. Pointing to the impact of political films like *Primary Colors* and the satirical *Wag the Dog*—not to mention the prospect of a messy impeachment trial—John was optimistic about the future of his magazine.

"All of a sudden the connection between politics and pop culture became vivid," he said. "You had these two movies and because of the current sensation in Washington, people are thinking of politics more. Suddenly, people were interested in the human component, which has always been our turf."

If anything, the growing perception of a moral vacuum in the nation's capital fueled speculation that John might enter the political fray. "John felt the strong sense of pressure and expectations," his friend John Perry Barlow said. "But he didn't like getting something he didn't feel he'd earned. John was also a free spirit in a lot of ways. He was used to one kind of scrutiny—the kind that was a nuisance but still allowed him to be John. He did not want to go into politics quite yet because of the very different, much more intense scrutiny it entailed. He was afraid if he ran for office, he couldn't go on being who he was."

That didn't keep his friends from occasionally needling him on the subject. At a joint awards banquet hosted by John and fellow philanthropist Paul Newman in May 1999, John thought it would be "amusing" to seat Barlow opposite him—and between the disparate likes of former Republican Senator Alfonse D'Amato and controversial rap superstar Puff Daddy.

"D'Amato and I tried to convince John to run for Mayor of New York City—as a Republican," Barlow said. "It was in jest at first, but John was really thinking it over. In many ways, John was quite conservative—socially I think he was more of a Republican than a Democrat. He had such a strong sense of what was appropriate behavior—John knew right from wrong. He would have made a great mayor. He really understood New York and he loved it dearly."

Ironically, John was a more polished campaigner than any of his politically active cousins. "Everybody who ever met him will say the same thing: 'He's a regular guy.' John had a way of getting people past the 'Oh my God it's *the* John' thing and getting people to look at *him*—the person," Barlow said. "He put you at ease instantly because he was genuinely fascinated with other people's lives. He wanted to know *your* story."

JFK Jr. made it clear to those closest to him that some day he would take the plunge. "He intended to run for office once he felt he'd earned it," Barlow said. "He thought he had a lot of time . . ."

John had confidently predicted that *George* would turn a profit in 1999, a full year ahead of schedule. But by October 1998, sales and ad revenue took another inexplicable dive. More than ever, John poured himself into the business. He often stayed at the office until dawn, and at times came in to work on the weekends.

Throughout the magazine's history, every employee from cleaning and security personnel to secretaries and copy editors regarded him as thoughtful and friendly. One night when *George* staffers were on deadline, John hopped on his bike, rode in the rain to the nearest Italian takeout place, and came back, soaking wet, with five pizzas. "He was the kind of person who would hold the elevator door open for you and always say hi," said a researcher at the magazine. "Just a warm, regular guy. To me, he was the perfect boss."

To drum up more advertising business from Italian designers, John traveled to Rome and Milan—without Carolyn. In a scene reminiscent of Princess Diana's trip to the Taj Mahal sans Prince Charles, John was photographed sightseeing in Rome, strolling through the Piazza Navona alone.

On the thirty-fifth anniversary of his father's assassination, John was alone again—this time ordering up Chinese food after taking Friday for a walk. A few days later, he celebrated Thanksgiving at Hyannis Port with the rest of the Kennedy clan. Carolyn, who had been so warmly embraced by the family, preferred to stay behind in New York and celebrate the holiday with several of her fashion buddies.

They appeared smiling and affectionate toward each other at a benefit at New York's Tavern on the Green that December, but the calculated attempt to lead separate but equal lives was beginning to take its toll on the marriage. John and Carolyn began seeing a marriage counselor in March 1999. There would be rumors of drug abuse on her part and a sexual estrangement that had lasted for months. One press report would depict John sitting over a Beck's beer at Walker's, a bar not far from his apartment, sobbing to a friend about Carolyn's addiction to antidepressants and cocaine. John also allegedly confessed that Carolyn had moved into the spare bedroom and that they had not had sex for a year.

There would also be rumors that Carolyn had had numerous affairs, and that out of desperation John cheated on his wife with at least two other women. But to many she seemed more content than ever in her role as Mrs. JFK Jr. One of the reasons, she told the *New York Daily News,* was that she stopped reading about herself in the newspapers. "I'm a happy person, and maybe a better person," she said, "for not knowing." At the White House Correspondents Dinner that May, she sat in John's lap as she had in the past and they laughed and nuzzled tenderly for the cameras.

There were problems in the marriage that final summer, unquestionably. But this seemed only consistent with the passionate, rollercoaster nature of their relationship. "They laughed a lot together," said Paul Wilmot, echoing the sentiment of many of their friends. "They were a very warm, happy couple." That was apparent when John and Carolyn dined at Chez Josephine, a French restaurant in New York's theater district. John got up from his table and requested a special tune from pianist Chris Curtis—Elton John's poignant ballad "Your Song."

Long before he met Carolyn, John had displayed the passionate nature that led to public battles with the other woman he felt serious enough about to consider marrying, Daryl Hannah. What Hannah apparently lacked, Carolyn had in abundance—a hot-tempered feistiness equal to his. This appeared to those who knew them as an ingredient essential to maintaining a level of passion in the marriage. "Carolyn was a tempestuous, passionate human being," Barlow said. "She could feel everything around her. The bottom line is that they really loved other deeply." Insisted Wilmot: "He had probably found his true soul mate in her."

Whatever the state of their union at any given time, John and Carolyn never wavered in their support of one another's friends, rising to the occasion when someone inside their charmed circle was in crisis. Lee's only son, Tony Radziwill, had been more to John than a cousin or his closest friend. Each, Caroline Kennedy once said, was "the brother the other didn't have."

For a decade, Radziwill had been battling cancer. But by 1998 it was plainly evident that he was losing. "Tony Radziwill's illness was really tearing John up for the last year," John Perry Barlow said. "He did everything he could for Tony, but he knew he was dying and they really loved each other."

John always spent time with his surrogate brother, but it was Carolyn Bessette-Kennedy who kept a ten-day vigil at Radziwill's side in his hospital room as he underwent debilitating chemotherapy. In a last-ditch effort to save Radziwill after conventional surgery, radiation, and chemotherapy had failed, Carolyn brought Radziwill to Dr. Gil Lederman at Staten Island University Hospital for stereotactic body radiosurgery—a revolutionary procedure that delivers precise doses of radiation to the cancer with pinpoint accuracy.

Carolyn accompanied Radziwill's wife Carole Ann to Dr. Lederman's office. "Carolyn sat shoulder to shoulder with the patient's spouse," he recalled, "their pinky fingers intertwined." Carolyn was with Tony when he arrived for each treatment and stayed to take him home afterward. "Her bright eyes and loving way gave him tremendous confidence," Dr. Lederman said. "She was soothing and reassuring." While she sat in the waiting room, Carolyn called John on her cell phone to keep him informed concerning his cousin's condition.

That summer, John and Carolyn insisted that Tony stay at Red Gate Farm while he continued to receive treatments on Martha's Vineyard. Like John, Radziwill was an irrepressible bike rider. Pale and thin, he astounded doctors by pedaling to and from his chemotherapy sessions at the local hospital.

While Jackie had seldom ventured from her own secluded Shangri-La, canoeing on one of her ponds, strolling the moors, or running along her 4,620 feet of private beach at secluded Red Gate Farm, her son was a fixture around Martha's Vineyard. On any given weekend during the summer months he could be spotted biking to the beach at Katama, Rollerblading past the Kelly House in downtown Edgartown, standing on the tiny ferry to Chappaquiddick, or cruising toward Menemsha in his vintage black Pontiac GTO convertible. He had also been a familiar sight in the skies over Martha's Vineyard, piloting his ultralight "flying lawnmower"—the Buckeye powered parachute—over the beach while locals, shielding their eyes from the sun, took bets on whether he would be blown out to sea.

More recently, John had taken to the skies over Martha's Vineyard in his new Piper Saratoga. "A beautiful young man" was the way longtime local resident Tony Di Lorenzo described him. "A great guy, but sadly he was a showboater. A lot of young guys are, I guess." According to Di Lorenzo, John had actually begun buzzing Red Gate Farm the previous summer in his Cessna with N529JK emblazoned on the fuselage. "All summer long," Di Lorenzo said, he would "buzz his mother's house. He would buzz it, go up, dive down and show all his friends where his house was."

But Kennedy was not the only young pilot to buzz property on the island, and he was popular enough with local residents that no one ever complained. Because of his mother's ties to the Vineyard, John made a point of contributing to local charities. In keeping with his philosophy of low-profile giving, his generosity went unpublicized. A rare exception was the 1996 auction to benefit Martha's Vineyard Community Services, in which a couple donated $12,500 for the pleasure of going on a bike ride with JFK Jr. around the island.

Nearly every weekend that summer, Carolyn and John would rendezvous at Martha's Vineyard—he flying up and she, more often than not, taking the ferry from Hyannis or a scheduled flight from LaGuardia. Resigned to her husband's flying but still worried that something might go wrong, Carolyn met with another nervous spouse—Harrison Ford's wife, Melissa Mathison—and the two women decided they would take flying lessons. Ford kept three planes, including his prized Husky, at New Jersey's Teterboro Airport, just a few minutes from John's Piper Saratoga at the Essex County Airport. (John had originally flown out of Teterboro, where John Travolta and Bill Cosby also park their planes, but moved to the smaller Essex Airport because the mood there was more relaxed.)

Both Carolyn and Melissa Mathison worried about what might happened if their husbands became incapacitated at the controls—a concern shared by Kennedy. "John and I spoke several times about Carolyn learning to fly," recalled his friend and fellow pilot David A. Green. "He wanted her to know how to take over the plane if anything went wrong. He even got Carolyn a book called *The Pinch Hitter's Manual,* a guide showing non-flyers how to pilot and land a plane in an emergency."

Toward that end, Carolyn and Melissa agreed to start their lessons in late July—a week after Rory Kennedy's Hyannis Port wedding. (In October 1999, Harrison Ford and his flight instructor would crash-land a Bell 206 Jet Ranger helicopter forty-five miles northwest of Los Angeles. Miraculously, both men would walk away unharmed.)

On Saturday, July 10, John and Carolyn went to dinner at the Wharf, a casual seafood restaurant in Edgartown. Later, they drove across the island to Oak Bluffs for a round of margaritas with friends at a sawdust-on-the-floor bar called the Lamppost.

When their friends paid the bill shortly after 1 A.M., Carolyn took waitress Meredith Katz aside. Handing her twenty dollars, Carolyn whispered to the twenty-year-old Tulane University student, "I know how expensive rents are here on the island."

As they left the Lamppost that night, their friends asked if they would be coming up to the Vineyard the following weekend as usual. No, John replied. "Next weekend is my cousin Rory's wedding in Hyannis Port. I promised I'd go."

We are tied to the ocean. And when we go back to the sea . . . we are going back from whence we came.

—*John F. Kennedy*

The next five years should have been the great years for them.

—*Paul Wilmot*

John's a good boy, but he's always getting himself in a jam.

—*Jackie*

9
=

The lone fisherman angling for striped bass off Squibnocket Pond on Martha's Vineyard looked up to see a small aircraft flying toward the island. Victor Pribanic, a forty-five-year-old Pittsburgh attorney who had been coming to the Vineyard for twenty years, thought nothing of it and went back to his fishing. Within moments, there was a loud bang—the sound of an explosion, perhaps, or something hitting the water—over Pribanic's right shoulder. When he turned there was nothing—just the inky surface of the Atlantic bleeding into the night sky. Pribanic scratched his crew-cut head, shrugged, and kept fishing until 1 A.M., reeling in a single striper before heading to bed.

Raucous laughter spilled out of the house and out onto the lawn of the Kennedy compound at Hyannis Port, where a billowy six-peaked wedding tent had been pitched for the next day's ceremony. Even for a Kennedy, Rory seemed to have endured more than her fair share of tragedy in her thirty years. Born six months after her father Robert's assassination, she was only fifteen when her brother

David died of a drug overdose. While her brothers ricocheted from one sordid scandal to the next, she, like the other Kennedy women, somehow stayed above it all. And it was Rory, now a documentary filmmaker in New York, who only eighteen months earlier had given mouth-to-mouth resuscitation to her dying brother Michael after he slammed headlong into a tree while skiing.

Outside, the same thick blanket of haze that had blinded John at the controls of his plane now settled over the white-shingled, green-walled compound. But inside the main house, where the rehearsal dinner for Rory's wedding to writer Mark Bailey was in full swing, no one was paying much attention to the weather. There were toasts and gifts—including a quilt with each square containing a handprint, a footprint, or a symbol that represented each member of the family. "Everybody was having a wonderful time," said one family friend. "It was a perfect evening, just perfect. Everyone was so happy for Rory."

John and Carolyn were not missed. Since they first had to drop Lauren Bessette off at Martha's Vineyard, it was understood that they would be arriving late at the rehearsal dinner that night.

But at tiny, wood-shingled Martha's Vineyard Airport, a couple who had come to pick up Lauren began inquiring as to the whereabouts of JFK Jr.'s plane as early as 8:30 P.M. An employee in the flight-operations office, Barry Bissaillon, had not seen John's plane, but checked with the control tower to see if Kennedy had in fact filed a flight plan. He hadn't.

Over an hour later, Lauren's friends again asked if anyone had seen or heard from JFK Jr. As was the case at countless small airports around the country, the tower at Martha's Vineyard airport had just closed at 10 P.M., leaving only Adam Budd, a twenty-one-year-old intern, on duty.

At 10:05 P.M., Budd, whose primary job was as a maintenance worker—a "ramp rat," in aviation parlance—called the Federal Aviation Agency's station in Bridgeport, Connecticut.

AN FAA AIR TRAFFIC CONTROL SPECIALIST   Good evening, Bridgeport Flight Service.

BUDD: Hi. I was wondering if you could track an airplane for me. Would you know about Teterboro or Westchester? There's two tail numbers.

FAA: OK, now, what's this all about now? Who are you?

BUDD: I'm with airport operations.

FAA: From where?

BUDD: Martha's Vineyard Airport.

FAA: OK.

BUDD: Actually, Kennedy Jr.'s on board. He's, ah, they wanna know, uh, where he is.

FAA: Well, is he on an IFR [Instrument Flight Rules] flight plan or what?

BUDD: They don't know.

FAA: You got an aircraft number?

BUDD: Yeah, there's two of them. It's either 529JK or 9253N.

FAA: OK, and who's this? Who [sic] are you calling from?

BUDD: This is from Martha's Vineyard Airport, and that's where they're headed.

FAA: Your name?

BUDD: Adam.

FAA: Adam what?

BUDD: Adam Budd.

FAA: Butt?

BUDD: Budd.

FAA: OK, well are you with operations there?

BUDD: Yeah. If it's not too much trouble.

FAA: Well, we don't give this information out to people over the phone.

BUDD: OK, well, if it's too much trouble, it's . . .

FAA: Okey-doke.

BUDD: I'll just have 'em wait.

FAA: What?

BUDD: All right, it's not a big deal.

FAA: All right.

BUDD: Take it easy.

The FAA official hung up the phone, still not convinced of Budd's identity and detecting no sense of urgency in the young man's voice. No action was taken.

Ted Kennedy had been in Washington that Friday, spearheading a fight in the Senate for a more expansive Patients' Bill of Rights. When a family friend called the senator shortly before 11 P.M. to say that John's plane had not yet arrived, Ted immediately called his nephew's TriBeCa apartment.

For a split second, he was relieved to hear someone pick up the phone. It was, it turned out, a friend of the couple whose air-conditioning was out; with temperatures in the nineties, John and Carolyn had invited the friend to stay in their apartment while they were away for the weekend.

"My nephew's plane is overdue at Martha's Vineyard," Ted asked. "Do you know if they left New York?"

Yes, came the unwanted reply. Yes, they did leave New York.

Ted and several other family members and friends burned up the phone lines between Cape Cod and Washington trying to locate John. At midnight the FAA, reacting to Senator Kennedy's inquiries, finally called the Martha's Vineyard communications center, which handles emergency 911 calls, and asked if John's flight had arrived. The night watchman at the airport, Paul Ronhock, checked the parking lot and reported back that Kennedy's plane was not there.

It was not until 2:15 A.M. that family friend Carol Ratowell called the coast guard operations center in Woods Hole. Her call, unlike Budd's, was urgent. They, in turn, contacted the First Coast Guard District Command in Boston—which contacted the FAA. Incredibly, only now did the FAA check to see if John's plane, like so many others caught in the disorienting haze that night, had rerouted to a different airport.

At 3 A.M., having failed to locate the missing plane, the FAA alerted both the coast guard and the Air Force Rescue Coordination Center at Virginia's Langley Air Force Base. Coast Guard cutters spent the next three hours on a wild-goose chase, checking out false reports of debris supposedly spotted off Long Island and a beacon deep in the waters beyond Montauk (Kennedy's plane was equipped with a transponder, but not one that could be counted on to work underwater).

A little after 5 A.M., the phone rang at the Bessette home in Greenwich, Connecticut. Ann Freeman "was hopeful for a while" that John might turn up safe with her daughter. "And then," said a family friend, "common sense prevailed."

Tony Radziwill tried to contact Caroline on vacation in Stanley, Idaho, but something was wrong with phones at the lodge where the Schlossbergs were staying. Eventually, he got through to Police Chief Philip Enright, the only law-enforcement officer in Stanley. Enright drove to the lodge and, at 4:30 A.M. local time (6:30 Eastern), woke Caroline up with news of an urgent call from Massachusetts.

Caroline and Ed had planned to celebrate their thirteenth wedding anniversary and his fifty-fourth birthday on July 19 by rafting through the region known as the River of No Return. Friday night, they had checked into suite 231 of the Mountain Village Resort to rest up for their adventure.

Tony was the first to tell Caroline her brother's plane was missing, triggering a series of calls to friends and family. When she finally got through to Teddy, he tried to reassure her that there was still a good chance that John had landed at some small airfield and just neglected to check in. "You know how John always manages to come out of these things," Ted told his niece. But from the beginning Caroline, who, like her mother had worried that something like this might happen if he learned to fly, appeared to harbor no illusions about her brother's fate. Caroline and Ed waited until 7 P.M. Saturday evening before heading back to New York aboard a private plane and driving directly to their weekend home in Bridgehampton, Long Island.

A half hour after Caroline was contacted, White House Chief of Staff John Podesta called Camp David and informed President Clinton that JFK Jr.'s plane was missing. Clinton, authorizing whatever measures were necessary to find the plane, asked to be briefed regularly as the search progressed.

By 7:45 A.M., an Air National Guard helicopter, a C-130 Hercules cargo plane, a UH-25 Falcon, fifteen Civil Air Patrol planes, and two Coast Guard HH-60 Jayhawk choppers had taken off in search of JFK Jr.'s plane. On the water, a flotilla of patrol boats, search-and-rescue vessels, and Coast Guard cutters scoured an area between Martha's Vineyard and the tip of Long Island.

Back in New Jersey, Kyle Bailey was just getting up. Bailey, who had decided that he would not take a chance and leave for the Vineyard that night, had watched the previous evening as John, Carolyn, and Lauren Bessette took off from Essex County Airport. When he called Saturday morning to see if conditions had improved, along with the recording was a report that a plane with the aircraft number 9253N was missing.

A few minutes later, Bailey was brushing his teeth when, he said, "I remembered seeing the letter N on the side of Kennedy's plane. Then it suddenly hit me—'Oh, my God, could it possibly be his plane?'"

Bailey drove out to the airport. "I was praying all the way," he recalled. "I assumed he had just forgotten to file his flight plan. Or maybe he just turned around when he saw that the conditions were so lousy."

When he arrived at the Essex County Airport, Bailey was relieved to see that John's white convertible was gone. "It wasn't where I saw him park it, so as far as I was concerned that meant he had come back and probably driven home to Manhattan. But then I looked around to see if his plane was there—and it wasn't."

It was then that Bailey spotted a policeman. "Hey," he asked the officer, "they're looking for John Kennedy, aren't they?"

The cop looked at him and replied stonily, "No comment." Bailey would later learn that when police first checked on John's car, they noticed something strange—a note left on the windshield. Fearing that the car might be booby-trapped, or that JFK Jr. had been kidnapped and that the scrap of paper left on the car was in fact a ransom note, they called in the FBI.

The car was towed to another spot on the airport grounds, and the note examined. It turned out that it was from seventeen-year-old Brooke Olitsky, one of the teenage girls who had spotted John buying a banana, Evian, and batteries at Jack's Friendly Service and Sunoco station. "He was on crutches when I saw him," Olitsky recalled, "so I just left a note saying, 'I hope your leg feels better, and it was nice to see you.' "

That morning, investigators paid a call on Olitsky. "I met with the FBI for an hour and a half," she said, "just to make sure I wasn't some lunatic who sabotaged his plane or something."

As the reality of what had happened slowly sank in, Bailey got this "spooky, eerie, sort of sickening feeling. It dawned on me that I might have been the last person to see them alive." He was.

After five fruitless hours, the CIA was called in on the search, employing three KH-11 photographic satellites to make a visual sweep of the area. At around 1 P.M., sleek-hulled yachts competing in the annual Edgartown Yacht Club Regatta sailed past the small armada of vessels now concentrating their search on a twenty-by-twenty-mile area seventeen miles west of Martha's Vineyard.

At the same time, the first bits of debris were beginning to wash up on Philbin Beach, virtually at the doorstep of the four-hundred-acre estate John and Caroline had inherited from their mother. A plane wheel was recovered, and a square aqua duffel bag. Damon Seligson, a Bostonian vacationing on the Vineyard, spotted something black bobbing in the surf and waded in to retrieve it. "I just had an awful feeling in my stomach," said Seligson. It was an overnight bag, its owner's business card clearly visible in a clear plastic pocket. The card read LAUREN G. BESSETTE. MORGAN STANLEY DEAN WITTER. VICE PRESIDENT.

By now, squadrons of police in all-terrain vehicles were scouring the beach for wreckage. Over the next several hours, the sea would yield more pieces of the puzzle—a piece of landing gear, broken pieces of Styrofoam insulation, a foam headrest from an airplane seat, a black cosmetics bag containing a prescription bottle belonging to "Carolyn Kennedy."

More ships joined the search. The ninety-foot *Rude,* a National Oceanic and Atmospheric Administration vessel, used state-of-the-art sonar to comb the sandy seabed one hundred feet below. Meanwhile, the U.S.S. *Grasp,* a navy salvage vessel with a grappling arm capable of lifting any large piece of wreckage, raced toward the presumed crash site.

All the while, Rory Kennedy and her guests in the family compound at Hyannis Port were glued to their television sets, praying for any sign that John and his passengers were all right. "They were saying, 'There's still hope,' " said a friend who was there. " 'Never say never.' "

Nevertheless, by 6 P.M. the decision was made to postpone Rory's wedding indefinitely. The bride-to-be stood on the front porch, managing a wan smile as she waved goodbye to her guests. Under the tent where Rory was to have been married, mass was said Saturday morning, and Saturday evening, and again Sunday morning.

Meanwhile, back in Wyoming John Perry Barlow was reading the e-mail John had sent him on Friday consoling his friend on the death of his mother. "It's so strange," he mused. "Our friendship started out with me being a father figure to him and ended up with him being a father figure to me. Now I went to *him* for advice. I came to realize that he was simply the finest man I had ever known."

Two weeks earlier, Barlow had a chance to let John know how he felt about him. "They kept telling him he had it in him to achieve greatness, but he asked, 'Isn't it more challenging to be good man?' I told him he was already one, and that in time he'd be the other."

Back in Hyannis Port, the grim reality was only beginning to sink in. "Let's take a sail," Ethel told her sons as Kennedys again faced the unexpected loss of one of their own. "We need to take a sail." Wearing white shorts, a blue button-down shirt and a navy blue baseball cap, son Maxwell and his wife, Victoria, at her side, a barefoot Ethel strolled down the dock toward a waiting sailboat.

Before they could reach it, a neighbor walked up and Ethel embraced her warmly. How was the family coping? the neighbor wanted to know. "We're keeping up," Ethel replied. "We're keeping up." Then Ethel and the others climbed into the boat and headed out to sea. Over the next few days several of John's cousins—Bobby Kennedy Jr., William Kennedy Smith, and Ted Kennedy Jr. among them—either sailed or swam or ran along the beach as a way of coping with their anguish.

Caroline also distracted herself with physical activity. Just as John had Rollerbladed along Park Avenue the day of his mother's funeral, his sister strapped on a helmet and in the blistering hundred-degree heat biked past the small army of photographers who had camped outside her house.

Across the nation and the world that Sunday, millions of people prayed that somehow John, Carolyn, and Lauren would turn up alive. But late that night, Coast Guard Rear Admiral Richard Larrabee reluctantly announced that, given the chilly sixty-seven-degree water temperature, there was no longer any hope of finding John, Carolyn, and Lauren alive. The mission was no longer "Search and Rescue," but "Search and Recover."

On Monday, Caroline and Ed Schlossberg would have celebrated their thirteenth anniversary. Instead, she went for another bike ride in the searing summer heat. Meantime, Uncle Ted arrived to console his niece and spent part of the afternoon in the driveway, shooting baskets with Rose, Tatiana, and Jack. It did not escape the senator's notice that this day also marked the thirtieth anniversary of Chappaquiddick.

Pope John Paul II, vacationing in the Italian Alps, said a special prayer for John and all the Kennedys. Aides listened as he recalled the sight of three-year-old John-John saluting the coffin of America's first and thus far only Roman Catholic president. "This is only the latest tragedy," the pope lamented, "that family has suffered."

The rusted metal steps outside 20 North Moore Street were transformed into a shrine as hundreds of mourners filed past police barricades to leave flowers, candles, cards, American flags, and notes of condolence. In Washington, meanwhile, a grim-faced President Clinton fought back tears as he offered words of support for the Kennedys and the Bessettes. "For more than forty years now, the Kennedy family has inspired Americans to public service, strengthened our faith in the future, and moved our nation forward," he said. "Through it all they have suffered much, and given more."

Monday night, John's grief-stricken kin finally gave up hope. In a statement issued from Hyannis Port, Ted Kennedy said, "We are filled with unspeakable grief and sadness by the loss of John and Carolyn, and of Lauren Bessette. John was a shining light in all our lives, and in the lives of the nation and the world that first came to know him as a little boy.

"He was a devoted husband to Carolyn, a loving brother to Caroline, an amazing uncle to her children, a close and dear friend to his cousins, and a beloved nephew to my sisters and me. He was the adored son of two proud parents whom he now joins with God. We loved him deeply . . .

"John had many gifts and gave us great joy," he went on, "most especially when he brought his wonderful bride, Carolyn, into our lives. They had their own special brand of magic that touched everyone who knew and loved them. We are thankful for her life and for their lives together."

As they had too many times before, the Kennedys now began making funeral plans. United as they were in their grief, Ted and Caroline once again clashed over the size of the memorial service. Only five years before, the senator had argued that Jackie should have a big funeral at St. Patrick's Cathedral, only to be overruled by Caroline.

Now Ted, both cognizant of the nation's affection for John and possessing the career politician's natural penchant for spectacle, wanted his nephew to be given a large public funeral. Caroline's aunt Eunice also lobbied with her niece for a mass at the imposing Fifth Avenue cathedral. But a media circus was the last thing Caroline wanted. And she specifically resisted St. Patrick's as a venue. "Caroline has vivid memories of Bobby's funeral there," a friend said. "It was very traumatizing and overwhelming for a ten-year-old girl, and she just didn't want to dredge all that up. That's why she didn't want her mother's funeral at St. Patrick's, and that's why she didn't want John's there either."

Instead, she insisted on a small, private service at St. Thomas More Church on East 89th Street off Madison Avenue—the small, neo-Gothic stone church where Jackie took her children to mass every Sunday, and where they always marked the anniversary of JFK's assassination. Eventually, a compromise was reached. A memorial service would be held at St. Thomas More, but the guest list would include the President, the First Lady, and other dignitaries. At Caroline's request Ted, who had been given the sad task so many times before, would deliver the eulogy.

It remained to be seen if the plane or its occupants would ever be recovered. Scores of divers braved sharks, the frigid temperatures, and the treacherous currents, but after four days the plane was still missing. Then, shortly before 11:30 P.M. on Tuesday, a remote-operated underwater camera spotted the fuselage of John's Piper Saratoga lying upside down at a depth of 116 feet some seven and a half miles southwest of Martha's Vineyard. John's crumpled body was clearly visible, still strapped into the pilot's seat. But there was no sign of either Carolyn or Lauren.

As dawn broke on Wednesday, the *Grasp* moored over the crash site. It was one of those brilliant summer days on the Vineyard when the sun's white-yellow rays transform the surface of the ocean into a carpet of diamonds. Considering the grim task at hand, the weather could not have been more inappropriate.

At 10:30 A.M., two navy divers went into the water using ROVs (remote-operated vehicles) to get to the wreckage. They discovered that the plane's wings had been ripped off and that there were several smaller pieces strewn up to 120 feet apart. But a ten-foot section of the cabin remained intact. Inside, John's body was strapped into his cockpit seat. The impact had been so great that the windshield had been sheared off. Working forty-minute shifts, the divers were finally able to locate Carolyn and Lauren several yards away on the ocean floor, still strapped into their seats.

By the time divers attached grappling hooks to the fuselage that afternoon, Ted Kennedy, along with his sons Ted Jr. and Rhode Island congressman Patrick Kennedy, had already been taken by coast guard tender to the *Grasp*. All unauthorized boats and aircraft were ordered not to come within five miles of the *Grasp* as it began to lift the plane out of the water. An ashen-faced Ted, wearing beige shorts, a blue-and-white polo shirt, and deck shoes with no socks, stood on the deck and watched as the cables slowly pulled the Piper Saratoga up from the ocean floor.

Shortly after 4:30 P.M., the first of the badly mangled bodies broke the glistening surface of the water. Ted, expressionless behind dark glasses, took a deep breath. One by one, they were brought up and placed on gurneys. Then the wreckage itself was maneuvered onto the deck of the *Grasp*. There was no doubt about the identities of the three victims, but Ted had promised Caroline he would be there when this horrible moment came. Tears streamed down the face of at least one crew member as others struggled to contain their emotions.

At about the same time the bodies were being recovered, President Clinton was fending off criticism that the extraordinary five-day search effort—the largest ever for a private plane—had cost the taxpayers millions. "Because of the role of the Kennedy family in our national life, and because of the enormous losses they have sustained in our lifetimes," he said at a press conference, "I thought it was appropriate to give them a few more days." He was not about to apologize for his decision. "If anyone believes that was wrong, the Coast Guard is not at fault, I am. It was the right thing to do under the circumstances."

The *Grasp* brought the victims' remains to Woods Hole, where they were placed in two vans from the Barnstable County Medical Examiner's office. Ted and his sons then climbed into waiting limousines that would be part of the motorcade accompanying the vans to Barnstable County Hospital in Bourne. Arriving at the hospital around 7:10 P.M., the bodies were wheeled into the morgue, where two coroners waited to begin the grim task of conducting autopsies on the bodies.

Portly, red-faced, exhausted from lack of sleep, Ted Kennedy still sought to exert control. It was agreed that only the pilot's body would receive a complete autopsy, but Ted clashed with local authorities on the question of whether photographs would be taken of the bodies—the normal procedure in such cases.

As had been expected, after the violent crash and five days at the bottom of the sea, the bodies were, in the words of one eyewitness, "in pretty bad shape." Ted and the rest of the family worried that any photographs of the victims might wind up in a tabloid or on the Internet. But state police were adamant. A compromise was reached: Autopsy photos were taken, as required by law—but the film would only be developed in the event of some future inquiry.

The four-hour autopsy on John was conducted by Chief Medical Examiner Dr. Richard J. Evans and his associate, Dr. James M. Weiner. All three victims, the medical examiners quickly concluded, had died instantly from multiple injuries incurred when the plane slammed into the water at more than sixty miles an hour. Beyond that, authorities would offer no details. Even before they began examining the bodies, Massachusetts Governor Paul Cellucci ordered Evans and Weiner to speak to no one.

Ted had consulted with Caroline and the grief-stricken Bessette and Freeman families, and everyone agreed that the bodies should be cremated as soon as possible. Shortly before midnight Wednesday, scarcely seven hours after they had been lifted out of the water, the bodies of John, Carolyn, and Lauren were rushed to the Duxbury Crematory in nearby Duxbury. Their ashes were then turned over to Ted Kennedy.

Ted's desire to keep gruesome autopsy photos from falling into the wrong hands was understandable. But the rush to cremate the bodies, as well as the decision not to do autopsies on the Bessette sisters, raised eyebrows.

Ever since Chappaquiddick, Ted had steered the family through one legal minefield after another. There had already been widespread criticism in the media of John's decision to fly that night, and charges that a congenital streak of Kennedy recklessness had cost John not only his life but the lives of his two innocent passengers. It was pointed out that John not only took off under questionable conditions and without an instrument rating, but that he also did so with a severely injured foot that may have made it difficult for him to operate the rudder and the brakes.

Advised that the Bessettes might indeed have the basis for a wrongful-death suit if it could be proven that John had acted irresponsibly—and undoubtedly eager to put the nightmare behind all the grieving relatives—Ted had moved quickly to facilitate a burial at sea.

Not surprisingly, many assumed that John would be interred at Arlington alongside his parents and his siblings. A call was made to the White House, and President Clinton personally approved plans to lay John to rest next to the eternal flame. But this invitation did not extend to Carolyn Bessette, and the Bessette girls' mother insisted from Greenwich that John and Carolyn must be interred together.

It was suggested that perhaps John could be buried with Carolyn at the Brookline cemetery that is the resting place of Joe, Rose, and other Kennedy family members. But again, the Bessette family pointed out that neither Carolyn nor Lauren had ties to Massachusetts.

Caroline, sensitive to the reality that Ann had lost two of her three children in a plane piloted by her brother, searched for a solution. It was then that she recalled John had once mentioned that he wished to be buried at sea.

The little girl who had once clung to her mother as JFK's riderless horse walked by seemed to have inherited Jackie's inherent sense of what was right in circumstances like these. She did not want to return yet again to Arlington, or wind up turning a private cemetery plot into some shrine à la Graceland. After talking it over with the Bessettes, it was agreed that the best way to avoid a circus atmosphere and preserve family privacy was to scatter the ashes of all three over the Atlantic.

At 9 A.M. Thursday, seventeen relatives boarded the cutter *Sanibel* and were taken to the *Briscoe,* a navy destroyer that had steamed up from training exercises off Virginia on direct orders from Defense Secretary William Cohen. Press helicopters were kept ten miles away as the *Briscoe* then steamed down Vineyard Sound, escorted by three cutters. On board, the family members carried with them three American flags, each folded in a triangle, three wreaths made of red, yellow, and white flowers, and three urns containing the ashes of John, his wife, and his sister-in-law. Caroline, her red eyes concealed behind dark glasses, sat down in a wooden slat-backed chair, head bowed.

After thirty minutes, the *Briscoe* stopped and turned toward Red Gate Farm in a symbolic salute to Jackie. Then it proceeded farther out to sea, stopping not far from where the *Grasp* was still going about its grim business of recovering pieces of John's plane from the sea floor.

It was then that the black-clad mourners, flanked by crew members in dress whites, moved toward the stern of the *Briscoe* and were seated as the flag was lowered to half-staff. Two Catholic navy chaplains assisted the Reverend Charles O'Byrne, the priest who had married John and Carolyn, in conducting the simple fifteen-minute ceremony. There were readings from the Book of Wisdom—"the souls of the just are in the hands of God, and no torment shall touch them"—and a brass quintet from the Newport Navy Band played "Abide with Me" and "For All the Saints."

An officer carried the three urns down a ladder to a platform just above the choppy surface of the water. Caroline, Ted, and the other family members followed, then, as the quintet played the Navy Hymn, scattered the ashes of their loved ones on the waves. "We commit their elements to the deep," intoned the navy's deputy chief of chaplains, Rear Admiral Barry Black, "for we are dust and unto dust we shall return, but the Lord Jesus Christ will change our bodies to be like his in glory, for he is risen the first born from the dead. So let us commend our brother and sisters to the Lord, that the Lord may embrace them in peace and raise them up on the last day . . ."

At the same time, a memorial service was being held off the coast of Virginia aboard the *John F. Kennedy,* the carrier christened by Caroline in 1967. After the crew of five thousand observed a moment of silence, the ship's chaplain, Lieutenant Commander Sal Aguilera, said a prayer. "We who are aboard the *John F. Kennedy* have a special kinship, and so we pray you console the hearts of the Kennedy family and all Americans who today mourn the loss of these young people."

"It was as if Jackie were orchestrating these ceremonies," said Tish Baldrige, praising the services for their elegant simplicity. Indeed, the hand of fate seemed to be in evidence everywhere on this blindingly sunny day in July. John's ashes were being spread within sight of his mother's house on what would have been Rose Kennedy's 109th birthday.

On a bluff not far from Red Gate Farm, several hundred people had gathered to watch the *Briscoe* set sail on its sad mission. Charlotte Cook of Sacramento said she was there to say goodbye to "America's child." All agreed that, given the Kennedys' historic ties to the sea, the ceremony was fitting. "What a gorgeous place to be buried," said Kathy O'Donogue of Rochester, Massachusetts. "It's the perfect place for a perfect guy."

A continent away in Los Angeles, the woman who had nearly become Mrs. John F. Kennedy Jr. spoke for the first time since the crash. "I find it so hard to believe that John is gone," Daryl Hannah said in a press release. "But now we must face reality and embrace the memory of his spirit and his voracious lust for life, which will live on. My heart goes out to both families."

From the steps of their apartment building in TriBeCa to the Vatican to the U.S. embassy in Paris to the Kennedy ancestral home in Duganstown, Ireland, makeshift shrines blossomed everywhere. None was more poignant than the simple cross on Philbin Beach made of driftwood tied together by grapevines. Beneath the cross, the names JOHN, CAROLYN, AND LAUREN were spelled out in small stones. On one of the stones someone had scratched the words TOO SOON.

As the *Briscoe* headed back to port, mourners released a blizzard of flower petals from the ship's fantail—blossoms that were originally intended to decorate the tables at Rory Kennedy's wedding reception. Tony Radziwill, in the midst of his own life-and-death struggle against cancer, had been pushed on board in a wheelchair. Now John's closest cousin and best friend—the man he had chosen to be executor of his will—sat with the others on the deck of the *Briscoe,* resting his head on a cane as he stared out to sea. "John is my brother," he said. "He made my life a lot brighter. I love and will miss him forever."

"It was very hard just being there," said an enlisted crew member. "A lot of guys got very emotional—especially two or three officers. They didn't cry or anything, but you could tell that they were really struggling."

That night in Hyannis Port, a drained Ted Kennedy worked on his eulogy until 1 A.M., then flew to New York the next morning and reworked it at the apartment of his sister Pat Lawford. Only a few hours later, 315 relatives, friends, and dignitaries filed slowly into St. Thomas More Church on Manhattan's narrow, tree-lined East 89th Street. The President, the First Lady, and their daughter, Chelsea, were there, as were John's childhood hero Muhammad Ali, a select few *George* staffers, Frisbee-playing pals from Central Park, old chums from Brown, and such New Frontier veterans as Robert McNamara,

John Kenneth Galbraith, and Arthur Schlesinger Jr. Nearly all had to present a printed invitation before being allowed inside.

Outside the sun shone brilliantly, but the interior of St. Thomas More was dark and solemn. What rays of sunshine did manage to struggle through the heavy stained-glass windows dappled the stone floor with an ethereal if muted display of light and color. On either side of the altar were two white hydrangeas.

Senator Kennedy stepped up to the pulpit, cleared his throat, and with grace and humor performed the task for which he had received far too much practice. "Once, when they asked John what he would do if he went into politics and was elected president, he said, 'I guess the first thing is call up Uncle Teddy and gloat.' I loved that," Ted said, cocking his head to one side. "It was so like his father."

His voice cracking, Ted invoked the memory of the little boy who scampered about the White House and saluted his father's flag-draped coffin. "But John was so much more than those long-ago images emblazoned in our minds. He was a boy who grew into a man with a zest for life and a love of adventure. He was a pied piper who brought us all along. He was blessed with a father and mother who never thought anything mattered more than their children."

Along the way, Ted paid tribute to Jackie's "unbreakable strength of spirit" that guided John "surely and securely to the future . . . Above all, Jackie gave him a place to be himself, to grow up, to laugh and cry, to dream and strive on his own.

"He had amazing grace. He accepted who he was, but he cared more about what he could and should become," Ted went on, pointing out that John drove his own car and flew his own plane because that was "how he wanted it. He was the king of his domain."

Ted praised John for founding *George* and Reaching Up and his work for the philanthropic Robin Hood Foundation, but quickly returned to the subject of John the son, brother, and husband. "John was also the son who was once protected by his mother. He went on to become her pride—and then her protector in her final days. He was the Kennedy who loved us all," Ted went on, his voice trembling, "but who especially cherished his sister, Caroline, celebrated her brilliance and took strength and joy from their lifelong mutual-admiration society."

Drawing on the phrase that so touchingly portrayed JFK's brief time as president, Ted continued, "And for a thousand days, he was a husband who adored the wife who became his perfect soulmate."

Ted took a long breath before going on. "John was one of Jackie's two miracles. He was still becoming the person he would be, and doing it by the beat of his own drummer. He had only just begun. There was in him a great promise of things to come."

Then the Kennedy paterfamilias pledged the Kennedys would hold an eternal wake for their prince: "He was lost on that troubled night, but we will always wake for him, so that his time . . . which was cut in half, will live forever in our memory and in our beguiled and broken hearts.

"We dared to think . . . this John Kennedy would live to comb gray hair, with his beloved Carolyn by his side. But like his father," Ted said, his voice catching, "he had every gift but length of years.

"We who have loved him from the day he was born, and watched the remarkable man he became, now bid him farewell. God bless you, John and Carolyn. We love you, and we always will."

As Ted stepped down from the pulpit, Caroline stood up to hug him. For all the undeniable eloquence of his eulogy, Caroline was the emotional focal point of the service. She recalled that Jackie had instilled a love of literature in both her children, and then recited Prospero's speech from Shakespeare's *The Tempest,* a play her brother had performed at Brown in 1981. "Our revels now are ended," she quoted. "We are such stuff as dreams are made on, and our little life is rounded with a sleep."

While hip-hop artist Wyclef Jean of the Fugees performed the Jimmy Cliff reggae song "Many Rivers to Cross" ("It was time for me to go home / And I'll be smiling in paradise"), Caroline's children, Rose, now eleven, Tatiana, nine, and six-year-old Jack lit candles. The moment was too much for many mourners, whose sobs were plainly audible above the music.

John's death had clearly dealt a hammer blow to the Kennedy family's fabled never-say-die spirit. "I've seen this family in other sad circumstances," said one of the mourners, "and I'm telling you, this was different. This gang is shell-shocked, blown away. This wasn't,

'Let's have ten family members get up and say the torch is passed, time for a new generation.' None of that. This was a funeral."

Yet, unlike several others at St. Thomas More that sunny Friday, Caroline never broke down. Remaining cool and in control, she greeted the other mourners warmly, and even put a comforting arm around relatives less adroit at masking their sorrow. Outside St. Thomas More, Caroline smiled wanly as she walked down the stone steps to the street. Her daughter Rose, on the other hand, did the sort of thing the eleven-year-old John-John might have done and stuck her tongue out at photographers. As Caroline's limousine pulled away from the church, she rolled down her window and waved to the thousands of onlookers who jammed the sidewalks.

The next evening, Caroline and Ted were among the twenty-five Kennedys present at the memorial for Lauren Bessette at Greenwich's Episcopal Christ Church. Ann Freeman handled all the arrangements; her sole surviving child, Lauren's twin, Lisa, was too overwrought to help in the planning. With good reason, certainly. At one point, Ann Freeman was walking with church secretary Mary Marks when they passed one woman telling another that she had recently given birth to twins. Ann turned to Marks and said quietly, "I used to have twins . . ."

Life went on, although over the next few weeks there would be constant reminders of what had been so suddenly, inexplicably lost. Ann and Richard Freeman went to the apartment at 20 North Moore and personally cleared out their daughter's possessions. At one point Dr. Freeman, his face etched with grief, walked to his car carrying a framed sequence of photographs showing Carolyn and John embracing. The Freemans also left with a Turkish copper-and-leather jewelry box—a memento of the Kennedys' honeymoon—Carolyn's beat-up hiking boots, and a cardboard box marked J.K.—MY BOOKS. Among the couple's collection of books were Bill Moyers's *Healing and the Mind,* Barbara Woodhouse's *No Bad Dogs,* and two cookbooks John had given Carolyn as a joke. Inside the front cover of each were inscribed the phone numbers of their favorite take-out restaurants.

Oddly, one of John's possessions would go unclaimed for eleven days following the crash. His white convertible remained parked at Essex County Airport until someone finally noticed it was still there and called to have it picked up.

Perhaps most confused by it all was Friday, the couple's beloved black-and-white Canaan. Ironically, Friday's life had been spared only because the dog hated to fly and had become impossible to handle in the cabin of John's plane.

After the accident, Friday was taken along with Carolyn's cat, Ruby, to Red Gate Farm to be cared for by Jackie's longtime butler, Ephigenio Pinheiro. "You can hear Friday crying at night," a neighbor said. "He can't understand why John doesn't come home." Pinheiro reportedly told a friend: "Friday's become very lethargic and won't eat. He's pining for John and I'm afraid he's going to die of a broken heart."

Donna Dodson, who sold John the dog, was also concerned. "John told me how much he loved Friday and how his dog had formed such a strong bond with him," she said. "It's distressing to me to think of the trauma that Friday is going through." Later, Friday would be taken to live with Caroline's young family on Park Avenue.

On August 2, two dozen guests looked on as Rory Kennedy and Mark Bailey were wed at the Greek villa of shipping tycoon Vardis Vardinoyannis. "It was the happy ending," said a member of the bride's family, "that they both deserved."

But there was to be no happy ending for Tony Radziwill. On August 10, less than three weeks after he attended John's funeral, John's surrogate brother lost his battle with cancer. (In another odd twist, Stanley Tretick, the photographer who took the famous pictures of John-John peering from beneath his father's desk in the Oval Office, died three days after John's plane went down.)

These human moments were all but ignored in the stampede to assign blame for the crash. The Piper Saratoga had had an excellent safety record, and after National Transportation Safety Board experts examined the wreckage, they determined that mechanical failure did not cause the crash. (The NTSB crated the wreckage and turned it over to Caroline. Fearing that pieces of the plane might find their way into the hands of souvenir hunters, Caroline planned to have what was left of her brother's Piper Saratoga destroyed.)

Several aviation experts suggested that perhaps John was actually not experienced enough to fly the Piper Saratoga, a high-performance plane with retractable landing gear. Others countered that the Piper Saratoga was, in aviation argot, quite "forgiving"—the sort of pilot-friendly aircraft that was by no means beyond the capabilities of a flyer with John's level of experience.

The FAA's false weather reports notwithstanding, consensus was building that the NTSB would blame the crash on pilot error, citing in particular the fact that after takeoff John did not once radio for help. Fellow aviators tended to chalk the crash up to a common—albeit fatal—mistake. "In all sincerity, he really worked at flying," said Andrew Ferguson, president of Air Bound Aviation, where John parked his Piper Saratoga. "He wasn't reckless. He made a stupid mistake. It's like going through a stop sign. But when a Kennedy goes through a stop sign, there always seems to be an eighteen-wheeler coming from the other side."

John's tragic "mistake" raised the question of whether pilots who are not instrument-trained should be allowed to fly at night under any conditions. Had he been in Canada, Great Britain, or most European countries, John would not have been permitted to take off that night or any other night until he learned to fly using only his instruments.

With a finding of pilot error in mind, Ann Freeman filed court papers in Manhattan asking to become the administrator of her daughters' estates (Carolyn's was estimated to be worth in the neighborhood of five hundred thousand dollars, Lauren's considerably more)—and seeking the right to file personal-injury and wrongful-death lawsuits in the future against "unknown" parties.

If anger was building in the Bessette–Freeman household over the possibility that John's negligence may have contributed to the crash, the contents of his will could not have helped matters. Filed on September 24, 1999, in Manhattan Surrogate Court, John's three-and-a-half-page will left the bulk of his one-hundred-million-dollar estate to a trust set up in 1983.

Of the fourteen heirs named in the will, Caroline and her children, Rose, Tatiana, and Jack, were the primary beneficiaries. But John also made bequests to Marta Sgubin, his nanny and later Jackie's cook; Jackie's butler, Ephigenio Pinheiro; John's assistant at *George*, RoseMary Terenzio; his cousins Robert F. Kennedy Jr. and Timothy Shriver; and two nonprofit organizations, Reaching Up and the JFK Library. Timothy Shriver was also named executor of the will, replacing John's first choice for the job, Tony Radziwill.

John left Caroline's children his half of Red Gate Farm. Had he had a son of his own, John would have specifically bequeathed him "a scrimshaw set previously owned by my father." But since JFK's only son died childless, little Jack Kennedy Schlossberg would receive the scrimshaw. There were two other minors mentioned in the will—Phineas Howie, then seven, and Olivia Howie, four, the children of his Andover classmate Alexandra Chermayeff and John's godchildren.

Oddly, had Carolyn survived, John had specified only that she would inherit his personal belongings and their TriBeCa apartment, valued at over $2 million. Since the provisions of the 1983 trust remained secret, it was probable that Carolyn would have been well provided for by the trust.

What was not open to speculation, however, was the fact that John's will, which left Carolyn the apartment "if she is living on the thirtieth day after my death," effectively cut his in-laws off without a cent. "John obviously had no relationship with his in-laws," said noted New York divorce lawyer Raoul Felder. "I think they will be very angry about this will."

In an effort to forestall a wrongful death suit, Caroline, who was also sympathetic to the feelings of Carolyn's parents, met with Ann Freeman and her surviving daughter Lisa Bessette over the next five months to work things out. "The two families—Ann Freeman and Caroline Kennedy Schlossberg—have managed to deal with everything on a very personal and cooperative basis," conceded Ann Freeman's lawyer Constantine Ralli. "I think the families will handle everything in a cooperative and nonpublic fashion." In the end, John's sister quietly arranged to pay Carolyn's family an estimated ten million dollars out of John's estate.

That she had forestalled a messy public trial was of little comfort to Caroline. Behind her Jackie-like mask of calm, John's sister was devastated—and, understandably, teetering on the verge of a breakdown. "Caroline was so close to John and she was crushed by his death—shattered," Marta Sgubin said. "She was weeping constantly. Many times after the funeral I saw Ted, without a word, put his arms around her and hold her as she wept onto his shoulders."

The loss struck her especially hard on November 27, 1999, her forty-second birthday. Memories of the joint birthday she and John celebrated—like the one only days after their father's assassination— came flooding back. Three days later, at a political fund-raiser for Ted, she nearly broke down. "Without Teddy," she conceded, "I don't think I could have gotten through the past few months." And he would still be there for his niece. "Caroline is still very sad," Sgubin said, "but at least with Ted there, she is never alone."

But Caroline *was* alone—the sole surviving member of a remarkable family of four who had endured unimaginable triumph and unspeakable tragedy. Yet she could take solace in the fact that untold millions shared in her sorrow and dismay—not because of anything John said or did, but simply because he existed. "From the first day of his life," his uncle Ted mused, "John seemed to belong not only to our family, but to the American family. The whole world knew his name before he did."

He was the Crown Prince of Camelot, the brightest star in the Kennedy firmament. He was also impossibly good-looking, charming, kind, and defiantly normal. It was the abiding sense that he was very much like us—or more accurately, like a son or brother or favored nephew, perhaps—that captured and held our interest.

While the rest of the planet watched, John simply went through the sometimes mundane, often thrilling, always perplexing business of living. From his much-heralded birth to his Oval Office antics to the heartbreaking salute, through Onassis and prep school and college and the bar exam and girlfriends and the death of his mother and the birth of his magazine and his fairy tale wedding, we looked on as any family member would: with interest, affection, and no small amount of hope.

As heartbreaking as they were, the images of the brave young widow and her two small children were still bright with promise. There was no doubt that this remarkable woman who held tight to those tiny hands would protect John and Caroline, and that one day they might fulfill their father's legacy.

From that day in Dallas onward, said Jackie's stepbrother, Yusha Auchincloss, "Jackie worried more about John than she did about Caroline, who matured quickly and was very influenced by her father. Jackie paid special attention to John." She was also careful not to suffocate her son, even urging John to test himself in the wilds of Africa and under the sea. But Jackie, whose own spiritual journey had taken her on annual pilgrimages to India, listened to her dreams and forbade him only the thrill of piloting his own plane.

Tragic as JFK's death was at forty-six, John's at thirty-eight seemed unfathomably so. Just as Jack and Jackie came together following the death of their infant son Patrick only to have it all ended by an assassin's bullet, John and Carolyn had weathered a crisis in their marriage and now appeared ready to start a family of their own.

If there was any solace to be had, it came from the fact that Jackie was not alive to endure the ultimate loss.

"I think the most interesting thing about him," John once said of his father, "is that you realize he was just a man, that he lived a life, like anybody else." JFK's son did just that—living life to the fullest and on his own terms, and at the same time cherishing his legacy.

Arthur Schlesinger Jr. once noted that there was a "characteristic gallantry" about Jackie. The same could be said for her son. Unlike other icons whose conflicts and contradictions confound and intrigue us, John was, like the national character itself, deceptive in his simplicity.

He held no high office, wrote no great books, created no masterpieces, performed no heroic feats. He cured nothing, discovered nothing. He didn't have to. From the very beginning, John was America's son.

ACKNOWLEDGMENTS

On Saturday morning, July 17, our eldest daughter Kate rushed downstairs and asked if we had heard the news that John Kennedy's plane was missing off Martha's Vineyard. Only two years earlier she had had the similarly unhappy task of telling my wife and me and our dinner guests that another remarkable young person, Princess Diana, had been killed in a Paris car crash.

As the author of *The Day Diana Died* and two previous best-selling books on the Kennedys, *Jack and Jackie* and *Jackie After Jack,* I harbored no illusions about the fate of John, his wife Carolyn, and Carolyn's sister Lauren. That the son of Jack and Jackie would die so tragically and so young seemed unbelievable, and at the same time completely predictable.

A tremendous amount of research is essential for any comprehensive biography, and this was particularly true for the final book in this Kennedy family trilogy. In essence, work began on *The Day John Died* six years ago, though I did not foresee the circumstances that would lead to its publication on the first anniversary of his death. That time was spent interviewing hundreds of family members, friends, classmates, teachers, co-workers, neighbors, colleagues, lovers, employers, fellow aviators, and employees, as well as photographers and journalists who covered John and his family over the years. Only a handful of these sources insisted that they not be identified, and I respected their wishes.

For the sixth time, I am blessed to be working with one of the finest teams in the publishing industry. I owe a special debt of gratitude to my editor, Betty Kelly, who brought the same insight and commitment to *The Day John Died* that she did to *The Day Diana Died*. My thanks extend to my entire family at Morrow and HarperCollins, especially Jane Friedman, Cathy Hemming, Lisa

Queen, Michael Morrison, Dominique D'Anna, Beth Silfin, Laura Leonard, Laurie Rippon, Richard Aquan, Brad Foltz, Rome Quezada, Betty Lew, Jo Anne Metsch, Michele Corallo, and Camille McDuffie of Goldberg-McDuffie Communications.

Eighteen books later, I am more convinced than ever that Ellen Levine is simply one of the finest literary agents that ever was—as well as that most treasured of commodities in the writing game, a wise and true friend. For almost as many years, it seems, I've owed a debt of gratitude to Ellen's formidable associates Diana Finch and Louise Quayle—and this book is no exception.

I am grateful, as always, to my mother Jeanette and my father Edward, to whom this book is dedicated on the occasion of his eightieth birthday. My daughter Kate, Oxford-bound at the time of this writing, is a never-ending source of pride and wonderment, as is her equally bedazzling sister, Kelly. Which should come as no surprise, considering the extraordinary woman who is their mother. My wife Valerie is, as she was when I met her more than thirty years ago, headstrong, beautiful, witty, brilliant, and utterly outrageous.

Additional thanks to John Perry Barlow, Pierre Salinger, Marta Sgubin, Kyle Bailey, David Halberstam, Keith Stein, Theodore Sorenson, Letitia Baldrige, Arthur Marx, Kitty Carlisle Hart, Arthur Schlesinger Jr., John Kenneth Galbraith, Angie Coqueran, Michael Cherkasky, Charles "Chuck" Spalding, Lloyd Howard, Sister Joanne Frey, Hugh "Yusha" Auchincloss, Julie Baker, Jamie Auchincloss, Peter Duchin, George Smathers, Lois Cappelen, Jacques Lowe, Rick Guy, Holly Owen, David McGough, Michael Berman, John Husted, the late Roswell Gilpatric, Helen Thomas, Larry Lorenzo, Tom Freeman, Frank Ratcliff, Oleg Cassini, John Marion, Ray Robinson, Priscilla McMillan, Anthony Hahn, the late Evelyn Lincoln, Wendy Leigh, Michael Gross, Anne Vanderhoop, James Hill, Paul Adao, the late Roy Cohn, Joseph Pullia, Ralph Diaz, Michael Foster, Paula Dranov, Dudley Freeman, Jerry Wiener, Larry Newman, Rosemary McClure, Ron Whealen, Steve Karten, the late Alfred Eisenstaedt, Joe Duran, Anthony Comenale, Tobias Markowitz, Jeanette Peterson, James E. O'Neill, Godfrey McHugh, Jean Chapin, the late Clare Boothe Luce, Lawrence Leamer, Mesfin Gebreegziabher, Lawrence R. Mulligan, Robert Drew, William Johnson, Alex Gotfryd, Valerie Wimmer, Wickham Boyle, the late Nancy Dickerson Whitehead, Aileen Mehle, Jonathan Soroff, Dr. Janet Travell, Ricardo Richards, Betty Beale, Megan Desnoyers, Farris L. Rookstool III, Bia Ayiotis, the late Theodore White, Charles Furneaux, Robert Pierce, Brad Darrach, Hazel Southam, Patricia Lawford Stewart, Cranston Jones, Vincent Russo, Dorothy Oliger, Betsy Loth, the late Doris Lilly, Earl Blackwell, Molly Fosburgh, June Payne, Jean Chapin, Jeanette Walls, Gary Gunderson, Janet Lizop, Michelle Lapautre, the Countess of Romanones, Ham Brown, Yvette Reyes, Norman Currie, the late Charles Collingwood, Michael

Shulman, Fred Williams, Denis Reggie, Bob Cosenza, Maura Porter, Patrice Hamilton, Debbie Goodsite, Ray Whelan, Jr., and Arlete Santos.

Thanks to the staffs at the John F. Kennedy Library and Museum, the National Transportation Safety Board, the Rockefeller Library at Brown University, Sothebys, the Robin Hood Foundation, Reaching Up, Phillips Academy, the United States Secret Service, the Federal Bureau of Investigation, the New York Public Library, the Columbia University Oral History Project, the Butler Library, the Redwood Library and Atheneum of Newport, the Barnstable Public Library, the Gunn Memorial Library, the Archdiocese of Boston, the Archdiocese of New York, St. Thomas More Church, Essex County Airport, Martha's Vineyard Airport, the Silas Bronson Library, the Southbury Library, the New Milford Library, the Brookfield Library, the Bancroft Library at the University of California at Berkeley, the New York University Law Library, Corbis, Corbis-Sygma, DMI, Archive Photos, the Coqueran Group, Gamma-Liaison, AP–Wide World, Reuters, Globe Photos, Retna, the Associated Press, Planned Television Arts, Barraclough Carey Productions, *The Folding Kayak,* the United States Coast Guard, St. David's School, Collegiate, the *Cape Cod Times,* the Edgartown Library, Design to Printing, and Graphictype.

SOURCES AND
CHAPTER NOTES

The following chapter notes are designed to give a general view of the sources drawn upon in preparing *The Day John Died,* but they are by no means all-inclusive. The author has respected the wishes of many interviewed subjects to remain anonymous and accordingly has not listed them either here or elsewhere in the text. The archives and oral history collections of, among other institutions, the John Fitzgerald Kennedy Library, the Lyndon Baines Johnson Library, and the libraries of Brown, Harvard, Columbia, and Yale Universities yielded a wealth of information. Obviously, there were thousands of news reports and articles on John over the course of the last four decades that serve as source material for this book—including press accounts of life in the Kennedy White House, the assassinations of JFK and Robert Kennedy and their aftermath, Jackie's marriage to Aristotle Onassis and the manner in which she raised John and Caroline, John's education, his law and publishing careers, and the fatal crash itself. These reports have appeared in such publications as the *New York Times,* the *Washington Post,* the *Boston Globe,* the *Wall Street Journal, USA Today,* the *Los Angeles Times,* the *New York Post,* the *New York Daily News,* the *Chicago Tribune,* the *Chicago Sun-Times, Vanity Fair, The New Yorker, Time, Life, Newsweek, Talk,* the *Times* of London, and *Paris Match,* and carried on the Associated Press, Reuters, Knight-Ridder, Gannett, and United Press International wires.

CHAPTER 1

Interview subjects included John Perry Barlow, Keith Stein, Kyle Bailey, Arthur Marx, Julie Baker, Lloyd Howard, Arthur Schlesinger Jr., Jack Tabibian, Mesfin Gebreegziabher, Larry Lorenzo, Jerry Wiener, Ralph Diaz, Anthony Comenale, Lois Cappelen, Anthony Hahn, Jeanette Walls, Anne Vanderhoop, Joe Duran, Bia Ayiotis.

Published sources included "He Was America's Prince," *Time,* July 26, 1999; "Tragic Echoes," *Newsweek,* July 26, 1999; Angie Cannon and Peter Cary, "The Final Hours," *U.S. News & World Report,* August 2, 1999; "Charmed Life, Tragic Death," *People,* August 2, 1999; Dr. Bob Arnot; "FAA False Visibility Reports: Lost in the Darkness and the Haze," *2000 Eye's* magazine, March 2000; "The Preliminary Report of the National Transportation Safety Board, NTSB Identification NYC99MA178," http://www.ntsb.gov/Aviation/NYC/99A178.htm.

CHAPTERS 2 AND 3

For these chapters, the author drew on conversations with John Kenneth Galbraith, Pierre Salinger, Letitia Baldrige, George Smathers, Chuck Spalding, Yusha Auchincloss, Theodore Sorenson, Jamie Auchincloss, Sister Joanne Frey, Jacques Lowe, Kitty Carlisle Hart, Oleg Cassini, Patricia Lawford Stewart, John Husted, the Countess of Romanones, Priscilla McMillan, Evelyn Lincoln, Willard K. Rice, Clare Boothe Luce, Dr. Janet Travell, Nancy Dickerson Whitehead, Betty Beale, Angier Biddle Duke, Alfred Eisenstaedt, Charles Furneaux, Theodore H. White, Larry Newman. The author also drew on numerous oral histories, including those given by Robert F. Kennedy, Rose Fitzgerald Kennedy, Richard Cardinal Cushing, Nancy Tuckerman, Eunice Kennedy Shriver, Maud Shaw, Janet Lee Bouvier Auchincloss, Pope Paul VI, Robert McNamara, Dave Powers, Dean Rusk, Betty Thomas, J. B. West, Admiral George Burkley, Paul "Red" Fay, Pamela Turnure, Walt Rostow, Peter Lawford, Father John C. Cavanaugh, Arthur Krock, Stanley Tretick, Douglas Dillon, William Walton, and Leonard Bernstein. Jacqueline Kennedy Onassis's oral history was done by Terry L. Birdwhistell in New York on May 13, 1981, as part of the John Sherman Cooper Oral History Project of the University of Kentucky Library.

Federal Bureau of Investigation, Secret Service, and National Security Agency files, newly released through the Freedom of Information Act, were of considerable value, as were White House staff files and the papers of JFK, Jacqueline Kennedy Onassis, Robert Kennedy, Rose Kennedy, Kenneth O'Donnell, Dave Powers, Lem Billings, Lawrence O'Brien, William vanden Heuvel, and Sir Alec Douglas-Home. Millions of words have been written about the assassination of JFK; thousands of articles published in the United States and abroad were consulted here. Among the published sources consulted: William Manchester, *The Death of a President* (New York: Harper & Row, 1967); *The Warren Commission Report* (Washington, D.C.: U.S. Government Printing Office, 1964); Arthur Schlesinger Jr., *A Thousand Days* (Boston: Houghton Mifflin, 1965); Ben Bradlee, *A Good Life* (New York: Simon & Schuster, 1995); Mary Barrelli Gallagher, *My Life with Jacqueline Kennedy* (New York: David McKay, 1969); Robert Sam Anson, *"They've Killed the President!": The Search for the Murderers of John F. Kennedy* (New York: Bantam, 1975); Lady Bird Johnson, *A White House Diary* (New York: Holt, Rinehart & Winston, 1970); Jim Bishop, *The Day Kennedy Was Shot* (New York: Funk & Wagnalls, 1968); Theodore Sorenson, *Kennedy* (New York: Harper & Row, 1965); Kenneth P. O'Donnell and David F. Powers with Joe McCarthy, *Johnny, We Hardly Knew Ye* (Boston: Little, Brown, 1970); Maud Shaw, *White House Nannie; My Years with Caroline and John Kennedy, Jr.* (New York: New American Library, 1965).

CHAPTERS 4 AND 5

Author interviews included George Plimpton, Peter Duchin, Yusha Auchincloss, Kitty Carlisle Hart, Aileen Mehle, Chuck Spalding, Jamie Auchincloss, Pierre Salinger, Ham Brown, Patricia Lawford Stewart, Marta Sgubin, Arthur Schlesinger Jr., George Smathers, David Halberstam, Jack Anderson, Roy Cohn, Roswell Gilpatric, Halston, Doris Lilly, John Marion, Mollie Fosburgh, Brad Darrach, Billy Baldwin, Earl Blackwell, David McGough.

Articles and other published sources for this period included Enid Nemy, "Here John Kennedy Jr. Will Be 'Just Another Boy,' " the *New York Times,* August 22, 1968; Nancy Moran, "John Kennedy Got into Collegiate School for Boys—Could *Your* Son?," *McCall's,* March 1969; Wendy Leigh, *Prince Charming* (New York: Signet, 1994); "John-John, Caroline Revisit White House," United Press International, February 5, 1971; George Vecsey, "And There Were Jackie, John and Caroline," the *New York Times,* September 1969; "The Curious Aftermath of JFK's Best and Brightest Affair," *New York Times Magazine,* July 9, 1976; Peter Evans, *Ari: The Life and Times of Aristotle Onassis* (New York: Summit Books, 1986); Robert Ajemian, "A Man's Week to Reckon," *Life,* July 3, 1964; C. David Heymann, *A Woman Named Jackie* (New York: Lyle Stuart/Carol Communications, 1989); Kitty Kelley, *Jackie Oh!* (Secaucus, N.J.: Lyle Stuart, 1979); William Manchester, *Controversy and Other Essays in Journalism: 1950–1975* (Boston: Little, Brown, 1976); Frank Brady, *Onassis: An Extravagant Life* (New York: Prentice-Hall, 1977); "The Happy Jackie, The Sad Jackie, The Bad Jackie, The Good Jackie," *New York Times Magazine,* May 31, 1970; Peter Beard, "John F. Kennedy Jr.—Images of Summer," *Talk,* September 1999.

CHAPTERS 6 AND 7

Information for these chapters was based in part on conversations with David Halberstam, James Young, Jack Anderson, Bobby Zarem, John Perry Barlow, Holly Owen, Frank Ratcliff, Rick Guy, Michael Cherkasky, Erika Belle, Carolina Herrera, Arthur Marx, Letitia Baldrige, Michael Gross, David McGough, Malcolm Forbes, Angie Coqueran, Alex Gotfryd, Paul Adao, John Marion, Howie Montaug, Anne Vanderhoop.

Among the published sources consulted: Peter Strafford, "U.S. Acts to Protect the Kennedy Children," the *Times* of London, May 4, 1972; Michael Ryan, "Barry Clifford's Zany Crew—Including JFK Jr.—Prove That Way Down Deep, They're Golddiggers," *People,* August 22, 1983; Wendy Leigh, "Caroline's Precious Legacy: What She Learned from Her Mother," *McCall's,* September 1994; "JFK Jr.'s Bash A Socko Show," the *New York Daily News,* November 28, 1978; Frank Rich, "The Jackie Mystery," the *New York Times,* May 26, 1994; "The Sexiest Man Alive," *People,* September 12, 1988; Marylou Tousignant and Malcolm Gladwell, "In Somber Ceremony Jacqueline Kennedy Onassis Is Laid to Rest," the *Washington Post,* May 24, 1994; Taki Theodoracopulos, "Jackie O: A Perfect Mom," the *New York Post,* May 23, 1994; Tina Brown, "A Woman in Earnest," *The New Yorker,* September 15, 1997; Annette Tapert, "Jackie's Dearest Wish," *Good Housekeeping,* July 1994; David Michaelis, "Great Expectations," *Vanity Fair,* September 1999.

CHAPTERS 8 AND 9

Interview subjects included John Perry Barlow, Marta Sgubin, Kyle Bailey, Lloyd Howard, Julie Baker, Lois Cappelen, Keith Stein, Ralph Diaz, Jeanette Walls, Larry Lorenzo, David McGough, Anne Vanderhoop, Edward Francis, Jerry Wiener, Jonathan Soroff, Rosemary McClure, Jack Tabibian, Wickham Boyle, Ricardo Richards, Joe Duran, Bia Ayiotis, Anthony Comenale, and Michael Gross.

Published sources included John F. Kennedy, "Don't Sit Under the Apple Tree," *George,* September 1997; Michael Gross, "Citizen Kennedy," *Esquire,* September 1995; Martha Brant and Evan Thomas, "Coming of Age," *Newsweek,* August 14, 1995; "Princess Carolyn," *W,* August 1996; Rebecca Mead, "Meet the Mrs.," October 7, 1996; Tom Squitieri, "Could a Kennedy Be Loosening Family Ties?," *USA Today,* August 12, 1997; "A Sad Goodbye," *Newsweek,* August 2, 1999; Rebecca Mead, "Does John Kennedy Sell Magazines?," *New York,* August 7, 1995; Peter Collier, "A Kennedy Apart: JFK Jr. Was His Own Man," *National Review,* August 9, 1999; "Charity Group Recalls John Kennedy Jr.," the *New York Times,* December 8, 1999; "John Kennedy,

New Yorker," the *New York Observer,* July 26, 1999; "Prince of the City," *New York,* August 2, 1999; Karen Duffy, "The Spell They Cast," *Glamour,* October 1999; "Kennedy Family Wanted Dignified Burial at Sea to Avoid Spectacle," the *Cape Cod Times,* July 26, 1999; Cindy Adams, "Report: John and Carolyn Spent Last Nights Apart," the *New York Post,* August 6, 1999; Anthony Wilson-Smith, "The Curse of the Kennedys," *Maclean's,* July 26, 1999; "John Kennedy: A Tribute," *George,* October 1999; "Aircraft's Reputation Called Good," Associated Press, July 18, 1999; "Sad Vigil," the *New York Daily News,* July 19, 1999; "Goodbye," *New York Newsday,* July 23, 1999; "Talk of the Town," *The New Yorker,* August 2, 1999; "Farewell, John," *Time,* August 2, 1999; Charles Gandee, "Goodbye To All That," *Vogue,* September 1999; "Goodbye, America's Little Prince," *Paris Match,* August 1999; Terry Pristin, "Families, Employees and Charities Named in Kennedy Will," the *New York Times,* September 25, 1999.

SELECTED BIBLIOGRAPHY

Acheson, Dean. *Power and Diplomacy*. Cambridge, Mass.: Harvard University Press, 1958.

Adams, Cindy, and Susan Crimp. *Iron Rose: The Story of Rose Fitzgerald Kennedy and Her Dynasty*. Beverly Hills, Calif.: Dove Books, 1995.

Amory, Cleveland. *The Proper Bostonians*. New York: E. P. Dutton & Company, 1947.

Andersen, Christopher. *Jack and Jackie: Portrait of an American Marriage*. New York: William Morrow, 1996.

——. *Madonna Unauthorized*. New York: Simon & Schuster, 1991.

Anson, Robert Sam. *"They've Killed the President!": The Search for the Murderers of John F. Kennedy*. New York: Bantam, 1975.

Anthony, Carl Sferrazza. *As We Remember Her*. New York: HarperCollins, 1997.

Baldwin, Billy. *Billy Baldwin Remembers*. New York: Harcourt Brace Jovanovich, 1974.

Baldrige, Letitia. *Of Diamonds and Diplomats*. Boston: Houghton Mifflin, 1968.

Beard, Peter. *Longing for Darkness: Kamante's Tales from "Out of Africa."* San Francisco: Chronicle Books, 1990.

Beschloss, Michael R. *Kennedy and Roosevelt: The Uneasy Alliance*. New York: Norton, 1980.

——. *Taking Charge: The Johnson White House Tapes, 1963–1964*. New York: Simon & Schuster, 1997.

Birmingham, Stephen. *Jacqueline Bouvier Kennedy Onassis*. New York: Grosset & Dunlap, 1978.

———. *Real Lace: America's Irish Rich*. New York: Harper & Row, 1973.

Bishop, Jim. *The Day Kennedy Was Shot*. New York: Funk & Wagnalls, 1968.

Blair, Joan, and Clay Blair Jr. *The Search for JFK*. New York: Berkeley, 1976.

Bouvier, Jacqueline, and Lee Bouvier. *One Special Summer*. New York: Delacorte, 1974.

Bouvier, Kathleen. *To Jack With Love: Black Jack Bouvier: A Remembrance*. New York: Kensington, 1979.

Bradon, Joan. *Just Enough Rope*. New York: Villard, 1989.

Bradlee, Ben. *A Good Life*. New York: Simon & Schuster, 1995.

———. *Conversations with Kennedy*. New York: Norton, 1975.

Brady, Frank. *Onassis*. Englewood Cliffs, N.J.: Prentice-Hall, 1977.

Brando, Marlon, with Robert Lindsey. *Songs My Mother Taught Me*. New York: Random House, 1995.

Bryant, Traphes, and Frances Spatz Leighton. *Dog Days at the White House*. New York: Macmillan, 1975.

Buck, Pearl S. *The Kennedy Women: A Personal Appraisal*. New York: Harcourt, 1969.

Burke, Richard E. *My Ten Years with Ted Kennedy*. New York: St. Martin's Press, 1992.

Burns, James MacGregor. *Edward Kennedy and the Camelot Legacy*. New York: Norton, 1976.

———. *John Kennedy: A Political Profile*. New York: Harcourt, 1960.

Cameron, Gail. *Rose: A Biography of Rose Fitzgerald Kennedy*. New York: Putnam, 1971.

Cassini, Oleg. *A Thousand Days of Magic*. New York: Rizzoli, 1995.

———. *In My Own Fashion: An Autobiography*. New York: Simon & Schuster, 1987.

Cheshire, Maxine. *Maxine Cheshire, Reporter*. Boston: Houghton Mifflin, 1978.

Clarke, Gerald. *Capote*. New York: Simon & Schuster, 1988.

Cohn, Roy. *McCarthy*. New York: New American Library, 1968.

Collier, Peter, and David Horowitz. *The Kennedys: An American Drama*. New York: Summit, 1984.

Damore, Leo. *The Cape Cod Years of John Fitzgerald Kennedy*. Englewood Cliffs, N.J.: Prentice-Hall, 1967.

Davis, John. *The Bouviers: Portrait of an American Family*. New York: Farrar, Straus and Giroux, 1969.

———. *The Kennedys: Dynasty and Disaster*. New York: McGraw-Hill, 1984.

Dempster, Nigel. *Heiress: The Story of Christina Onassis*. London: Weidenfeld & Nicolson, 1989.

DuBois, Diana. *In Her Sister's Shadow: An Intimate Biography of Lee Radziwill.* Boston: Little, Brown, 1995.

Duchin, Peter. *Ghost of a Chance.* New York: Random House, 1996.

Evans, Peter. *Ari: The Life and Times of Aristotle Socrates Onasis.* New York: Summit, 1986.

Exner, Judith Campbell, as told to Ovid Demaris. *My Story.* New York: Grove, 1977.

Fay, Paul B. Jr. *The Pleasure of His Company.* New York: Harper & Row, 1966.

Fisher, Eddie. *Eddie: My Life, My Loves.* New York: Harper & Row, 1981.

Fontaine, Joan. *No Bed of Roses: An Autobiography.* New York: William Morrow, 1978.

Frank, Gerold. *Zsa Zsa Gabor, My Story.* New York: World, 1960.

Fraser, Nicolas, Phillip Jacobson, Mark Ottaway, and Lewis Chester. *Aristotle Onassis.* Philadelphia: Lippincott, 1977.

Frischauer, Willi. *Jackie.* London: Michael Joseph, 1967.

———. *Onassis.* New York: Meredith, 1968.

Galbraith, John Kenneth. *Ambassador's Journal: A Personal Account of the Kennedy Years.* Boston: Houghton Mifflin, 1969.

Gallagher, Mary Barelli. *My Life with Jacqueline Kennedy.* New York: David McKay, 1969.

Giancana, Antoinette, and Thomas C. Renner. *Mafia Princess: Growing Up in Sam Giancana's Family.* New York: William Morrow, 1984.

Goodwin, Doris Kearns. *The Fitzgeralds and the Kennedys: An American Saga.* New York: Simon & Schuster, 1987.

Granger, Stewart. *Sparks Fly Upward.* New York: Putnam, 1981.

Halberstam, David. *The Best and the Brightest.* New York: Random House, 1969.

Hall, Gordon Langley, and Ann Pinchot. *Jacqueline Kennedy.* New York: Frederick Fell, 1964.

Hamilton, Nigel. *JFK: Reckless Youth.* New York: Random House, 1992.

Heymann, C. David. *A Woman Named Jackie: An Intimate Biography of Jacqueline Bouvier Kennedy Onassis.* New York: Lyle Stuart/Carol Communications, 1989.

Kelley, Kitty. *His Way: The Unauthorized Biography of Frank Sinatra.* New York: Bantam, 1986.

———. *Jackie Oh!* Secaucus, N.J.: Lyle Stuart, 1979.

———. *Nancy Reagan: The Unauthorized Biography.* New York: Simon & Schuster, 1991.

Kennedy, John F. *Profiles in Courage.* New York: Harper & Row, 1965.

———. *Why England Slept.* New York: Wilfred Funk, 1940.

Kennedy, Rose Fitzgerald. *Times to Remember.* New York: Doubleday, 1974.

Kessler, Ronald. *Inside the White House.* New York: Pocket Books, 1995.

Klein, Edward. *Just Jackie: Her Private Years.* New York: Ballantine, 1998.

Koskoff, David E. *Joseph P. Kennedy, A Life and Times,* Englewood Cliffs, N.J.: Prentice-Hall, 1974.

Krock, Arthur. *Memoirs: Sixty Years on the Firing Line.* New York: Funk and Wagnalls, 1968.

Kunhardt, Philip B. Jr., ed., *Life in Camelot.* Boston: Little, Brown, 1988.

Lash, Joseph P. *Eleanor and Franklin.* New York: Norton, 1971.

Latham, Caroline, with Jeannie Sakol. *The Kennedy Encyclopedia.* New York: New American Library, 1989.

Lawford, Patricia Seaton, with Ted Schwarz. *The Peter Lawford Story.* New York: Carroll & Graf, 1988.

Lawliss, Charles. *Jacqueline Kennedy Onassis.* New York: JG Press, 1994.

Leamer, Laurence. *The Kennedy Women: The Saga of an American Family.* New York: Villard, 1994.

Leigh, Wendy. *Prince Charming: The John F. Kennedy Jr. Story.* New York: Signet, 1994.

Lilly, Doris. *Those Fabulous Greeks: Onassis, Niarchos, and Livanos.* New York: Cowles, 1970.

Lowe, Jacques. *Jacqueline Kennedy Onassis: A Tribute.* New York: Jacques Lowe Visual Arts, 1995.

———. *JFK Remembered.* New York: Random House, 1993.

Mailer, Norman. *Of Women and Their Elegance.* New York: Simon & Schuster, 1980.

———. *Marilyn.* New York: Grosset & Dunlap, 1973.

Manchester, William. *The Death of a President.* New York: Harper & Row, 1967.

———. *Portrait of the President: John F. Kennedy in Profile.* Boston: Little, Brown, 1962.

Martin, Ralph. *A Hero for Our Time.* New York: Ballantine, 1984.

Moutsatsos, Kiki Feroudi. *The Onassis Women.* New York: Putnam, 1998.

McCarthy, Joe. *The Remarkable Kennedys.* New York: Dial, 1960.

Montgomery, Ruth. *Hail to the Chiefs: My Life and Times with Six Presidents.* New York: Coward-McCann, 1970.

O'Connor, Edwin. *The Last Hurrah.* New York: Bantam, 1970.

O'Donnell, Kenneth P., and David F. Powers, with Joe McCarthy. *"Johnny, We Hardly Knew Ye."* Boston: Little, Brown, 1970.

O'Neill, Tip, with William Novak. *Man of the House: The Life and Political Memoirs of Speaker Tip O'Neill.* New York: Random House, 1987.

Ogden, Christopher. *Life of the Party: The Biography of Pamela Digby Churchill Hayward Harriman.* New York: Warner Books, 1994.

Oppenheimer, Jerry. *The Other Mrs. Kennedy*. New York: St. Martin's, 1994.

Parmet, Herbert S. *J. F. K.: The Presidency of John F. Kennedy*. New York: Dial, 1983.

———. *Jack: The Struggles of John F. Kennedy*. New York: Dial, 1980.

Parker, Robert. *Capitol Hill in Black and White*. New York: Dodd, Mead, 1987.

Pepitone, Lena, and William Stadiem. *Marilyn Monroe Confidential*. New York: Pocket, 1979.

Reed, J. D., Kyle Smith, and Jill Smolowe. *John F. Kennedy Jr.: A Biography*. New York: People Profiles/Time, 1998.

Reeves, Richard. *President Kennedy: Profile of Power*. New York: Simon & Schuster, 1993.

Reeves, Thomas C. *A Question of Character: A Life of John F. Kennedy*. Rocklin, Calif.: Prima Publishing, 1992.

Salinger, Pierre. *P.S.: A Memoir*. New York: St. Martin's, 1995.

———. *With Kennedy*. Garden City, N.Y.: Doubleday, 1966.

Schlesinger, Arthur M. Jr. *A Thousand Days*. Boston: Houghton Mifflin, 1965.

Sgubin, Marta. *Cooking for Madam: Recipes and Reminiscences from the Home of Jacqueline Kennedy Onassis*. New York: Lisa Drew/Scribner, 1998.

Shaw, Maud. *White House Nannie: My Years with Caroline and John Kennedy, Jr.* New York: New American Library, 1965.

Shulman, Irving. *"Jackie"!: The Exploitation of a First Lady*. New York: Trident Press, 1970.

Sidey, Hugh. *John F. Kennedy, President*. New York: Atheneum, 1964.

Sorenson, Theodore C. *Kennedy*. New York: Harper & Row, 1965.

Spada, James. *Peter Lawford: The Man Who Kept the Secrets*. New York: Bantam, 1991.

Spignesi, Stephen. *The J. F. K. Jr. Scrapbook*. Secaucus, N.J.: Carol, 1997.

Stack, Robert, with Mark Evans. *Straight Shooting*. New York: Macmillan, 1980.

Storm, Tempest, with Bill Boyd. *Tempest Storm: The Lady Is a Vamp*. Atlanta: Peachtree, 1987.

Summers, Anthony. *Goddess: The Secret Lives of Marilyn Monroe*. New York: Macmillan, 1985.

Swanson, Gloria. *Swanson on Swanson*. New York: Random House, 1980.

ter Horst, J. F., and Ralph Albertazzio. *The Flying White House*. New York: Coward, McCann & Geoghegan, 1979.

Thayer, Mary Van Rensselaer. *Jacqueline Bouvier Kennedy*. Garden City, N.Y.: Doubleday, 1961.

Thomas, Bob. *Golden Boy! The Untold Story of William Holden*. New York: St. Martin's, 1983.

Thomas, Helen. *Dateline: White House.* New York: Macmillan, 1975.

Tierney, Gene, with Mickey Herskowitz. *Self Portrait.* New York: Simon & Schuster, 1979.

Travell, Janet. *Office Hours: Day and Night.* New York: World, 1968.

Vidal, Gore. *Palimpsest: A Memoir.* New York: Random House, 1995.

Warhol, Andy. *The Andy Warhol Diaries.* Ed. Pat Hackett. New York: Warner Books, 1989.

The Warren Report. New York: Associated Press, 1964.

Watney, Hedda Lyons. *Jackie.* New York: Leisure, 1971.

West, J. B., with Mary Lynn Kotz, *Upstairs at the White House.* New York: Coward, McCann & Geoghegan, 1973.

White, Theodore H. *In Search of History.* New York: Warner, 1978.

———. *The Making of the President 1960.* New York: Atheneum, 1961.

Wills, Garry. *The Kennedy Imprisonment.* Boston: Atlantic/Little, Brown, 1981.

INDEX

Agnelli, Gianni, 100
Aguilera, Sal, 271
Albaz, Alber, 21–22
Albright, Madeleine, 224
Alderman, Ellen, 192
Ali, Muhammad, 224, 272
Alson, Peter, 225
Amanpour, Christiane, 14, 171, 247
Amory, Cleveland, 137
Anderson, Harold, 27
Anderson, Marian, 44
Archer, Jeffrey, 154
Arnot, Dr. Bob, 20, 30
Auchincloss, Hugh D. (grandfather), 53, 74
Auchincloss, Hugh "Yusha" (uncle), 48, 93, 223, 280
Auchincloss, Jamie (uncle), 58, 63, 71, 75, 79, 102, 107, 144, 146–147, 197, 203, 228–229
Auchincloss, Janet (aunt), 75, 90, 102, 180
Auchincloss, Janet (grandmother), 38, 53, 63, 71, 72, 74, 142
Aviznienis, Audra, 194–195
Ayiotis, Bia, 233

Bailey, Kyle, 21, 26–29, 32, 262–263
Bailey, Mark, 258, 276

Baker, Julie, 16, 194–195, 212
Baldrige, Letitia (Tish), 43, 46, 48, 49, 50, 51–52, 58, 59, 147, 172, 229, 271
Baldwin, Billy, 89, 120–121
Banderas, Antonio, 222
Bardes, Georges, 208
Barlow, John Perry, 12, 19, 23, 27, 158–159, 161, 179, 186, 191–192, 204, 213, 218, 225–226, 227, 230, 237, 238–240, 248, 250, 251, 264
Barron, Brian, 105–106
Barrymore, Drew, 228
Bartlett, Charlie, 71, 83
Bartlett, Martha, 83
Beard, Peter, 130–131
Becker, Ted, 138
Bedford Stuyvesant Restoration project, 180
Beiser, Edward, 165
Bellamy, Black Sam, 174
Bemelmans, Ludwig, 109
Benetton, Alessandro, 219
Bening, Annette, 203
Bergen, Candice, 225
Bergin, Michael, 220, 236
Berman, Michael, 206–207, 212, 221, 223, 237, 239–240

Bernstein, Leonard, 113
Bessette, Lauren (sister-in-law), 10–11, 19,
  23–24, 25–33, 218, 247, 257–270,
  275
Bessette, Lisa (sister-in-law), 218, 230, 235,
  275, 278
Bessette, William (father-in-law), 218
Bessette-Kennedy, Carolyn
  background, 22, 217–219
  burial at sea and memorial, 270–275
  career, 202–203, 219–220
  education, 218–219
  fear of John's flying, 2–3, 11–12, 13,
    14–15, 21–22, 243, 244, 252–253
  last flight, 10–13, 26–33, 257–270,
    276–277
  marriage
    courtship, 202–203, 204, 212–213, 220
    prenuptial agreement, 228
    problems in, 15–16, 22–23, 235,
      249–250
    proposal, 222–223
    wedding, 229–233
  press and, 225–226, 234, 235–236, 242,
    243, 250
Beyer, John, 140–141
Biederman, Jay, 15
Billings, Lem, 54
Bissaillon, Barry, 258
Black, Barry, 271
Blair, Tony, 244
Bouvier, Black Jack (grandfather), 47, 53, 62
Bowman, Patricia, 195
Boyen, Sandy, 178
Bradlee, Ben, 50, 53, 55, 59–60, 64, 72, 83
Bradlee, Tony, 37, 64, 72
Brady, James, 125
Brinkley, Douglas, 13
Brooks, Garth, 224
Brooks, Mel, 138
Brown, Ham, 80
Browne, Jackson, 190, 194, 196, 198, 201,
  212
Bubby's (restaurant), 232–233
Budd, Adam, 258–261
Buggy, Richard, 139
Bundy, McGeorge, 83
Burke, Richard, 146
Burton, Richard, 133
Bush, George, 152

Callas, Maria, 108, 116, 128, 137
Campbell, Judith, 55, 187
Capote, Truman, 126

Cappelen, Lois, 245–246
Carlin, Eugene, 218
Carragher, Owen, 191
Carter, Jimmy, 162
Castro, Fidel, 224, 242
Cavanaugh, Laura, 243
Cellucci, Paul, 269
Cerruti, Nino, 230
Charlotte, Grand Duchess of Luxembourg,
  61
Cherkasky, Michael, 191, 194
Chermayev, Alexandra "Sasha," 155, 278
Chermayev, Serge, 155
Christian, Jenny, 155, 156, 168
Christina (yacht), 64, 77, 108, 110, 111, 120,
  121, 123, 124, 135
Clark, Kemp, 69
Clay, Cassius, 104–105
Clemens, Roger, 7
Cliff, Jimmy, 274
Clifford, Barry, 140–141, 174
Clifton, Peter, 103
Clinton, Bill, 211, 241, 244–245, 247–248,
  262, 265, 267–270, 272
Clinton, Chelsea, 272
Clinton, Hillary, 10, 210, 241, 267, 272
Cohen, William, 270
Cohn, Roy, 134
Collins, Jaimie, 233
Cook, Charlotte, 271
Coqueran, Angie, 235–236
Corkery, Richard, 160
Cosby, Bill, 252
Cramer, Bob, 132
Crawford, Cindy, 224
Crespi, Vivian, 169
Crosse, Natalie, 190
Cruise, Tom, 246
Cullen, John, 218–219
Cunanan, Andrew, 238
Cuomo, Andrew (cousin), 193
Cuomo, Kerry Kennedy (cousin), 193
Cuomo, Mario, 193
Curtis, Chris, 250
Cushing, Cardinal, 63, 100, 109

Dallas, Rita, 89–90, 109–110, 127
D'Amato, Alfonse, 248
Davis, John, 178, 240
Davis, Peter, 163
Death of the President, The (Manchester), 104
De Celis, Luis, 151
DeChiara, Peter, 172
de Gaulle, Charles, 46, 78

De Niro, Robert, 189
d'Estaing, Valéry Giscard, 144–145
Diana, Princess of Wales, 22–23, 235, 238
Diaz, Ralph, 198
Diba, Empress Farah of Iran, 58
Dickinson, Angie, 44–45
Dillon, Matt, 189
Di Lorenzo, Tony, 252
Di Marzo, Bobby, 219
Dodson, Donna, 21, 276
Donovan, Dean Bruce, 165
Doubleday, 154
D'Souza, Christa, 236
Duchin, Peter, 135, 136, 140, 146, 161, 172
Duffy, David, 200
Duke, Angier Biddle, 87

Eisenhower, Mamie, 41, 42
Elizabeth, Queen of England, 97–98
Enright, Philip, 261
Erhard, Ludwig, 78
Essex County Airport, 24–29, 252, 262, 275–276
Evans, Richard J., 269
Exner, Judith Campbell, 55, 187

Farrakhan, Louis, 224
Fay, Paul "Red," 44–45
Felder, Raoul, 278
Ferguson, Andrew, 277
Fitzgerald, John Francis "Honey Fitz," 221
Fitzwilliam, Earl, 11
Flynt, Larry, 133
Ford, Harrison, 16, 252, 253
Ford, Joan, 14
Foster, Bob, 78, 82, 91–92
Francis, Edward, 32–33
Fraser, Hugh, 148
Freeman, Ann Marie Bessette (mother-in-law), 218, 275, 277, 278
Freeman, Richard (father-in-law), 218, 275
Freeman, Tom, 30–32
Frey, Sister Joanne, 47, 65, 79, 87, 89–90, 92
Friel, Brian, 177–178
Frischauer, Willi, 120

Galbraith, John Kenneth, 272–273
Galella, Ron, 126–127
Gallagher, Mary, 47, 63, 84
Gambaccini, Sciascia, 219–210
Garvin, Venard, 194
Gebreegziabher, Mesfin, 24–26
George magazine, 8–10, 12, 13, 15–16, 18–20, 206–207, 212, 221–226,

228–229, 237–238, 239–240, 247–248
Getty, J. Paul, 111
Gibbons, Euell, 158
Gibson, Barbara, 155–156
Gillon, Steve, 165–166
Gilpatric, Roswell, 62, 95, 107
Goddard, Paulette, 108
Gomez y Gomez, Antonio, 151–152
Goode, Eric, 220
Goodwin, Doris Kearns, 180
Graham, Billy, 224
Gray, Richard "Stretch," 174
Green, David A., 253
Griffith, Melanie, 222
Gromyko, Andrey, 59
Gross, Michael, 179
Guy, Rick, 167

Haag, Christina, 171, 177–179, 187, 189, 190, 194
Hachette-Filipacchi, 8, 16, 18, 221, 224. See also George magazine
Haddad, Bill, 90
Hageman, Hans, 115
Hahn, Anthony, 7
Hairston, James, 193
Halberstam, David, 146
Hamill, Pete, 154–155, 163
Hannah, Daryl, 189–190, 194, 195, 196, 198–205, 208, 209–210, 211–212, 218, 226–227, 236, 241, 250, 272
Hare, John, 171
Harriman, Averell, 82, 83, 88–89
Hartington, Kathleen "Kit" Kennedy (aunt), 11
Hay, Couri, 177
Hayden, Brenda, 2
Hayes, Rutherford B., 52
Heart of the City program, 206
Hearts and Minds (film), 163
Hennessy, Luella, 40, 42, 43
Hepburn, Katharine, 156–157
Heron, Nye, 178
Hill, "Mother," 197–198
Hine, Robert, 25
Hirsh, Jacqueline, 83
Holmes, Oliver Wendell, 152
Hoover, Herbert, 48
Hope, Judith, 10
Howard, Lloyd, 233–235
Howard, Ralph, 2
Howie, Olivia, 278
Howie, Phineas, 278

Huber, Oscar, 70
Hughes, Howard, 111
Hume, David, 103
Humphrey, Hubert, 109
Hurley, James, 223
Hussain, Munir, 25
Hutter, Lynn, 160

In Our Defense (Alderman and C. Kennedy), 192
Irons, Jeremy, 189
Isaacson, Walter, 185

Jacobson, Max, 54–55, 89, 154
Jagger, Mick, 131
Jean, Wyclef, 274
Jenkins, Marion, 70
JFK (film), 196
John, Elton, 238, 250
John F. Kennedy Library, 93, 162–163, 193, 227–228, 278
John F. Kennedy Profile in Courage Awards, 198
John Paul II, Pope, 265
Johnson, Lady Bird, 81, 210
Johnson, Lyndon, 75, 81, 82–83, 108, 110–111
Jonson, Ben, 163–164

Katz, Meredith, 253
Kelley, Pam, 145–146
Kennedy, Caroline. *See* Schlossberg, Caroline Bouvier Kennedy
Kennedy, David (cousin), 145–146, 175–176, 240, 257–258
Kennedy, Edward (uncle), 38, 63, 105, 112–113, 154, 159–160, 171, 173, 185, 195, 209, 241, 246–247, 260, 266–269, 271–274, 279
    Chappaquiddick incident, 125, 142, 180, 265
    discouragement of John's flying, 11–12, 18, 244, 245
    eulogies for family members, 110–111, 159, 210–211, 272–274
    plane crash of 1964, 11, 93–94, 142
Kennedy, Edward, Jr. (cousin), 201, 265, 267
Kennedy, Ethel (aunt), 11, 70, 83, 90–91, 109–111, 120, 145, 146, 147, 155–156, 159–160, 175, 196, 221, 240, 264–265
Kennedy, Joan (aunt), 109
Kennedy, John F., 37–82
    affairs, 44–45, 55, 187

Cuban Missile Crisis, 60, 173, 242
    death, 69–82
    inauguration, 44–45
    marriage, 47–48, 55
    relationships with children, 46–47, 51–52, 54–66
Kennedy, John F., Jr.
    acting in, 171, 174, 175, 176, 179
        family productions, 156
        Irish Arts Theater production, 177–178
        Murphy Brown episode, 225
        Saturday Night Fever invitation, 164–165
        school productions, 131, 156–157, 163–165, 172
    Alexandra Chermayev ("Sasha") and, 155, 278
    Aristotle Onassis and, 112, 116, 121–124, 128, 141
    Bedford Stuyvesant Restoration Project and, 180
    Bill Haddad and, 90
    birth, 39–40, 42, 43, 45
    birthdays, 77, 79, 96, 159–160
    Bob Foster and, 91–92
    burial at sea and memorial, 266–267, 270–275
    career
        bar exam, 190, 191–192, 193
        42nd Street Development Corporation, 175
        George magazine, 8–10, 12, 13, 15–16, 18–20, 206–207, 212, 221–226, 228–229, 237–238, 239–240, 247–248
        interest in journalism, 137–138, 206–207
        Justice Department clerkship, 185–186
        Manhattan District Attorney's office, 190–195, 200
        summer at Manatt, Phelps, Rothenberg, and Phillips, 185–186
    Carolyn Bessette and, 202–203, 204, 212–213. *See also* Kennedy, John F., Jr., marriage
    Christina Haag and, 171, 177–179, 187, 189, 190, 194
    daredevil nature, 13–14, 17, 58–59, 60–61, 101–102, 198
    Daryl Hannah and, 189–190, 194, 195, 196, 198–205, 208, 209–210, 211–212, 218, 226–227, 236, 241, 250, 272

and death of father, 69–82, 127–128
and death of mother, 208–211
dedication of John F. Kennedy Library,
    162–163
early years, 45–82
education
    Brown University, 161–162, 163–164,
        165–169, 172–174
    Collegiate School, 113–115, 123–124,
        131, 138, 156
    New York University Law School,
        180–181, 185–186, 190, 191
    Phillips Academy, 152–153, 156–158,
        159
    religious, 65–66
    St. David's, 97, 99, 102, 103–104, 113
    University of New Delhi, India, 175
Edward Kennedy and, 11–12, 18, 105,
    159, 171, 244, 245, 246–247
exhibitionism, 177, 186
flying, 18, 100–101, 252
    Alexander Onassis and, 124
    Buckeye powered parachute, 1–3, 8,
        233–235, 237–238, 252
    early years, 56–57
    last flight, 10–13, 20–21, 24–33,
        257–270, 276–277
    lessons, 172–173, 243, 245–246
Jenny Christian and, 155, 156, 168
John F. Kennedy Profile in Courage
    Awards and, 198
John Walsh and, 160
Julie Baker and, 16, 194–195, 212
Kennedy Fellows, 205–206
Madonna and, 187–189, 224
marriage
    courtship, 202–203, 204, 212–213, 220
    problems in, 15–16, 22–23, 235,
        249–250
    proposal, 222–223
    wedding, 229–233
Maurice Tempelsman and, 17–18,
    206–207, 208
Peace Corps in Guatemala and, 151–152
Peter Beard and, 130–131
pets, 21, 48–49, 64, 75, 122, 124, 128,
    130, 226, 235, 276
political activities, 240, 248–249
    press conference at Center for
        Democratic Policy, 171
    speech at Democratic National
        Convention (1988), 185–186
press and, 82, 87, 94, 98, 106, 126–127,
    128, 130–131, 160, 180, 186–187,

    188–189, 191–192, 195, 196, 209,
        224–227, 229, 231–233, 235–236,
        238–239, 243
Reaching Up program and, 205, 206,
    273, 278
rebellion, 138–140, 143–144, 153–154,
    158, 165, 166–167, 175–176
relationship with father, 51–53, 55–66,
    111–112
relationship with sister, 20, 58, 129, 131,
    201
Robert Kennedy and, 70, 77, 90–91, 97,
    100, 105, 107–109, 111
Robin Hood Foundation and, 10, 139,
    205–206, 273
Secret Service and, 48, 50, 56, 58, 66, 80,
    82, 83, 91–92, 95–99, 102, 113–115,
    131, 132–133, 137, 138–140, 152,
    153, 160
as Sexiest Man Alive, 186–187
social service, 105, 159, 171, 205–206,
    252
South African Group for Education and,
    170
sports, 7–8, 104–105, 123–124, 176
    biking, 251–252
    family football games, 146–147, 195
    scuba diving, 140–141, 146
    skating, 180, 197, 251–252
threats to self and family, 42–43, 69–71,
    102–103, 132–133, 138–140
travels, 97–99, 100–102, 105–106,
    144–145, 146, 158–159, 170, 175,
    180, 198
    with Carolyn, 225, 227, 231–232, 238,
        241–242, 247
    National Outdoor Leadership School
        trek in Kenya, 161
    Outward Bound program in Maine,
        158
    Vast Explorer diving expedition,
        174–175
    White House years, 39–82, 128–130,
        244–245
Kennedy, Joseph II (cousin), 145–146, 147,
    239–240, 241
Kennedy, Joseph P., Jr. (uncle), 11, 206
Kennedy, Joseph P., Sr. (grandfather), 11, 38,
    42, 47, 49, 59–60, 80, 89–90,
    109–110, 127, 270
Kennedy, Kerry (cousin), 91, 193
Kennedy, Michael (cousin), 11–12, 91, 147,
    221, 239–240, 241, 243, 244, 258
Kennedy, Patrick (cousin), 195, 267

Kennedy, Patrick Bouvier (brother), 42,
    62–64, 73, 74, 88, 211, 280
Kennedy, Robert, Jr. (cousin), 145, 147,
    265, 278
Kennedy, Robert F. (uncle), 11, 63, 70, 77,
    79, 82–83, 90–91, 97, 100, 105,
    107–109, 112, 115, 125, 175, 180,
    266
  death, 110–111
  Senate campaign, 93–94
Kennedy, Rory (cousin), 10, 20, 21, 180,
    243, 253, 257–258, 264, 272, 276
Kennedy, Rose Fitzgerald (grandmother),
    47, 58, 79–80, 131, 155–156, 193,
    221, 270, 271
Kennedy, Rosemary (aunt), 205
Kennedy Fellows, 205–206
Kerouac, Jack, 19
Kesey, Ken, 156
King, Martin Luther, Jr., 109
Klein, Calvin, 219–220
Klein, Edward, 158, 175, 201
Klein, Kelly, 219
Klein, Marcie, 219
Kliger, Jack, 18–19
Koch, David, 221
Koch, Ed, 192
Konviser, Jill, 191
Kopechne, Mary Jo, 125
Kotite, Toni, 195

LaLanne, Jack, 46
Larrabee, Richard, 265
Lawford, Chris (cousin), 145
Lawford, Pat Kennedy (aunt), 93, 120, 146,
    196, 272
Lawford, Patricia Seton (aunt), 171, 176
Lawford, Peter (uncle), 93, 101, 171, 176
Lawford, Sydney (cousin), 120, 146
Lederman, Gil, 251
Leeves, Jane, 198
Leigh, Wendy, 167
Lemmon, Jack, 152
Lerner, Alan Jay, 81
Lewinsky, Monica, 247–248
Lilly, Doris, 133
Lincoln, Abraham, 77
Lincoln, Evelyn, 57, 64, 75, 84
Littell, Rob, 171
Livanos, Athina "Tina," 108, 141–142
Livanos, Stavros, 108
Lopez, Robert, 138–139
Lord, Sterling, 19–20

Lorenzo, Larry, 26
Louis-Dreyfus, Julia, 198
Lowe, Jacques, 50

MacLaine, Shirley, 155
Madonna, 187–189, 224
Manchester, William, 104
Mankiewicz, Frank, 109, 147
Manocchia, Pat, 18
Marks, Mary, 275
Marshall, Leslie, 9–10
Marx, Arthur, 14, 172–173
Matchett, Chris, 219
Mathison, Melissa, 252, 253
McCray, Wilson, 143–144, 152–153
McDonnell, Marjorie "Peggy," 106,
    115–116
McDonnell, Murray, 106
McGough, David, 242, 245
McNamara, Robert, 272
Mehle, Aileen, 112, 132, 169
Mehta, Gita, 175
Meir, Golda, 78
Mellon, Bunny, 99, 100, 159–160
Mellon, Paul, 99, 100
Merrill, Dina, 228
Meyer, Andre, 113
Meyer, Johnny, 141, 142
Meyer, Mary Pinchot, 55
Millay, Edna St. Vincent, 210
Miller, Melody, 230–231
Minnelli, Liza, 189
Miske brothers, 101–102
Monroe, Marilyn, 55, 187, 188, 228
Moody, Rick, 164
Moran, Nancy, 113, 115
Morgenthau, Robert, 190–191
Moutsatsos, Kiki Feroudi, 119, 120, 122,
    123, 125, 131–132
Moynihan, Daniel Patrick, 10
Munro, Sally, 168–169
Murphy Brown episode, 225

National Outdoor Leadership School, 161
Neal, Carolyn, 197
Newman, Larry, 145
Newman, Paul, 248
New York Daily News, 154
Niarchos, Stavros, 112, 141–142
Nichols, Mike, 210
Nicholson, Jack, 156
Nixon, Julie, 129, 231
Nixon, Pat, 128–130

Nixon, Richard, 75, 129–130, 245
Nixon, Tricia, 129
Noonan, Billy, 19, 24
Norman, Jessye, 210
Novak, Kim, 45
Nureyev, Rudolf, 175
Nye, Joseph, 244

O'Byrne, Charles J., 230, 271
O'Donnell, Kenneth, 39, 62
O'Donnell, Rosie, 225
O'Donogue, Kathy, 271
O'Leary, Mugsy, 113, 114
Olitsky, Brooke, 263
Onassis, Alexander (stepbrother), 11, 120,
    124, 134–135, 136, 141
Onassis, Aristotle (stepfather)
  death, 141–143
  death of son, Alexander, 11, 134–135,
    136, 141
  illness, 136–137
  relationship with Jackie Kennedy, 64, 77,
    107, 108–113, 116, 119–128,
    132–137, 140
  wealth, 17, 108–109, 111, 141, 143
Onassis, Athina "Tina" Livanos, 108
Onassis, Christina (stepsister), 108, 120, 124,
    134, 137, 141–142, 143
Onassis, Jacqueline Bouvier Kennedy
  and Aristotle Onassis, 64, 77, 107,
    108–113, 116, 119–128, 132–137,
    140
  career, 154, 206
  death, 17–18, 208–211
  and death of Aristotle Onassis, 141–143
  and death of John F. Kennedy, 69–82,
    92–93, 95, 100, 103, 104
  financial issues, 88, 112–113, 120–121,
    125, 134, 141, 143, 169–170,
    200–201, 220–221, 227–228
  Georgetown mansions, 82–90
  illness, 202–203, 204–205, 207–208
  and Maurice Tempelsman, 17–18,
    169–170, 173, 199–200, 201, 202,
    204, 206–209, 227, 229–230
  near-fatal accident, 106–107
  and Pete Hamill, 154–155
  pregnancies, 37–38, 39–40, 42, 62–63
  press and, 40, 41, 49–51, 98, 105, 121,
    122–123, 125–127, 133–134
  tributes, 227–228
  White House years, 37–82, 128–130,
    169

Oswald, Lee Harvey, 242
Outward Bound, 158
Owen, Holly, 153–154

Pangan, Domingo, 152
Papadimetriou, Stelios, 135
Paparo, John, 229
Papert, Frederick, 210
Paredes, Providencia "Provi," 99
Parker, Sarah Jessica, 195
Paul VI, Pope, 100
Pavlick, Richard P., 42–43
Paz, Veronica, 152
Peace Corps, 151–152
Pecker, David, 221
Pei, I. M., 162
Penn, Sean, 187–189
Perón, Evita, 108
Philip, Prince of England, 78
Philips, Elsie, 44
Phillips, Samuel, 152
Pinero, Miguel, 164
Pinheiro, Ephigenio, 276, 278
Plimpton, George, 1, 99–100, 124, 154,
    159–160
Podesta, John, 262
Powers, Dave, 63, 79, 83, 89, 104–105
Presidential Medal of Honor, 82–83
Pribanic, Victor, 257
Price, Seth, 233
Prounakis, Sylianos, 142–143
Puff Daddy, 248

Rabe, David, 164
Radziwill, Christina (cousin), 98, 120
Radziwill, Lee (aunt). See Ross, Lee
    Radziwill (aunt)
Radziwill, Stanislas "Stas" (uncle), 92, 98,
    110
Radziwill, Tony (cousin), 98, 120, 130, 212,
    229, 251, 261, 272, 276, 278
Ralli, Constantine, 278
Ratcliff, Frank "Rat," 197
Ratowell, Carol, 261
Rauch, Sheila, 239
Rautbord, Sugar, 199, 200
Reaching Up program, 205, 206, 273, 278
Red Gate Farm, Martha's Vineyard, 1, 200,
    251, 252, 276
Reno, Janet, 19
Richards, Ricardo, 25
Richardson, Ashley, 195
Robards, Jason, 113

Robin Hood Foundation, 10, 139,
    205–206, 273
Rodriguez, Narciso, 230
Ronan, Marion, 200
Ronhock, Paul, 260
Roosevelt, Eleanor, 81, 163
Roosevelt, Franklin, Jr., 53
Roosevelt, Franklin D., 52, 77
Ross, Herb, 189–190, 212
Ross, Lee Radziwill (aunt), 63, 64, 90, 92,
    93, 98, 107, 120, 124, 189–190,
    229, 251
Rubin, James, 14, 247
Rusk, Dean, 60

Salinger, Nicole, 135–136
Salinger, Pierre, 40, 43, 50, 51, 77, 111, 120,
    135–136, 142, 211, 222, 240
Saturday Night Fever, 164–165
Sawyer, Diane, 17, 203
Schlesinger, Arthur, Jr., 12, 50, 108, 202,
    273, 280
Schlossberg, Caroline Bouvier Kennedy
    as author of book, 192
    birth, 38–39
    children, 20, 192, 199, 204, 207,
        229–230, 265, 274, 275, 277
    death of brother, 261–262, 265,
        268–270, 274–275, 277–280
    death of father, 69–82, 89–90
    death of mother, 208–211
    education
        Brearley School, 126, 178
        Columbia Law School, 180–181
        Concord Academy, 132, 134, 136, 141,
            147–148, 168
        Convent of the Sacred Heart, 94, 99,
            126
        Radcliffe College, 159
        religious, 47, 65, 79, 89–90, 92
    internship at New York Daily News, 154
    internship at Sotheby's, London, 147–148
    marriage to Ed Schlossberg, 180–181
    threats to self and family, 42–43, 69–71,
        102–103, 147–148
    White House years, 38–82, 128–130
Schlossberg, Edwin Arthur (brother-in-
    law), 20, 170, 180–181
Schlossberg, Jack (nephew), 20, 199, 204,
    229, 265, 274, 277, 278
Schlossberg, Rose (niece), 20, 192, 204,
    229, 265, 274, 275, 277
Schlossberg, Tatiana (niece), 20, 192, 204,
    229, 265, 274, 277

Seinfeld, 198
Selassie, Haile, 78
Seligson, Damon, 263
Sesam, Gabriel, 152
Sgubin, Marta (governess), 113, 120,
    124–125, 147, 155, 156, 197, 200,
    207–208, 230, 277–279
Shall We Tell the President? (Archer), 154
Shaw, Maud (nanny), 38–39, 41, 44, 45–47,
    53–56, 58, 59, 61, 71, 72–74, 76–79,
    82, 84, 88, 97–99, 104, 120, 129,
    147, 197
Shepard-Turner, Hilary, 186–187
Shikler, Aaron, 128
Shriver, Bobby (cousin), 145
Shriver, Eunice Kennedy (aunt), 145, 146,
    159–160, 196, 205, 266
Shriver, Maria (cousin), 145, 146, 180
Shriver, Robert (cousin), 24
Shriver, Sargent (uncle), 145, 196
Shriver, Timothy (cousin), 145, 151–152,
    171, 278
Shusteroff, Shelley, 177
Sirhan, Sirhan, 110
Skakel, George, Jr., 11
Smathers, George, 38, 59
Smith, Bessie, 197
Smith, Bubba, 104–105
Smith, Jean Kennedy (aunt), 93, 120,
    195
Smith, Steven (uncle), 93
Smith, William Kennedy (cousin), 97, 98,
    195–196, 240, 246, 265
Socrates (restaurant), 233
Sokol, Susan, 219
Sorenson, Theodore, 53
South African Group for Education,
    170
Spalding, Betty, 83
Spalding, Chuck, 83, 101, 147, 163, 217
Special Olympics, 205
Spender, Stephen, 162–163
Springsteen, Bruce, 238–239
Stein, Keith, 8–10, 23, 206
Steinbrenner, George, 7
Stern, Howard, 227
Stevenson, Adlai, 169
Stigwood, Robert, 164–165
Sting, 238
Stone, Oliver, 196
Stone, Sharon, 222
Stoughton, Cecil, 56, 57
Straus, Billy, 13
Strayton, Dana Gallo, 228

Stronach, Belinda, 8–9
Styles, Steven, 208
Susskind, David, 107
Swanson, Gloria, 108
Synge, J. M., 164

Taylor, Elizabeth, 133
Tempelsman, Lily, 169
Tempelsman, Maurice, 17–18, 169–170,
      173, 199–200, 201, 202, 204,
      206–209, 227, 229–230
Terenzio, RoseMary, 278
Theroux, Alexander, 156, 157
Thyssen, Fiona, 134
Tito, Marshall, 61
Travell, Janet, 42
Travolta, John, 252
Tretick, Stanley, 50, 51, 52, 57, 276
Trudeau, Pierre, 9
Tuckerman, Nancy, 94, 138, 141, 202,
      227–228
Tyson, Mike, 12–13

Van Dyk, Ted, 193
Vast Explorer diving expedition, 174–175
Versace, Donatella, 247
Versace, Gianni, 238
Viking Press, 154

Wallace, George, 224
Walsh, John, 39, 42, 62, 102, 107, 139–140,
      160

Walters, Barbara, 137, 186, 225
Warhol, Andy, 162, 170
Warnecke, John, 101
Warren, Earl, 44
Weiner, James M., 269
Wells, Mary, 199
Wescott, Gail, 40
West, J. B., 41, 46, 48, 75
Wexler, Haskell, 189
Wexler, Jerry, 189, 198–199
White, Theodore, 77, 80–81, 125
Whitehead, John, 13
Wiese, Richard, 12, 166, 167, 186,
      217–218, 220, 237–238,
      246
Wilcox, Thomas, 157
Williston, Beverly, 137
Wilmot, Paul, 250
Wilson, Woodrow, 52
Winfrey, Oprah, 225
Winners (Friel), 177–178
Wise, Shirley, 231
Wolff, Michael, 8
Worrell, Geoffrey, 115
Wrightsman, Charles and Jayne,
      92

Xuxa, 195, 196

Young, Andrew, 170

Zogby, John, 240